Feeding Winter Birds

Feeding Winter Birds

Bob Waldon

Voyageur Press

Printed and bound in the United States
91 92 93 94 95 5 4 3 2 1

Library of Congress Cataloging-in-Publication Data

Waldon, Bob, 1932–
[Prairie guide to feeding winter birds]
Feeding winter birds / Bob Waldon.
p. cm.
Reprint. Originally published: A prairie guide to feeding winter birds.
Saskatoon, Sask. : Western Producer Prairie Books, © 1990.
Includes bibliographical references and index.
ISBN 0-89658-166-7
1. Birds. 2. Birds—Feeding and feeds. 3. Bird feeders.
4. Birds—Wintering. I. Title.
QL685.5.P73W35 1991
598.29712—dc20   91-13601
CIP

Published by
Voyageur Press, Inc.
P.O. Box 338, 123 North Second Street
Stillwater, MN 55082 U.S.A.
In Minn 612-430-2210, Toll-free 800-888-9653

Voyageur Press books are also available at discounts for quantities
for educational, fundraising, premium, or sales-promotion use.
For details contact the marketing department. Please write or call
for our free catalog of natural history publications.

Contents

To Dr. Harold Waldon,
who with a few soft words
could turn the common things
of nature into objects of wonder

Acknowledgements

As a lifelong naturalist it has been my pleasure to have worked with staff and members of the National Audubon Society, at both the state and national levels. In accumulating the background information that in time led to this book, these relationships were valuable for the knowledge and information they imparted, and for the encouragement they afforded.

I must also extend thanks to the Cornell Laboratory of Ornithology, especially Erica Dunn, Coordinator of Project Feeder Watch. Through participation in their many programs and services, and through personal communications, I have grown and benefited as an observer of the world of birds.

Over the many years that I have known artist and wood-carver Peter Sawatzky, the illustrator of this book, I have greatly enjoyed both his work and his friendship. Working with Peter is a pleasure not only because of the high level of his interpretive skill, but also because he brings to his profession a good business sense and an enthusiasm for developing new projects and working in a partnership.

Introduction

This is a nontechnical, nonacademic book. It is intended for the information and enjoyment of the thousands of householders in the Upper Midwest who feed birds in winter and whose bird watching is done mostly through a picture window. With their counterparts in the adjacent Prairie Provinces of Canada, for whom the first edition of this book was written, they share the rigors of an unforgiving midcontinental winter. As a result, the vast majority of their birds migrate. Those few resident species that stay behind are joined by nomadic and partially migratory birds from farther north. They are treasured for their beauty, admired for their tough self-reliance, and cherished for the life and vitality they add to our winterscapes, all the more because there aren't that many of them.

As a feeder of birds it was impossible for me to watch them throughout our fierce winters without wondering how such tiny creatures could survive the cold and the wind on the other side of the sheltering pane of glass that separated us. My own search for answers led to the discovery of much that was fascinating in the world of birds and, in time, to the idea that other people would be interested in hearing what I found out. There seemed to be a place for a handy-sized reference focusing on a region and a season that had not yet been featured together. And it seemed especially fitting to supply such a bird guide for folk who can appreciate survival since they themselves spend close to half of every year preparing for, coping with, or recovering from, winter.

The coming of spring and the warm weather of summer are the seasons we naturally associate with birds. Why, then, a book about birds in *winter*?

It may seem contradictory to point out that, in fact, far more people spend far more time watching greater numbers of birds in winter than is the case in summer when there are far more species around. In summer the birds are scattered throughout their habitat, busy and concealed by foliage. To seek them out demands getting up before dawn and prowling tangled habitat amidst the dew and the mosquitos. This is admirable beyond words, but exceeds the resolve of most of us. Besides, many of us are just as busy in summer as are the birds.

1

But winter, though it banishes most of the birds, also strips the concealing foliage from the vegetation and changes the remaining birds' social habits. Many wintering species gather into large flocks, roving widely in search of food. Most of these will congregate readily around feeders that can be placed near a convenient window where the birds can be continuously, closely, and comfortably observed. In effect, instead of having to seek out birds, winter birders can manipulate the birds into seeking out *them!*

Selecting the species of wintering birds to be included in a book is an absorbing subject for a would-be author. At first blush there would seem to be embarrassingly few. For the casual Upper Midwest birder a midwinter day's list numbering twenty or more species is a real accomplishment. Short as it is, this list could include species such as gulls, owls, and perhaps waterfowl that don't qualify as "feeder" birds.

With some scanning of Christmas Bird Count results from across the Upper Midwest, however, the list of candidate species lengthens considerably. In addition to the resident, nonmigratory regulars that can be expected in each zone, there are the nomadic northern finches that might, or might not, show up during the course of any winter. Then there are the rather hesitant north-south migrants like juncos and goldfinches, parts of whose populations occasionally do only a partial migration and winter in the region. Holdovers are another group composed of a small percentage of a normally migratory population that stays behind. These include robins, White-throated Sparrows, flickers, grackles, and others.

To complicate the problem of choosing species, there are the decidedly winter birds, such as Horned Larks and longspurs, that don't as a rule visit feeders, and shrikes, owls, and some hawks that call only with ulterior motives in mind. In the end, at the risk of appearing inconsistent, which I am, and of offending some readers by leaving out their favorite bird, which I regret, I mustered my biases and made arbitrary choices.

To these, perhaps in the minds of some bird-lovers adding insult to injury, I added a small contingent of mammals, the "Walk-in Trade." These rarely get respectful treatment in bird feeder books, even though some of them play a major role in the activity around feeding stations. Their natural history is, to me, just as fascinating as that of the birds.

In the end the total came to forty-seven species of birds and six of mammals, plus twenty family and group write-ups. The advantage for the reader of having a reference with only forty-seven bird species is that there is less thumbing-through-pages than there is for the major, continentwide guides. Further, when you've found what you're looking for, there's room for it to be discussed in much more detail than is possible in a guide that must cover over 650 species. For the writer there is also the luxury of being able to include family write-ups in which all manner of stimulating new material can be included.

This of course is not the *only* bird guide. In fact, many readers will already have one of the major field guides. My intent was that this reference and the more comprehensive guides would complement each other. To this end, I have listed in each species write-up the page numbers where that species can be found in the most recent editions of the most popular field guides, and in Robert B. Janssen's *Birds in Minnesota.*

Writing this book has been a lot of fun, an admission one probably ought not to make. My research was essentially painless, consisting of foraging through the popular literature, constantly on the sniff for those neat bits of lore that we information junkies love to collect. Such sources are readily available to anyone with the time and interest to assemble them. But not everyone has the time to wade through a pile of books. What I have done is saved my readers a lot of sometimes repetitious reading, and in the process distilled out what I hope will be a truly absorbing collection of information.

There are few references as to source; most of my searching was from books and periodicals whose authors and writers themselves gave no sources. It was therefore a matter of relying on my own judgment, and comparison with many sources, to determine the reliability of the information I selected. Where material was obviously an author's own, or in rare cases where the statements bent credulity a little, I accorded in-text credit.

As well as bird lore, the content of this augmented guide includes practical information on the "how-to" aspects of winter feeding. There are things to do, and things not to do, that will help you maintain a station with less effort and enhance your viewing pleasure.

On a final word about content, I follow what appears to be the most widely practiced, though by no means unanimous, convention regarding capitalization of the common names of species. For the full, recognized common name, both words are capitalized. Obsolete, regional, or partial names are not, and neither are names of groups; hence we have: "The House Sparrow isn't really a sparrow, but a weaver finch."

In conclusion, this is not the work of a scholar, nor even of a respectable birder. Rather, it is the offering of a writer with an abiding sense of excitement about nature and a shameless compulsion to infect others with it. I hope my fellow window bird watchers enjoy reading this book as much as I enjoyed writing it.

CHAPTER 1

Principles of Feeding

Why Feed Birds?

Self-satisfaction is probably at the root of most people's decision to start feeding birds. Most of us respond to the plight of fellow creatures struggling to get through hard times and feel good about helping them out. It is easy charity; the gifts are small, and the response is immediate and obvious, sometimes overwhelmingly so.

Along with the instant gratification and all those positive vibes, the happy giver gets a ringside seat at an ongoing natural wonder, winter survival. When you develop a knowing relationship with birds, you can't help but marvel how such tiny, fragile creatures are able at all to live through our savage midcontinent winters. We also cater to our own aesthetic sense by filling our environs with beautiful creatures that may be the only signs of life and color in an otherwise deep-frozen, monochromatic landscape.

There can be intellectual stimulation as well. Even the most casual of us will develop a keener appreciation for wildlife. And if we give our sense of curiosity at least half a chance, we'll find ourselves learning more about these engaging creatures and how they fit into their environment. Feeding birds has, in fact, converted some of its unsuspecting beginners into lifelong students of nature.

Charity, entertainment, and intellectual growth acknowledged, there is as well a gut-level element of self-esteem involved. A forlorn, unattended feeder stands for the expectant beginner as a symbol of rejection, a minor one, to be sure, but perplexing. Doubts smoulder as time passes: Is there something wrong with my feeder? the seeds? Are the birds all over at the neighbors'? What are they doing better than I? But let the first chickadee alight on that brand new feeder, and a moment of triumph ignites and every doubt is forgotten. You've been accepted!

That feeling persists, with variations, for as long as you feed birds. Even those of us who consider ourselves hard-bitten and jaded develop a bit of an ego trip from having a yardful of all the northern finches, every nonmigratory regular in the book, perhaps a holdover robin, a visiting pheasant, and maybe a goshawk or shrike that swoops in from time to time. The feeling of superiority is keenest if one's bird-feeding associates are not quite so well blessed. Even the highest-minded charity isn't immune to the taint of one-upmanship.

Those who like to think of themselves as part of a long tradition could point to Saint Francis of Assisi who lived in Italy from about 1181 to 1226. As well as founding the Franciscan Order, he is renowned for his love of wild birds and his mystical powers of attracting them; there are countless medieval paintings of "Saint Francis and the Birds." His day is October 4, a fitting day for a winter-bird-feeders' patron saint, since it could serve as a last-date reminder to us northerners that our stations should be readied for action.

Ethics of Feeding

While I'm on the subject of saints and good deeds, it is appropriate to clear up questions that often crop up in discussions on bird feeding.

Will offering food to birds prompt some of them to delay migration until it's too late for them to leave, thus luring them to an untimely death from cold and starvation?

Much as we like to think how important our feeding stations are to the birds, we probably have a minimal effect on the movements of truly migratory species. In some years great numbers of goldfinches or juncos, among others, will elect to winter in parts of their breeding range, well north of their usual winter haunts. Whether these are the locals that simply stayed put, or birds from farther north that undertook a partial migration, we usually can't tell. The reasons aren't entirely clear either; a protracted, mild fall, a superabundance of natural food, or the lack of it, could trigger a holdover.

Once the birds have settled into their wintering mode they will certainly take advantage of whatever suitable human-source feed is available, to the delight of captivated bird feeders. Since the birds are challenging a winter that could ultimately tax them far more than a presumably milder one farther south, many that might otherwise succumb on scarce natural forage will pull through thanks to rich, plentiful food at feeders.

Rare, solitary holdovers of confirmed migrants such as robins may have stayed behind because of some abnormal factor in their behavior or physiology. An unfit bird may not have the vitality to join the hustle and commotion of large premigratory flocks and will simply "miss the boat" when the rest of its fellows abruptly vanish on some frosty, moonlit autumn night. Most of these unfortunates die. A few, lucky enough to find good shelter and a plentiful source of food, will survive to greet the reduced ranks of their returning relatives the following spring.

Another question is whether you are morally bound to keep at it once you've started feeding. If you stop, won't the birds that have come to rely on your food starve to death?

My initial answer is a definite "yes!," you *are* morally obliged; qualifiers come later. In the severe climate of Manitoba where I do my wintering, even the hardiest birds are tested to the ultimate. Hanging on from day to day on the slimmest margin between life and death, they don't need the added uncertainties of on-again-off-again feeding. If an "off" happens to coincide with a blizzard or a spell of really deep cold, the delay they suffer in relocating to another feeder or in switching back to natural food could be fatal.

This obligation is particularly pressing if your feeder is the only one for some distance around, as at a rural homestead or a backcountry cottage. Here, you will probably attract a large number of birds, many of them a long way from their home territories and hence more critically dependent on you than those from close by. In this situation, in a region of harsh winters, you really do have a moral obligation to see to it that your feeders are kept stocked once you've started.

However, the farther south you are, the closer your bird-feeding neighbors are, the less binding is your obligation to be consistent. If you must stop feeding, perhaps for a midwinter holiday, it will be easier on the birds to pick a mild spell well before you leave. Avoiding the awful moment of total withdrawal by simply leaving may be easier on you than facing the forlorn gaze of your birds as they sit on your now-empty feeders. But if your cop-out coincides with the worst blast of the winter, some of your trusting little dependants could be not only forlorn, but dead.

A Touch of Analysis

One can spoil a first flush of enthusiasm with an overdose of sober reflection. At its basic level, feeding birds is blessedly uncomplicated. It can remain that way and be easier in the long run, however, if you take stock before heading off to the shopping center on a late fall afternoon to fetch a bag of seeds. Depending upon where you live, with whom, and who your neighbors are, questions could arise to cloud your apparently innocent intentions.

What about the mice and rats that spilled seeds will attract? What about weed seeds from your feeders that will infect your flowerbeds? What about the noise of the birds? What about sanitation, like droppings and disease? Will we now have to put the cat in solitary confinement?

If you live in a small village or lakeside cottage, or on a farm or spacious acreage where you have only your own household to answer to, most of the queries are irrelevant. But on a street in a town or suburb, the questions should be addressed honestly. There *have* been cases where bird lovers in these locations have brought the hostility of their neighbors, and civic wrath, down upon themselves by going overboard with their enthusiasms.

Some advice on how to head off difficulties, and how to deal with them if they occur, is offered in chapter 4, "The Downside." All considered, however, problems are the rare exceptions; millions of urbanites happily feed birds winter after winter without a single hitch in neighborly relations.

You can actually have a little fun doing a pre-audit of your prospects, preferrably on a summer's day long before the first chickadee has cracked a single sunflower seed. This assessment can proceed from the general to the specific, i.e., from zone to habitat to site.

Zone assessment   The Upper Midwest is a fascinating mosaic of geological and vegetative zones. From the Great Lakes beech-maple forest of the east to the high, dry plains of the west, from the boreal forest of the north to the long-grass prairie of the south, it presents a huge variety of habitats. Very adaptable mammals and birds can find a place in all of these, particularly since settlement has drastically altered almost all the landscape. But the more specialized species may be limited to one or two zones, and it would be highly unusual for them to show up in the others. It will be helpful to check the species write-ups, which give the seasonal ranges for each bird.

Habitat assessment   Is your neighborhood within a quarter mile of a lake, river, marsh, or tract of undeveloped woodland? In such places, unless compulsive civic tidiness, heavy recreational vehicle abuse, or overgrazing have denuded them, there should be ribbons or patches of good cover. Shoreside and/or floodland willow, scrubby gullies, or blocks of forest with an understorey of shrubbery are good bird habitat. So is a large park with generous plantings of hedges and ornamental trees. The closer your house is to tangled tracts of the wild country that birds require, the better are your chances of attracting some of them to your yard.

Is your immediate neighborhood well-blessed with tall trees, thick hedges, an occasional vacant lot, plenty of ornamental shrubbery? As subdivisions age, the trees get bigger, hedges and ornamentals expand. If you live on a circular bay where all the back yards and perhaps a little park or playground combine to provide a modest continuum of shrubby growth and reasonable tranquility, your chances of getting some action are improved.

The less your neighborhood resembles any of the foregoing, the poorer are your chances of attracting winter birds. Prepare yourself for modest returns if you live in a spanking-new subdivision where every square foot of natural growth has been landscaped out of existance, where the neat ornamentals are barely out of their root-ball diapers and the boulevard trees are spindly adolescents still in braces. If the wildest land around is the convenience store in the mall, you may have to be content with a gang of sparrows and some starlings.

Site assessment   If your review of the area is encouraging, and other bird feeders in the vicinity report good results, your own property has potential.

If you can, look at the place from a small bird's point-of-view on a January morning when it's five below and the windchill factor, thanks to a brisk northwesterly, is forty below. The main thing you'd want to do is find shelter from that nose-freezing wind as quickly as possible and stay there. If there was a cafeteria in that sheltered spot, you'd want a place to stand back and wait your turn, and a spot to sit down once you'd picked up your tray.

The best windbreak on most lots is the house itself, and in this latitude of prevailing westerlies, the best shelter is on the south or southeast side. An alcove formed by walls on the west and north is ideal. The waiting places, in the bird world, are simply trees or shrubs where they can perch, out of the worst of the wind, above the reach of cats. They might have to wait their turn in their own flock, as chickadees do, the "alpha" one first, the others in descending order of dominance. Or, they might have to bide their time while the big guys—Blue Jays, Evening Grosbeaks, or a squirrel—have finished pigging out.

There are easy ways of augmenting the bird-friendly features of your yard. Putting up a temporary holdover zone of dead trees or branches, making a brush pile, propping up discarded Christmas trees, or tacking up a plywood baffle to cut the wind are all Good Deeds we can perform. However, unless your yard is truly bleak, before rushing off to muster the raw materials it might be just as well to wait and let experience, i.e., the birds themselves, suggest specific, short-term local improvements.

For long-term modifications such as fences, hedges, and plantings, the Reference section lists books that give yard plans and varieties of trees and shrubs that will attract birds.

Basic Needs

Reduced to the fundamentals, the basics are: 1) feed and 2) something to serve it on. Both have been, and will continue to be, the subjects of endless debate in birding circles. They are dealt with in detail in the chapters "Seeds and Feeds" and "Feeders and Shelters."

To get started, most of us simply clump into the grocery or hardware store and pick up a bag of "Wild Bird Seed." But before doing that it is a good idea to find out what other local feeders are using, how much they go through in a winter, where they get it, and the cost. If there is a naturalist club around, or a nature columnist in a local paper, they will be your best source of advice. This information could come in handy if you find yourself in a winter when the northern finches visit in great numbers and you want to respond. Thus, instead of putting away the unused portion of your lone "birdseed" bag next spring, you could be buying armloads of them every few weeks all winter. There is a list of state wildlife bureaus, naturalist groups, and nature centers in the Appendix.

Storage should be considered. Stored seeds must be kept dry and out of reach of rodents or raccoons. It is also nice to have them convenient to the feeder(s). The vessel that does this best for me is a metal garbage can with a tight-fitting lid. For seeds on reserve, I stack extra bags in a rodent-proof metal shed.

This may seem to be a bit overcautious, except to someone who has caught a bad dose of mice or rats, or whose garage, back porch, workshop, or attic has been hit by break-and-enter squirrels. Once rodents discover a source of good food it is extremely difficult to keep them out of it. They can dig or gnaw their way into wooden sheds with ease, chewing holes in bags or boxes and gleaning nesting materials from whatever valuables are stored there. With a reproductive capacity that is truly awesome, two mice can rapidly become a horde.

Birds and mammals are not the only animals that exploit the nutritious bounty of seeds; thousands of species of insects do so as well, some adapted to take special advantage of stored grain. Almost any sample of bulk seeds will have its share of these, plus a few accidental ride-alongs. In a warm environment they can multiply at a rate that makes even mice seem straightlaced. Keeping your seeds outside in winter completely cools the reproductive capacity of these stowaways.

The answer to undesirable preemption is found in the ounce-of-prevention homily: Keep the seeds out of reach, outside. Sweep up any spills, put lids back on. I keep my trusty garbage can conveniently under my window shelf feeder. Anything that spills is picked up by the birds or other foragers that stay where they belong . . . out!

I refer again to chapter 4, "The Downside," for more suggestions on how to keep control of the situation and still be a generous host.

CHAPTER 2

Seeds
and Feeds

The "KISS" Principle

Although I am taken up with the idea and pleasures of feeding birds, there are other things in my life that have a justifiable claim on my time. Therefore, I have avoided getting too fussy about feeds, operating on the "KISS" principle: "Keep It Simple, Stupid." To those who take pleasure in melting suet twice, in cooking and mixing bird cakes, in rolling balls of suet and peanut butter in cornmeal and chopped almonds, I say "go for it!"

To demonstrate my open-mindedness on the subject, I have provided a few tantalizing bird recipes in the Appendix, under the heading "The Non-KISS Gourmet." One of these is "bird stone," a classic that will test the greatness of those who really get off on unusual mixtures. I found it in a bulletin published in 1932 by National Parks of Canada. The writer, R. Owen Merriman, attributes it to one Baron von Berlepsch. Have fun!

What to Feed?

The most primitive form of feeding is found in the householder who tosses a handful or two of breadcrumbs out the back door and lets the sparrows pick them off the snow. Offering breadcrumbs is sometimes a very good way of initially baiting birds in, since the white fragments of bread are eye-catching. And although the nutritional value of white bread leaves a lot to be desired, many winter birds do enjoy it, and there is usually no problem later in making the switch to seeds.

Baits and switches notwithstanding, the very best attractant to a feeder is a bird already busy at it. Chickadees, nuthatches, titmice, and Downy Woodpeckers commonly form loose foraging flocks in the bush. When one of these discovers your feeder the others are quick to get in on the action. Their activity, in turn, will attract other foragers like Blue Jays and the finches. How long they stay with you, and in what numbers, depends on the quality of the setting and the quality and quantity of the feed.

As pointed out in the previous chapter, what you feed may depend on what is available locally at a reasonable price. If you have a choice, however, there are good reasons for making deliberate selections. Manipulation of the kinds of feeds and where you offer them enables you to control, within limits, where various species will congregate around your yard. More on this subject later. Nutritional worthiness of any given feed is academic if nobody likes it, so I have listed relative feeder food preferences for each species in their separate write-ups.

On "Expert" Advice

There is a strong urge, particularly if one is writing a book, to play the sage and solemnly hand down pronouncements as if from the Mount. But almost certainly, if you begin to talk in terms of absolutes about animals, they will do something to make a fool of you in the eyes of your readers.

Take the subject of rapeseed. In Canada a variety more easily processed into cooking oil was developed some time ago and (perhaps just as well) renamed "canola." My own experience, and all the books, tell me that nothing, except for partridges scratching for it in a field, will eat it. Bird-feeding friends of long experience have hooted at the idea of offering birds rapeseed. And yet I read recently in Cam and Joy Finlay's column, "Birdwatching" in the *Edmonton Journal*, that their feeding station had attracted a flock of over one hundred redpolls, and that every day they had to lay on fresh feed, "one large can of rapeseed." Perhaps the new "canola" is also more palatable to the birds!

Just a few hours before writing this, on a sunny day in early March, a cat demonstrated convincingly that there is nothing to behold that doesn't have an exception to it. This beast clambered up over the wire around my window feeder and sat there for a good half hour eating sunflower seeds! I had plenty of time for pictures. Aside from an exploratory sniff and a half-hearted lick, the cat ignored a small block of rendered suet and a fragment of chicken fat.

If I were compiling statistics, that cat's strange tastes would produce some interesting pronouncements, such as: "17.3 percent of the cats observed during March of 1990 ate sunflower seeds." But since I'm not, I'm left musing on the cause. The cat was obviously not starved, being sleek and fit-looking. She might have been pregnant and responding to the sort of dill-pickles-with-ice-cream compulsion that besets human ladies-in-waiting. I think not, however, for the sounds she made from time to time suggested that she was interested in *becoming* pregnant. Perhaps her state of hormonal excitement explains her peculiar tastes.

Seeds

The Noble Sunflower

Cultivated sunflower seeds come in several varieties, all of them arising from a Eurasian species *Helianthus annuus*. The familiar ones we munch are referred to in the grain and processing trades as "confectionary" sunflower seeds. Whole seeds are large, up to 5/8 in (1.5 cm) long, striped lengthwise in buff and dusty black. Roasted, salted, or unsalted, they are sold as a confection everywhere, the infamous "spits" so hated by pool hall, bowling alley, and arcade operators across the land. In a quite different role, hulled, roasted or raw, with or without salt, they are standard items in the bulk bins of organic food shops.

Confectionary seeds are universally relished at feeders. But their size and thick hulls make them awkward for birds smaller than Purple Finches to husk, especially if they get damp and turn leathery. Hulled or cracked they are of course supremely palatable, but even at wholesale prices are relatively expensive.

Until 1975 the confectionary seed was the unchallenged choice of those who chose to feed sunflowers. In that year a particularly heavy crop of small, black sunflower seed pushed its way into the birdfeed market, and quickly moved into dominance. This was "oilseed," which means it is grown for processing into cooking oil.

The acceptance of oilseed sunflowers as birdseed was helped by the widely publicized findings of Dr. Aelred D. Geis of the U.S. Fish and Wildlife Service, who scientifically assessed the food preferences of wild birds that visit feeders. Among other things, Dr. Geis discovered that all birds tested except Tufted Titmice, Common Grackles, and Blue Jays selected oilseeds over confectionary when given a choice between the two. It is now accepted that oilseed sunflowers are eaten readily by at least forty species of birds and are the first preference of many.

Oilseeds are about half the size of the confectionary seeds, and their much thinner hulls make them manageable by birds right down to siskin size. They are cultivated extensively in the Upper Midwest—North Dakota leads the nation in sunflower acreage—so they are readily available. Bought directly from a farmer or at the elevator, they are reasonably economical.

Not quite so economical are the sunflower "hearts" (or "harts") that are advertised for sale by most seeds suppliers. Unlike peanut hearts, which are the germs of peanut seeds, sunflower harts are the damaged and undersized kernels culled during the preparation of sunflowers for human consumption, mainly confectionary seeds. Hulls are discarded, but there is a small percentage of bits and milling debris mixed in.

Not that the birds care. As an experiment I obtained a few pounds of hulled and cracked oilseeds, hulls still in the mixture, from a processing plant and tried them on my birds. My window feeder is separated into two halves by a low divider. I put the crushed seeds on one half, whole on the other. That winter the dominant visitors were siskins, and they overwhelmingly selected the cracked seeds over the whole. This is quite understandable; the cracked seeds are much easier to feed on, especially for siskins, the most diminutive feeder visitors. I would expect other small species to make the same choice.

Anyone fortunate enough to live close to a processing plant has the best chance to get this premium feed at reasonable prices. Failing this, an alternative would be to have your own seeds custom-ground, or to do it yourself. I know of one ingenious bird feeder who cracks sunflower seeds with his power mower. He just strews them on the concrete floor of the garage, cranks up, and collects them in the grass catcher.

An advantage of hulled and cleaned (no hulls) seed is that there is no pile of husks under the feeder to contend with in spring. A disadvantage is that cracked sunflower seeds weep oil—the finer the crush, the faster the loss. That oil very quickly turns rancid in mild weather. I would think that cracked seeds, with the hulls left in the mixture, might keep a little better since the husks would tend to absorb the oil. With or without the hulls, however, broken sunflower seeds should not be stored over the summer except in the deep freeze.

Short of being downright smug, I feel very good about feeding oilseed sunflowers to my birds (and squirrels). In that little black package is the closest to a universal feed that is commonly available. With over 40 percent oil content, plus a wholesome component of carbohydrate, protein, and minerals, they are richly nutritious. Their excellent palatability is supported not only by the scientific findings of Dr. Geis, but by users of mixed seed who complain that much of it is wasted by birds flicking through it to pick out the sunflowers, like a guest who eats all the cashews and filberts and leaves the peanuts in the bowl.

Ironically, the very attractiveness of the seeds to birds could in time affect their availability to bird feeders. Farmers are often plagued by hordes of blackbirds raiding their fields of ripening sunflowers. To curb this depredation, varieties of sunflowers have been developed that are less vulnerable to birds in the field. One variety being tested tastes unpleasant to birds but doesn't affect the flavor of the oil or meal it yields. Although still in the experimental stage, bird-repellent varieties of oilseed sunflowers bear noting by bird feeders, for obvious reasons. If they take over in future as the dominant field crop, bird-palatable seeds will become a very minor factor in the overall market and will be grown only as a specialty crop by a few farmers. This means very much higher costs and much-reduced availability. In the meantime, those who buy from producers should make sure they don't unwittingly stock up on seed the birds won't eat.

Mixed Seed

This is variously marketed as "Wild Bird Seed," "Wild Bird Mix," and so on. Compositions vary, but millet (red and/or white) usually dominates, with cracked cereal grain (wheat, oats, barley), cracked corn, milo (sorghum), canary seed, and black sunflowers added in differing ratios. There are no regulations setting what wild-bird mixes should consist of, nor for printing the content percentages on the label. Buying the components separately and mixing them yourself is the only way of being absolutely sure of what you're scooping into your feeders.

On the subject of mixtures, acceptable bird fodder can be dished out in the form of "screenings." This is the weed seeds, damaged and undersized kernels, dust, and other debris winnowed out of grain when it's cleaned. It's usually very cheap, but you take your chances on what it contains. Not that the birds mind; weed seeds are part of the regular diet of many of our winter species. But many of the seeds are lightweight and blow far and wide in the winter wind, sowing the possibility of a bumper crop of objectionable weeds and neighborhood resentment.

Millets

Common or proso millet, *Panicum miliaceum*, comes in white or red, and is the major constituent in commercial wild bird mixes. It is grown as human food in Asia and Europe, and as poultry and livestock feed here. The seeds are small, round, fairly thin-hulled; the white variety is slightly favored over the red in selection tests. House Sparrows love millet, and it is highly acceptable to most finches, after the sunflowers are all gone.

Canary Seed

This is a European grass, *Phalaris canariensis*, now cultivated in parts of the Upper Midwest as a specialty crop. The seeds are flat, small, spindle-shaped, gray-buff with a polished, slippery coat, like flax. Free-flowing, it is excellent for tube feeders used as alternates for daintier clients. Thus, while a feeding frenzy of Purple Finches or Evening Grosbeaks is devouring commoner fare by the pound at the main tray, the goldfinches and siskins will be extracting the high-priced canary seeds one at a time from the dainty little ports in the tube feeder. Or so the theory goes.

Cracked Grains

Oats, barley, rye, and feed wheat, particularly if you get them from a farmer, are very cheap bird feed. Whole, they are acceptable to grouse, partridge, pigeons, Mourning Doves, rodents of all kinds, and deer. Cracked, they become more palatable as well to finches, buntings, and House Sparrows. In my view the main advantage of grain is not its limited value as a bird feed, but as cheap lure fodder for uninvited, heavy eaters.

For example, hard winters may drive deer to venture into yards to browse on ornamentals, glean fallout from bird feeders, or paw into compost heaps. Hunger overcomes fear; frightened off, they return when vigilance lapses. They quickly learn to rear up and strike with their front hooves at elevated feeders. Whether moved by sympathy or self-preservation to feed them, you'll find that once you begin, the word spreads and others arrive. If you shovel bird seed at them, it can get very expensive. Policies vary from state to state and year to year, but some game management bureaus supply free deer chow—usually alfalfa pellets—to people willing to dispense it. Otherwise, the cheapest whole grain you can get is the best alternative. There are other hearty eaters you might wish, or be forced, to cater to. These include porcupines and rabbits or hares, in which case a protective collar of wire or sheet metal around your favorite trees and shrubs is a wise precaution, even as you lay on the oats. In fall and early spring raccoons can become prime nuisances, cleaning you out of sunflower seeds and suet in one raid. Improved security measures for these goodies, combined with a diversionary offering of grain, could be the answer.

Rapeseed (Canola)

The little black seeds of rapeseed, *Brassica napus*, look as if they should be good bird feed, and in many agricultural areas of the Upper Midwest there is lots of it around. Some birds, especially grouse, partridge, and pheasant, will eat it if there's nothing else on the plate, but given a choice all birds tested completely ignored it.

Corn

Zea mays can be offered on the dry cob, as whole kernels, or cracked and ground to various consistencies. Whole, it is attractive to birds like grouse, pheasants, and pigeons, and it is reportedly acceptable to Blue Jays, grackles, and cardinals. Cracked, it is much more widely accepted by the smaller species, including finches and House Sparrows. There is, of course, its advantage of being abundant throughout the area. However, damp cracked corn cakes up and spoils quickly. Birds feeding on musty grains can inhale the spores of *Aspergillis* mold and contract a lethal respiratory disease. An alternate, less risky use of crushed or cracked corn is as an addition to suet and/or peanut butter to make them more palatable.

Milo (Sorghum)

Sorghum vulgare originated in Africa and is a very important crop in the U.S. as both fodder and grain for livestock and in cereal for humans. Two to three times the size of millet, the round, reddish seeds are tough-coated and can be handled readily by pigeons, grouse, and partridge, but otherwise are not popular at all at the feeder. In times when millet or other palatable seeds are high priced, sorghum may find its way into commercial birdseed mixes as a filler. Watch for the telltale reddish hue to the mix; if it isn't small red proso millet, skip it.

Peanuts

It would be surprising indeed if peanuts *weren't* high on the palatability list of birds and mammals, since we humans relish them so. *Arachis hypogaea* are tasty, rich, and as bird feed, damnably expensive. There is a small knuckle that sticks out from the inside surface of one end of the seed half when you separate it. In the manufacture of peanut butter these "peanut hearts" are discarded. At one time they were fairly readily available for bird feed. They were never cheap, but one could afford a small sack to use in a pinch-penny feeder for the small species, as a treat, or to add to mixed concoctions.

Nowadays, most of us buy a few in the shell, string them on a wire or cord, and hang them where the jays and chickadees can get at them. Once they've discovered what they are, and if the squirrels don't get there first, it's a diversion to watch the antics of the birds trying to shell them out.

Safflower

Safflower is an oilseed crop grown here and there in the Midwest, but not extensively. In some locales it is referred to as "cardinal bait," in spite of the fact that cardinals now prefer sunflowers three-to-one. *Carthamus tinctorius* is also accepted by pigeons, Purple Finches, Evening Grosbeaks, and House Sparrows. Some station operators see as an advantage the fact that it is not readily eaten by Gray Squirrels.

Thistle

Guizotia abyssinica is also referred to as niger seed and, depending on which literature you read, is either a member of the thistle family or isn't even closely related. Whatever the case, these small black seeds have long been a mainstay of cage birds, and are a highly desirable item with the smaller finches. They are usually considered too expensive to be served from large, generous hopper feeders or on tables. Most people use tube feeders, some designs for which are even called "thistle" feeders. You can also purchase a "thistle bag" with mesh tight enough to hold the seeds but large enough to permit their being pulled through by small, probing bills. Being an unrepentant sunflower advocate, I have never felt the need to own a thistle bag, but read they don't always work and can be leaky and wasteful. Niger seed, as the name suggests, is grown in Africa, which explains the price.

Feeds

Power Feeding and Beyond

If palatable, reasonably priced seeds are available to you without too much bother, and you are satisfied they provide a balanced diet, you needn't worry about extras. I have noticed that my chickadees continue to forage for their natural foods between trips to the sunflower seeds. I suspect that many other species do the same, and that this rounds out any deficiencies in the seed diet.

I supplement my sunflower seeds (no reflection on them) with suet, partly because it may provide an extra boost of critical energy during especially cold periods, and partly because it is particularly tempting to nuthatches and jays and is the main feed item for woodpeckers, including the magnificent pileated.

Extra feeds, novelty items, treats, and such really come into their own in suburbia, where bird-feeding neighbors vie with each other to see who can get the most birds. Serious competition calls for power feeding, the laying on of as many tempting goodies as you can buy or invent, dished up in a dazzling array of dispensers. It is, usually, a harmless outlet in which the real winners are the birds and the local bird-feed retailers.

Peanut Butter

A jar of peanut butter that's been a little too long at the back of the fridge is usually the source of my use of it for feed or bait. Otherwise, I find it too expensive, especially when the squirrels catch on. However, others look for bargains and buy it for their birds. It is rich nourishment, and can be handled somewhat like suet, smeared into open pine cones and holes in suet logs. Some writers make the claim, disputed by myself and others, that it can be dangerous because it can clog up birds' mouths and throats and suffocate them. If you want to be certain that no such fate befalls your birds, mix peanut butter with softened suet, corn meal, flour, or cooking grease.

Suet

Suet is the fat deposited around the kidneys and loin of cattle and sheep, in the body cavity. It comes from the carcass as rounded white globs held together with light sheets of clear connective tissue. Cold, it tends to break easily, and its flakey texture makes it easier for small birds to peck out bits of it even when it's frozen solid.

You may be able to get bulk suet from your local butcher shop. If you live near one, an abattoir or packing house is the cheapest source for large amounts. Most feed, pet food, and nature center shops sell it in one form or another.

Suet can be put out as it comes from the butcher. Pure suet won't rot, although it will get rancid and very stale-smelling in warm weather. Bits of meat in the suet will of course spoil, so it is a good idea to pull the globs apart and strip away most of the connective tissue and bits of meat. Plastic mesh onion bags, wire screen baskets, or similar dispensers will permit birds to peck through for small bits but prevent its being carted off wholesale by jays or crows.

"Suet logs" are made by boring holes into a stick of firewood, filling them with suet, and hanging it up. Making suet logs is a time-honored way of giving youngsters, and their grandparents, a way of occupying themselves constructively and, for the most part, harmlessly.

Some writers worry that birds' feet, eyes, or tongues will stick to the frozen metal of wire suet baskets. Having in childhood stuck my own tongue to the pump handle I can sympathize. But I know of no direct account of this having happened to birds; their feet are dry and their reflexes so quick I doubt very much if their eyes or tongues are at hazard. A panicked bird or one that is ill *might* be vulnerable. If it worries you, prepare yourself for a price shock and buy liquid latex and coat the wire or metal parts of your suet baskets with it.

If you're not sufficiently fulfilled by hanging raw suet out in an onion bag, it can be refined by rendering. Suet melting should be done with care since it is inflammable and can burst into a very hot, stubborn fire if mishandled. A double boiler is safe, but seems to take forever; a slow fry over direct heat is my way, gently pressing the chunks to get all the oil out as the meltdown proceeds. Fished out, the crunchy brown "cracklings" are themselves a tasty bird treat. I just scatter a few on the feeder among the seeds every now and then, breaking them up so the Blue Jays can't immediately cart everything off in big chunks.

The oil is then poured into molds for cooling. Any container with an appropriate shape and size, and preferrably of destructible material, can be used: aluminum-foil bowls, waxed-paper cups, melon shells, grapefruit rinds. For variety, peanut butter, seeds, corn meal, crushed grains, or dried fruit can be added and stirred in as the mixture cools.

In my own view, suet and seeds are not best mixed together because grease-soaked seed hulls are harder to husk. And a suet-seed mixture attracts suet-lovers to the fat, others to the seeds, and you have a crowded point of conflict where somebody has to wait. You can accommodate both simultaneously by offering these feeds in the usual manner, in separate containers.

There are two advantages to rendering. One is that if suet is to be fed in warmer weather, melting it down twice will make it harder when it's cooled the second time. The other is that liquifying the suet makes it easy to fish out nonfat fragments that would rot quickly at warm temperatures. For any bits that you miss, the heat of rendering has a sterilizing effect that slows down the decay process.

Suet will continue to be eaten by some species well after the arrival of warm weather. Softened and rancid it can saturate the facial feathers of birds and result in infected follicles and feather loss around the beak and eyes. Since the high-energy feeds become less crucial in warm weather, and since natural foods like insects become available then, it is better to withdraw suet once spring has truly set it.

Suet is, of course, attractive to predators, including raccoons, weasels, coyotes, and the like. Hanging it six feet up in the air will keep it out of the reach of these animals, plus the ones who'll likely be the biggest nuisances, dogs.

One final word on this excellent bird food. If you buy a prepared ball of frozen, ready-to-serve suet mixed with what-have-you, keep an eye, and your nose, on it as weather warms. I got one of those cute bells for Christmas, parked it on the woodshed roof, and found, around about Mother's Day, that it had transformed itself into a putrid blob.

Slab Fat

Forms of animal fat other than suet can be offered successfully. In the trimming process butchers slice slabs of fat off the outside surface of sides of beef. This fat is tougher, much stringier, and lacks the flakiness of suet. It can be rendered or served by simply nailing a chunk to a tree trunk. Slabs of pork fat, with or without the rind, can be treated similarly. "Slab" fat (my name for it) can be useful in keeping heavy users like crows or ravens diverted from the higher-quality stuff in the fragile onion bags where the chickadees feed.

Cooking Grease

Residue cooking fat is highly nutritious and very palatable providing it isn't charged with particularly hot spices. It can be saved in a mold and either presented by itself in a solidified cake or mixed with suet or peanut butter.

Bones

The birds that take suet seem to be strongly attracted to large, raw bones; some prefer to hammer away at them for the tiny shreds and scraps their labors produce rather than take easier pickings from a nearby suet bag. Such scavenging probably evolved at predator kills. Hence, nuthatches, woodpeckers, and chickadees may get an atavistic satisfaction in picking at bones that hanging on a plastic onion bag can't afford. If I come by a beef, horse, or deer hip, or a large leg bone, I park it in the snow on top of the back shed. By the time it has turned from its quite startling red to a more somber brown, the birds will have pulled all but the toughest shreds of sinew from it.

Meat/Carrion

There are two majestic birds that turn up erratically in winter that can be enticed to feed within view if the right kind of setup is offered to them. I refer to the eagles. Golden Eagles will drift south and eastward from their nesting grounds in the mountains and the far north, cruising the forests and farmlands for snowshoe hares, cottontail rabbits, and game birds. Bald Eagles will now and then stay over, especially near open water, living off the plentiful supply of carrion in gut piles, dead and wounded deer, and crippled waterfowl left over from the hunting seasons.

  Several years ago, noting the presence of both these great raptors near my country place in southern Manitoba, I erected a stout shelf on a post, high enough off the ground so the coyotes couldn't reach a chunk of road-killed deer that I lashed onto the tray. Magpies were the most numerous visitors, until one morning a dark, hulking bird had banished them. It was a golden, and it came only two or three times.

In two succeeding winters I have had Bald Eagles, one adult and one immature. Between visits from these big predators, my "eagle feeder" out in the meadow gives the neighborhood magpies something to do besides gang up at the suet feeders in the yard.

Baked Goods

A restaurant, retail bakery, or doughnut shop can be a good source of stale stock and leftovers. Doughnuts, cakes, and pastries are tasty-rich in carbohydrates and fats, just the ticket for winter calories. But take care not to get carried away by the generosity of donors; some outlets create leftovers in awesome quantities and are pleased to give it to anyone who'll cart it off for them.

Before you start strewing these goodies about the yard and making regular runs to the garbage dump with the stuff the yard won't hold, go to the dump ahead of time and survey the clientele there. In the bird department we're talking starlings, House Sparrows, pigeons, crows, gulls, and ravens—lots of ravens—if we're in their range. Amongst the ground crew are rats, mice, raccoons, stray cats, and dogs of no fixed address.

The point is that leftover baked goodies could turn your yard into a satellite garbage dump. Done discretely, you can dispense this rich, tasty food to some of the regular clients that will learn to relish it, if they haven't already developed the taste. Keep it well up off the ground; the local dogs will smell it out quickly and, if they can reach it, may become constant nuisances.

Fruit

Dried fruit, especially raisins because of their size and easy availability, has been frequently used as a specialty or treat food. Waxwings, if they stick around long enough for you to get their attention, will take raisins with enthusiasm. Wintering robins are said to sustain themselves mainly on tree-dried berries. I have seen a backyard crabapple in early spring surrounded by dozens of robins gathered to feed on the fallen fruit. The interesting bit was that neighboring crabs, having borne just as abundantly, were totally ignored. The hint here is that if you discover such a tree, gather a basket or two of the fruit in the fall. Keep it frozen and offer them to the mockingbirds in winter and to the returning robins in spring.

The literature regularly mentions frozen banana, orange, apple, straw-berry, raspberry, and other fruits as being accepted, but these writers report from latitudes more southerly than the Upper Midwest. Mockingbirds, blackbirds, grackles, and holdover robins might find these items much to their liking.

If, in any particular summer, there was a particularly abundant crop of wild fruit, such as serviceberries, highbush cranberries, chokecherries, elderberries, or mountain ash, one might gather a few buckets. They could be kept at the ready in the deep freeze against the appearance of a flock of waxwings.

Grit

Most birds require grit of some kind in their gizzards to grind up their food; it is particularly important to seed-eaters. I've never supplied it for my birds, since I believe the adjacent gravel roads to be a more-than-adequate source. So, I read, is the grit that washes out of the asphalt shingles on my roof. However, if you live in what you believe to be a grit-deficient neighborhood, you can do your part for avian digestion by putting a shovelful of gravel or coarse sand out where the birds can get it. Feed companies sell poultry grit in three or more sizes; "chick" grade would be most suitable for the small-caliber plumbing of most feeder species. Crushed oyster shell, even the "pullet" size, would likely be too coarse except for grouse, pheasants, and pigeons.

Salt

Crossbills are frequently seen picking at the ashes around barbecues and fire pits, presumably due to a craving for the minerals they contain. Many of them are killed by traffic when they flock onto roads for the salt scattered there in winter. A small pan of coarse salt mixed with ashes, grit, or soil might be an interesting addition to your offerings, particularly if you have a flock of crossbills. I have never fed salt, but if I did I would not follow the advice of a writer who solemnly bid his readers mix salt with snow!

Water

A good supply of water is essential to the well-being of birds. In the winter they get it by eating snow. This is a long-established adaptation, so I don't agree with those authors who worry at length about the necessity of installing a heated watering pan for birds. In my own city water mains occasionally burst in midwinter, creating ponds of steaming water on the street. If the local birds craved water, they'd be flocking to it. But I have yet to see a single one come to drink at these breaks.

The one situation where they might be stressed could be during a protracted fall freeze-up when the sources of open water would be iced over and there would be no snow. In this situation there might be a case for maintaining a bird bath or pan of warmed water. The heat source could be a light bulb, heat lamp, battery warmer, or submersible heating coil sold specifically for keeping bird waterers and baths warm.

I have no experience as to whether water, kept warm in very cold weather, would deceive birds into trying to bathe in it. One writer recounts the observation of a householder who noted that starlings bathed in the warmed water he supplied, and then promptly froze to death! Other references suggest that birds can bathe in water and suffer no afterchill, but I suspect the references come from places where winter isn't favored quite so often by those cold fronts that Canada sends down.

CHAPTER 3

Feeders
and Shelters

First Considerations

There are two beneficiaries to consider in setting up a feeding station: birds and people, in that order. This basic priority suggests a sequence of things to ponder. Of primary importance are (1) accessibility to the birds, (2) easy visibility for the people, and (3) shelter from the wind. Secondary considerations are (1) ease of filling and maintaining feeders, (2) feeder capacity (frequency of filling), (3) shelter from snow and/or rain, and (4) vulnerability to cats.

Site (yard) assessment, already discussed, will suggest the kinds of feeders you should use, i.e., table, window shelf, post-mounted, or hanging. If you have a big window facing into an alcove on the southeast side of the house, with ample shelter from the prevailing northwesterlies, there are no priorities to sort out, since this is a setup in which everybody wins. But if your best window faces west or north, and there is no shelter worth the name between it and Siberia, you have some adjustments to make.

The All-weather Yard

My own option would be to put up a nice feeder on the ledge at the big window and fit raised sides on the windward edges so the seeds wouldn't be scattered with every passing gust. On calm days, or when the wind was brewing up a storm from the opposite side of the house, the birds could feed at the big window without being subjected to punishing windchill. But I would put up another feeder, a table or pole, in the place most sheltered from the prevailing westerlies; whether or not there was a window view of this alternate site would be a secondary consideration.

This combination, with perhaps a couple of hanging seed feeders and a suet bag at various selected spots, would make my yard an all-weather feeding haven, with birds more likely to congregate, and remain, there in all kinds of weather. My big window might be deserted on days when our

23

continental westerlies whistled against it, but the feeders out back would keep everybody around until things calmed down.

Feeders

From the Ground Up

The most basic feeder of all is the ground itself. Many species, such as House Sparrows, juncos, pigeons, grouse, starlings, and the blackbirds much prefer to feed on the ground. Others—redpolls, chickadees, goldfinches, Evening Grosbeaks, Purple Finches—also feed there but are just as happy with something higher up.

Throwing feed on the ground might not be as simple as it first appears. It can be wasteful; seeds get mixed in with soft snow and disappear. Repeated snowfalls, or windblown snow, bury everything. In spots close to shrubbery or other hiding places, birds on the ground are most vulnerable to ambush by cats. From a high window, it may be awkward to see birds on the ground. If I'm feeding on snow-covered ground, or wish to minimize waste of seeds spilled from an overhead feeder, I pack the snow first by patting it down with a shovel or rolling it flat with a large plastic pail.

A piece of plywood, an old door, or something of the sort can be used as a modest improvement on bare ground or snow. It cuts waste somewhat, and cleaning it off is merely a matter of up-ending it and giving it a kick, or flopping it over.

The Table—Next Step Up

If you take your plywood or old door and nail legs under the corners, you have yourself a table feeder. Putting a low rim around the edges stiffens it and helps keep seeds in place. You can make a neater job of sweeping it off if you leave gaps in the rim at the corners. A further modification that lets rain or meltwater run off better is to give the table top a slight tilt by cutting two of the legs on a long side a bit shorter. The water will drain off through the gaps you've providently left in the edging.

The height of the table is a matter of taste and/or convenience, as is its size, or both may be determined by the scrap lumber at hand. A general rule is that the bigger your feeder(s), the more birds you'll attract, particularly the sociable species like finches. A full 4×8-ft sheet of plywood can accommodate a mob of redpolls, Purple Finches, and/or Evening Grosbeaks. But in years of real abundance, a modest feeder no more than 1×2 ft can attract an astonishing crowd of visitors.

At this point in the setting-up stage one might as well face the fact that in any location where there are neighbors there are going to be cats, sometimes a whole parade of them. It will be better for the birds, and your state of mind later on, to take preventive action now to minimize the cat problem. Recommended measures are to be found in chapter 4, "The Downside," under the subhead, "Frustrating the Felines."

For now, I should point out the space under a low table feeder can provide a custom-made ambush for lurking cats. The birds are baited right to the place of concealment, and spilled seeds bait the birds to the ground right in front of the cats' noses. Not only this, but cats quickly master another lethal trick. They pinpoint the location of birds on the platform overhead from the sounds of their feet, and when one is near the edge, pounce over and grab it. My own experience is that the best way of preventing your table from becoming a cat-treats bar is to tack wire screen or wooden slats to the legs all the way around so they can't get underneath.

Pole Feeders

One of the more pleasing arrangements, from both the birds' and their observers' points of view, is the pole feeder. This is basically a shelf-on-a-stick, with infinite variations. It can be made or bought.

Many manufactured feeders come with metal tubes that fit cleverly together in sections. The bottom end of the lowest section is crimped to a rough point, and to set the device up you simply tap it into the ground, *straight* into the ground, if possible. Don't beat on the top of the tube with a hammer or some other steel bludgeon; you'll crimp or bend the rim and it won't take the small end of the next section. Put a piece of soft wood on the top of the tube and thump on that.

The sectional rod idea is doubly convenient, since the feeders bolted to the top section are usually of the hopper variety and stretching up to fill them *in situ* can be awkward. You simply rotate and pull off the feeder, plus the attached top section of pipe, recharge it at convenient working height, then replace it. To make sure it detaches at the first section below the feeder, I apply a lubricant to that joint so that it comes apart easiest. If that doesn't work, I wrap a little tape around the other joints to hold them in place. Most store-bought pole feeders, by the way, come with a squirrel baffle, a cone- or Frisbee-shaped metal disc loosely fixed to the pole just below the feeder.

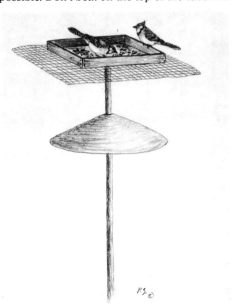

Simple Pole Shelf *Note the squirrle baffle and anti-cat screen*

If you're making your own, the pole can be anything sturdy enough to hold whatever you intend to fix to the top: metal or polyvinyl chloride (PVC) pipe, posts, two-by-fours or other dimension lumber, or a slender tree trunk. My largest feeder is mounted on a 10-ft (3-m) section of cedar telephone pole. The 7 ft (2 m) above ground are clad top to bottom in sheet metal. The hopper on the platform at the top is made of a 30-in (76-cm) section of 18-in (46-cm) culvert. It looks like a small water tower designed for Dogpatch, and has been described somewhat uncharitably as an eyesore. But it stands out behind the cottage in the country where few, save myself, the critic, and the birds, rarely see it. I have to fill it from a stepladder, but since it holds upwards of 88 lb (40 kg) of seeds, this isn't too frequent a chore, and I can go away for a fortnight or more and not have to worry about my birds running short. Among its other sturdy virtues my tower is squirrel-, raccoon-, and deer-proof.

Beer-carton Craft   As I have already mentioned, the variations that can be worked into the basic pole-and-shelf pattern are infinite. The most primitive can be large berry-baskets, twelve-pack beer cartons, or small cardboard boxes nailed on their sides to the tops of fenceposts. A refinement to this is a small scrap of plywood used as an oversized washer so the nail won't rip through the cardboard in the wind. It's crude, but the birds don't care, and the materials can be gleaned out of any roadside ditch. At this level of technology you are thus not only benefiting the birds, but helping to keep roadscapes litter-free.

Opposite to crude can be a finely crafted, multistorey platform with several hoppers, one or two sides made of plexiglass, little balconies for baked scraps and other treats, eye screws on little booms for suet bags and thistle feeders, all tucked under a trimly shingled roof. Such a feeder doesn't have to be very big to accommodate a large number of birds at once. With rustic natural finish, or tastefully selected paint, a station like this can be a quaint and attractive centerpiece to the yardscape. My only word of caution is that if you're just starting out, begin near the primitive end of the technology and let experience, coupled with decorative ingenuity, guide your hand.

How High?   Your pole feeder may be a lesson in simplicity or the architectural pride of the neighborhood. Either way, squirrels and your attitude to them may dictate basic features of construction.

If you want to keep them off your pole feeder, as most people seem to, it must first be high enough to prevent their jumping directly up to it. For Gray Squirrels, this means a *minimum* of 5 ft (1.5 m). Depending on snowfall in your area, allow extra height for the snow pack under the feeder. It must also be set far enough away from trees or other launch points to prevent squirrels jumping across to, or down onto, the roof. Horizontally, that means a span of 8 ft (2.4 m), more for a launch point higher than the top of the feeder. For Red Squirrels, take a foot to 18 inches (30 to 45 cm) off these clearances.

Obviously, elevation is only one way of deterring squirrels, superbly adapted climbers that they are. Preventing them from shinnying up the pole has taxed the skill and patience of countless backyard artificers, and the battle goes on. Some of these countermeasures are described in "A Gnawing Problem" in chapter 4.

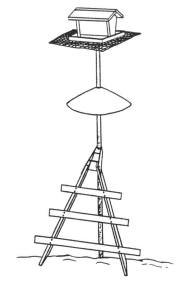

Low-rise Ladder   For the moment, the question of a pole feeder's being high enough to deter squirrels means that top-loading hoppers will be awkward to fill for people of average height. If the pole is fitted with telescoping joints, as described previously, there is no problem. But for a solid pole one should have a sturdy wooden box or something solid to stand on. An old chair or stool is most untrustworthy on packed snow; the legs have a tendency to suddenly poke through the crust when you're teetering aloft.

My own answer is a 3-ft (1-m) ladder. The sides are set very wide apart at the bottom, very close together at the top, an

Three-step Ladder *Convenient access to tall top-loading pole feeders*

exaggeration of a library ladder; it looks like an isosceles triangle. The idea is that the close-set ends at the top rest loosely against the sides of the pole while the splayed bottom affords a very secure base. You can augment this simple design with an extension set at an angle to the top. With this resting against the pole you're set back more comfortably from your work. See the accompanying diagram.

My squatty ladder is very light and also comes in handy for filling or cleaning high window shelf feeders, servicing bluebird houses, cleaning windows, and doing other odd jobs at modest elevations where a full-sized ladder is awkward.

Window Shelves

Factors of shelter and serviceability permitting, a window shelf feeder offers the ultimate in closeup viewing and photography. I say "shelf," but several makes of commercial window feeders exploit windows to the ultimate in other ways.

One commercial model mounts directly onto the glass with suction cups. The birds are about as close as you can get and still be outside. But I hear that the suction cups lose their grip and the feeders tend to fall off, usually when they're being filled. I should imagine that the loss of vacuum in the little cups would be aggravated by our severe cold.

Another idea, the ultimate attempt at cozy intimacy, is a plexiglass box that is installed, like an air conditioner, into the window frame. The outside end is open, the rest of it, in effect, extends a bit of the outdoors into your home. The room-side surface is coated with reflecting film to dim the birds' view of the occupants. A neat hinged door opens on the inside for easy access. One could construct a version of this with a suitably sized aquarium.

Whether commercial or home-crafted, for our winters one should use some accessories for this alcove-in-a-window idea. I would make a snug-fitting panel of rigid foam to close the open side at nights. When I wasn't actually watching the birds, I'd cover the feeder with a foam box fitting over it from the inside. Without these modifications, our infamous wind chills would turn this novel feeder into a chronic heat hemorrhage. There might also be the problem of condensation, excessive frost accumulation, and dripping. The measures suggested later in this chapter under "Window Management" could be helpful.

Shelf Control   For most of us, attaching a simple shelf to the outside of the windowsill is quite sufficient. For a small shelf, bracing and bracketing are easy problems since seeds and birds don't weigh much. The bigger the shelf gets, the sturdier the supports will have to be. And any shelf should be anchored solidly enough to allow for vigorous action when you have to scrape or chop away ice and crusted snow. Whatever the size, I leave 1 in (2.5 cm) of space between the glass and the near side of the shelf so that snow and seeds won't collect there and form an icy crust that is messy looking and awkward to chip away.

If the platform is close enough to the ground for cats to leap up to it, i.e., 6 ft (1.8 m) or less, staple a fringe of woven wire around the three outside edges before you install it. If stucco or chicken wire is aesthetically displeasing to you, buy the decorative wire border trim that garden shops sell.

Simple Window Shelf *The anti-cat screen is important here*

The shelf must have a rim about 1 in (2.5 cm) high around all the edges; otherwise the wind and the birds will waste most of the seeds. It will be much easier to sweep snow and seed leftovers off the shelf if you leave the outside corners open by a couple of inches or more. And when you make your plans, allow for a moderate slope to the outward edge so that rainwater and melting snow will run off through the corner openings.

Baffled   For either tables or shelves in exposed places, you'll lose a lot less seed, and make it better for the birds, if you contrive to divert the force of the wind. If the problem is really serious, you can set up a large baffle upwind, separate from the feeder. I have quite effectively used a long, heavy table propped up on one end against the house wall. I nail the top edge of the table to a slat screwed to the wall (this is at the back of the house), and there it remains all winter, secure against the roughest gales. A sheet of plywood, sufficiently well braced to the house, a tree, or some other sturdy anchor point, could also be used as an effective baffle.

The feeder can be partially self-protecting with higher sides on the upwind edges. How high? The amount of downwind shelter afforded by a horizontal wall is proportional to its height. A four-inch-high wall would provide sufficient shelter for a shelf one foot square, but would be less than adequate for one four feet square.

You want protection, but you don't want to go overboard and create a deep, enclosed box. Birds feel trapped in constricted spaces where vision and escape are cut off. Leaving one side with just its low rim helps dispel that claustrophobia. Even for a single side, the higher it is the more the birds will constantly startle each other as arrivals abruptly flutter onto it from the blind side. Your own sense of proportion, observation of the behavior of the birds themselves, and the action of the wind will ultimately be your best guide.

The measurements of the actual shelf are matters for your own taste and ambition to play with. Most are ultimately governed by the size of the window. And bear in mind that whisking snow off and chipping crusted ice away are chores directly proportional to the size of the feeder.

Finish and color   When all these heavy matters have been pondered through to a conclusion, and the sawing and nailing are done, you might want to paint your creation. I favor a finish rather than leaving the wood bare, even though this is less "natural." My choice is more practical than decorative; with a coat of good quality paint the smoother surfaces are easier to clean, water runs off them more readily, and ice doesn't bond to a smooth paint finish nearly as tenaciously as to the exposed fibers of bare wood.

For the feeding surface of the shelf I pick light colors that absorb less of the sun's radiation, and hence are slower to melt accumulated snow into what will later freeze into a thick crust of ice. Black seeds also tend to show up better on a light base.

Photogenic Feeders   While you're thinking paint, you might consider what tones would complement color photography, particularly if there are raised sides on the edges of your feeder. Bright ones will reflect light and have to be allowed for on your exposure meter readings. Depending on the angle of sunlight, they will provide fill-in lighting to soften the hard shadows. They will also enter into the composition of your photographs, adding or detracting from them with their shape, texture, and color.

These are things you might not notice in the excitement of fiddling with your camera to get that super closeup of a beautiful bird before it takes off. But there is nothing more annoying, when you get your slides back, than discovering that a scrappy-looking or off-color slab of plywood sticks out like a sore thumb in all of them.

Window Management

The charm of a window feeder—the closeness of the birds—can turn into its chief disadvantage under some circumstances. If there is a lot of activity inside the room, the birds might be constantly startled away. Some species are more flighty than others, while some individuals seem to quickly grow accustomed to the activity inside and ignore it altogether.

If there are drapes or venetian blinds on the window, leaving them partially closed for the first few days that a feeder is in use and then gradually opening them will enable the birds to get used to the signs of movement inside. It helps, as you move about or draw closer for a better look, if you are wearing neutral-colored or dark clothing.

For my own feeder window I installed a temporary curtain of dark netting across the lower half—*dark* net, because the lighter it is the more difficult it is to see through, especially with the sun shining on it. Black netting obstructs the birds' view of the room, which during most days will be darker than the outdoors, and it allows you a somewhat hazy view of them. When I want a clearer look I clip the bottom of my screen to the curtain rod. For pictures from concealment I cut several strategically placed vertical holes just big enough to poke the camera lens through.

Unless you enjoy the paramilitary association of camouflage netting, it hasn't as good see-through qualities as black.

Solar Films   A partially mirrored or tinted effect can be added to window glass with a thin sheet of reflective or tinted mylar film, the same stuff used for office building and vehicle windows. Accordingly, it is available from glass-specialty dealers or auto-accessory shops. In the event you're willing to follow directions, it can be applied by the do-it-yourself method. It goes on the inside.

You should be aware that the silvered film, which imparts a semi-mirrored effect, could precipitate window collisions in some locations. Try it, and if this is a problem, see the section on "Window Pain" in chapter 4. The only reaction from my birds that a newly installed film prompted was in a chickadee that challenged its own reflection a few times before dismissing it as no threat. Other than this minor reaction, there have been no complications and I find that during full daylight, with my study lights on, I can move about on my side of the window without alarming those on the other side.

Both the tint and mirroring will cut down on the amount of light passing through the glass, and the tint will slightly affect the color values of photos taken through it. There is also some loss of clarity, but this isn't a critical handicap for the super closeups you can get with good telephoto lenses and the close proximity of your subjects at window feeders.

Frost and Ice   Frost on the inside of the glass can be a problem, particularly in kitchens or rooms close to the bathroom. Scraping at frost or wiping away vapor is a waste of time and frightens away the birds. I have a frost shield installed on the inside of one window at the cottage. This works well for mild conditions. But on really cold days if we're doing a lot of cooking it will frost over. Another of its failings is that it distorts light so much I can't take acceptably clear pictures through it.

One alternative is a fan. It can be quite small, and it needn't have a built-in heater. All it needs to do is move enough warm room air past the glass and the frost will disappear very rapidly. On severely cold days it will begin to re-form soon after you turn the fan off.

At full speed the whirling blades are invisible to the birds. But when you turn it off so you won't stick your elbow into it while preoccupied with a camera, remember that in the last couple of revolutions the flash of the slowly rotating blades could scare your subjects. My fans have pliable plastic blades that won't harm straying fingers or inquisitive noses.

Hanging Feeders

It's possible to suspend a shelf, with a hopper and roof, from some overhead point and let it swing in the breeze. But most hanging feeders are compact, self-enclosed, and act best as satellites to larger feeders. Hanging feeders make it easy to diversify with special feeds and to cater to smaller species. They can also be the cheapest and easiest to contruct.

The commercial manufacture of hanging feeders lends itself to the whims of the plastic molder's craft. They are marketed in globe, hemisphere, toadstool, space station, and animal shapes. Some no doubt appeal to the birds. Many, however, seem to have been crafted to catch the eye of buyers who know nothing of feeding birds but know "cute" when they see it. Some of the resulting baubles are fit to hang nowhere but on Christmas trees.

Classic Clorox   Consider the homemade end of tacky, the classic bleach bottle. Numberless backyard *improvisarios* have rescued them in the nick of time from the garbage, hacked holes in their sides, charged them with seeds, and hung them by the neck from a tree limb for the winter. Their children have carted them off to school science fairs as proud evidence of their parents' inventive ingenuity.

Of equal honor are empty cardboard milk cartons.

Deserving of their historic place as the bleach bottle and milk carton are, I have nevertheless abandoned both in favor of the larger and more  conveniently squared-off shape of the one-gallon windshield washer fluid jug. The accompanying diagram shows how to use the flap of plastic as a little roof over the cut-out hole, and to attach the cord through a hole in the cap. The handle (not shown) is ever so convenient when you pour the seeds in through the holes.

Some writers recommend putting in little perches just below the holes. But for this kind where the birds go inside to pick up seeds, I found that the only ones seeming to appreciate perches were House Sparrows. If the holes are around 2 or 3 in wide by 3 in high (7 by 8 cm), the small birds have no difficulty getting in. I wasn't surprised to see that the acrobatic chickadees took only a pass or two to get the knack of managing the relatively small hole and slippery plastic rim. With a bit more practice they could fly right in. What did surprise me was that nuthatches, redpolls, Purple Finches, and goldfinches also quickly mastered the trick.

Windshield Washer Jug
Note that the holes are cut high on the sides to max-imize carrying capacity

So did the squirrels, by sliding down the string. To satisfy their gnawing urge for improvements they enlarged my neat little doors to gaping, ragged holes, chewed away the clever little flaps, and cut the string holding them up. Then somebody learned to cut the main cord and collect the seeds on the ground. When I substituted a length of wire, they cut the branch. None of this bothers me particularly; the source of free bottles is infinite, the string is discarded baler twine, and the wire old coat hangers. It takes about five minutes to make a new one.

Thistle Feeders   There are a number of commercial hanging feeders that are basically a cylinder with a number of small feeding ports in the side. Inside baffles over each one allow the birds to pick out seeds but control flow. The birds don't go inside, and since the slippery plastic sides don't allow them to cling, there are little perches below each hole. The cap at the top functions as both a roof and filler hole.

As a group these are often referred to as "thistle" feeders because that's the feed they are often used for. Thistle, or niger, seed is much prized by some birds but rather expensive for the average station operator to shovel out in bulk on a come-one-come-all basis. Since the small, smooth seeds dispense well in tube feeders, and can be extracted only one or two at a time from each hole, feed and feeder are a nice combination for the person wanting to cater to the smaller birds on a somewhat selective basis. While the siskins and goldfinches are on the perches, daintily extracting the costly imports from their little hideaways, the heavy eaters like Evening Grosbeaks, Blue Jays, and Purple Finches are elbowing each other over less expensive fodder at the communal table or shelf.

Canary seed and millet work equally well in these tube feeders. Depending on the length and diameter of the cylinder, they can hold quite a lot of seed and don't need constant filling. The top ports run out first, of course, but the feeder isn't empty until the lowest one is exhausted. Many of the commercial varieties are made of clear plastic so the level of seeds can be easily seen.

Keep in mind that squirrels, if they can reach hanging feeders (and in all but rare situations they can), won't be content with licking up little seeds one at a time through the dinky little holes. If the material is gnawable, and the ports aren't reinforced with metal, they'll chew holes in it to suit themselves and ruin a feeder that is expensive to buy or time-consuming to make. Retrofitting holes with metal is a fussy and awkward bit of frustration. The provision of an easily-accessible alternate supply of seeds is the simplest way of trying to beguile squirrels into leaving the hanging feeders alone. But if you have no faith in this ploy, make your thistle feeders out of galvanized stove or drain pipes. In one important respect they are much easier to make, since the baffles and the holes can be made by making horizontal cuts with a hacksaw in the side of the cylinder and pushing the top flaps inward.

If you're looking for the ultimate in quick and cheap thistle-style feeders, the plastic container comes to the rescue again. This time it's pop bottles; any size will suffice, but the 2-liter size is best. Make a one-port feeder by slicing a 3-in (8-cm) cut through the side of the bottle along the top of the plastic base. If you push in the wall of the bottle just above the cut it will pop back out again. You can make it stay in if you just pinch the plastic between thumb and finger at each corner just above the cut, making permanent creases. Punch or burn a hole through the cap, run a piece of string through with a stop-knot, and . . . voila! . . . a neat hanging feeder.

For birds new to this clever device, just fill it and set it on the ground or feeder shelf until they discover it, then hang it up. A strip of fabric tape stuck to the lip of the port gives the birds a better grip. I'm quite happy with the one-hole model, but you can make a multi-port feeder by slicing more holes, as in the accompanying diagram. And your fertile imagination has no doubt already come up

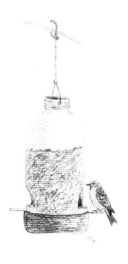

An ordinary plastic pop bottle can be made quickly into a tube feeder

with the idea of cutting off the top of another pop bottle to use as a custom-sized filler funnel, so I needn't mention this.

This type of feeder is the ultimate in free-swinging, gyrating instability, even in a light breeze. It's amusing to watch how quickly the birds master their timing, however, and dock with the moving lip with off-hand precision. Many authors of bird-feeding books reassure their readers that such an unstable feeder is not to the liking of House Sparrows. My sparrows might not *like* them, but they damn well learned how to get used to them! This past winter they lined up to use my pop-bottle feeders, even with shelf feeders handy. They just persisted until they had their docking technique down pat.

Suet Dispensers

Suet can be dispensed in any way, including leaving chunks of it on a table or shelf. There are several good reasons for not doing this, the law of supply and demand being one. If there are crows, ravens, or raccoons around, your place could become a bulk station supplying suet for miles around. Another is economy and control, and the easiest way of achieving these virtues is to put your suet into a net bag and hang it well up.

Mesh Bag Suet Holder *A good way to recycle onion bags*

What could be handier and cheaper than the plastic net bags that onions or peanuts are sold in? The chunks are tucked in, the neck tied to a hank of cord, and the lot looped onto a tree branch or a hook on some overhead structure where the birds, but not roving mutts, can reach it. The birds that love suet—all the woodpeckers, chickadees, nuthatches, and jays and their relatives—have no trouble clinging to the bag while they peck fragments of suet from between the strands of netting.

The netting is strong enough to prevent the jays from chopping off big chunks and carting it off wholesale, which they'll do if given the chance. As the suet is eaten, the bag collapses around it and the remnants remain available until there's nothing left but strands of stringy tissue.

A supposed hazard of the onion-bag feeder that one might hear occasionally is that birds can entangle their claws in the netting and die struggling to free themselves. It's possible, but I've only heard speculation on this; none of my contacts, nor my own experience, backs it up.

The major shortcoming of the onion bag is that there is a limit to the amount of bulk you can cram into it, and if you have crows or ravens to contend with, they'll rip it apart and clean you out in no time. In that case, the answer is wire mesh, the armored equivalent of the plastic net. As with most classes of feeders, you can buy commercial suet cages, generally made of wire, often coated with latex.

If you wish to make your own, the raw material that I have found most useful is hardware cloth with either quarter-inch or half-inch mesh. Respectively, it's called "4×4" and "2×2" in the trade, which means four squares or two squares per inch. In spite of the name, the "cloth" is actually made of good stiff wire soldered together at the joins. It can be bought off a roll at some building- or hardware-supply retailers; you might have to phone around a bit.

Match Size to Demand   With a pair of tinsnips you can cut your hardware cloth to conform to an imaginative array of dispensers. Size depends on the anticipated use. In the city, I feed at most only 2 to 4 lb (1 or 2 kg) of suet during most winters, but in the country that amount would last only a few days.

In town, therefore, I have a neat little cage that measures about 6 in (15 cm) square by 3 in (8 cm) deep. It is "2×2" mesh on four sides. Only the back, a solid 1-ft (30-cm) piece of rough 1×6 in (2.5×15 cm) and the lid, a piece of scrap plywood, are made of wood. It is tacked to the side of the house which, since it is made of logs, makes such add-ons easy. Whether it's the solid feel of the cage, or the bigger mesh, the chickadees, Downy Woodpeckers, and nuthatches use the cage much more than the onion bag hanging from the lean-to roof over my window shelf feeder.

In the country I have built a much larger feeder based on a 3-ft slab of 2×6 in (5×15 cm) plank. The screen is cut to form a semicircular cage against the wood, large at the top, narrowing down to a very close fit at the bottom, like a very long, narrow funnel. This is to give the birds continued access to the suet. As they peck it away it tends to slide down into the constricted bottom of the cage where they can still reach it through the mesh.

This feeder holds about 9 lb (4 kg) of suet, and it is gone in two weeks thanks to the magpies, a family of Blue Jays, a large clan of chickadees, several Hairy and Downy woodpeckers, and at least one pair of White-breasted Nuthatches. I can't use onion bags any more because the magpies tear them apart.

For the next time the urge to be handy comes over me, I have a plan to devise a box or tube suet feeder with access through wire mesh only at the bottom. This will be no inconvenience to the woodpeckers, nuthatches, and

Heavy-duty Suet Feeder *If you tack a small shelf to the bottom it will catch fall-out, but give the magpies a place to stand*

chickadees, since they are just as happy clinging upside down as rightside up when they eat. But it will put a crimp in the Blue Jays' access, and (I hope) shut out the magpies entirely.

If you want to coat wire, I have already referred to liquid latex in the previous chapter under the "Suet" subhead. It comes in ordinary and aerosol cans. It would make snaggly wire, or any metal, more comfortable to handle in cold weather. As a safety factor for birds it is unnecessary in my view. Northern birds have to deal with superchilled ice in various forms, which will also do an instant freeze-on if touched with something damp.

Hoppers

It is probably to our poultry-raising forebears that we owe the invention of the hopper, or "self-feeder." This is merely a storage container with a hole near the bottom opening over a tray or trough. The hole is constructed so that the feed trickles out only as fast as it is eaten. The hopper protects the reserve of feed from the weather, and from the animals themselves, and saves the bother of having to attend them at every feeding time. Clever, those ancestors!

What the hopper does for those who feed wild birds is ensure a reserve of feed if they can't be on hand to dish it out every day. It helps them observe the rule of keeping up the critical supply of feed to birds that have become dependent on it.

Most commercially built feeders, and the plans for homemade ones, incorporate a hopper of some kind. Most will give the capacity of the hopper in volume. Given a choice between two models with similar features, I tend to pick the bigger.

Buckets and Bottles   The simplest hopper, and one that can be very useful in combination with a table or good-sized shelf, is merely a container filled with seeds and inverted over boards set so the rim sits snugly on them, except for spaces between them where the seeds can run out only as fast as they're eaten. With a larger container it takes a bit of nerve and practice to whap the open container upside down over the boards in just the right place and not spill seeds all over. Once that trick's been done, it's a good idea to put a rock or other weight on the container to hold it in place when the contents run low and no longer anchor it against the wind or pushy squirrels.

The size of the container can vary according to the area of the feeder; a big table could take a five-gallon bucket, a small shelf a two-quart juice can or plastic pop bottle. The latter would have to be wired or taped in place to a solid upright, with the hole a half inch above the shelf surface to let the seeds dribble out at just the right rate.

For filling bottles and other small-port receptacles, homemade funnels can be easily contrived. You can also buy scoops in the form of funnels with a gizmo that closes off the spout until you've got it into the hole.

Prevention being superior to cure, it is best to simply avoid the curse of the itty-bitty filler hole when either buying or building feeders. Not all designers are aware of the joys of playing thread-the-needle with a can, a funnel, and an awkward filler hole after dark in a wind that lowers the equivalent temperature to fifty below. You can, by the way, make a very good scoop/funnel, complete with convenient handle, by cutting the bottom 4 to 6 in (10 to 15 cm) off a one-gallon windshield washer fluid jug.

The Basic Bin   For hoppers built of wood the standard design is a small bin, the sides of which, viewed from the end, form a V. This shape simply means that most of the seeds will run out of the hole or slot at the bottom, and there won't be many left beyond reach when the supply runs out. Whatever its shape, the roof or part of it comes off or is fitted with a hinge for filling.

A bin like this can be an integral part of a feeder or can be added onto a table or shelf. If you have a big table catering to an enormous number of birds, a really large hopper will keep them supplied without too much waste and without your constant attention. It will also allow you to leave for a period of time without breaking the "once started, never stop" rule.

Roofs

A roof can be both a decorative and useful addition to a table or shelf feeder. Shingles, shakes, thatch, and other novel materials have been used to add that quaint touch. The benefit is, of course, the protection offered from snow and rain.

If you get a couple of inches of snow on the feeding surface, most birds will have a hard time getting down to the seeds. Woodpeckers, chickadees, and nuthatches haven't got the knack of burrowing yet. If someone doesn't sweep the snow off and replace the seeds, they will perch and peer in expectant befuddlement, not realizing that food is right beneath their feet. Redpolls will poke little holes in the snow, but the best burrowers around are the squirrels. They'll dig in and scatter enough seeds around to see everyone else through until you can clear the deck properly.

Recalling that birds are rather claustrophobic creatures, don't build the roof too low. For adequate weather protection, therefore, give it lots of overhang.

Maintenance Kit   I'm an advocate of roofs. They save work and waste, since clearing the deck off means sweeping away the seeds with the snow. I have a permanent shade over my window feeder. It doubles nicely as a passive solar control in the summer when the sun is high. But my shade doesn't keep wind-driven snow off the window shelf, so I am faced with the occasional task of sweeping it off. Being cheap, I hate to whisk the sunflower seeds onto the ground where most of them are trampled into the snow and wasted. Therefore, as well as a stiff-bristled little hand brush for whisking off the feeder, and a putty knife for chipping away crusty snow, droppings and (occasionally) frozen squirrel urine (keep your mouth shut as you hack away), I have a screen seive, the largest I could find.

All three hang in a neat row on the outside wall, beside the feeder. Come a snow problem, I mount my stubby ladder (remember it?) and sweep the snow and the seeds off the feeder through the open corners (remember them?) and into the waiting seive. With a bit of vigorous shaking and winnowing, the snow and smaller fragments are gone, and the seeds are replaced on the feeder. Voila!

I repeat the process until all the seeds are separated from their admixture of snow. Then I hang my tools back up in their neat row and retire, enormously satisfied that this little ritual would be the best-organized part of my daily routine, if I had one.

Shelters

A shelter, as meant here, is basically a winter birdhouse, except that it isn't used for nesting. Many of our birds, notably chickadees, titmice, nuthatches, woodpeckers, House Sparrows, and starlings use cavities of one sort or another both for nesting and as nighttime roosts. These are so important that some tree-hole nesters that do not excavate their own remain paired over the winter in order to maintain property rights to a territory that has the all-important, second-hand nesting/roosting hole.

Every winter I am told by puzzled bird feeders that they began putting out feed early, attracted a nice clientele of chickadees, nuthatches, and sparrows, but that with the first onset of cold weather and/or snow, the chickadees vanished. I have no pat answers to this problem, except to speculate that the reason may be that there were no suitable winter quarters close at hand, and that the chickadees may have moved to another part of their territory where there was a feeder close by a den tree.

If this notion is true, then it might be worthwhile to provide an artificial tree hole in the form of a box or a length of hollow tree trunk. Chickadees excavate their own holes, pecking the soft, punky wood from decayed branch sockets in dead or aging trees. Nuthatches may either do this or take over a vacated woodpecker hole. I have even had a Downy Woodpecker, a bird quite able to excavate a tree cavity, take up winter quarters in a bluebird house.

If you already have bluebird houses at hand, shelters can be made quickly by taking the fronts off, turning them upside-down so the holes are near the bottom, and tacking them on again. It would be helpful to put several pegs or some twigs in for roosts and to plug all holes and cracks other than the entrance. They should then be set up in trees, preferably conifers, dense hedges, or in some other natural growth that offers the best shelter from the wind.

The literature suggests that chickadees really feel better about clearing out their own quarters, so if you fill a bird house with sawdust that they can empty out, they'll be more likely to take your offering seriously. Titmice are apparently not so fussy.

Lacking a store of disused birdhouses, you can of course go to work and construct custom-made shelters. I refer you to the Appendix for specifics.

CHAPTER 4

The Downside

Feeding birds and other drop-ins should be a happily benevolent pastime. But anyone who elects to live close to animals of any kind invites possible aggravation. Animals do not come to our feeders to be cute and entertaining; they are there because it helps them survive. Therefore, they deal with us, our dwellings, and our handouts on *their* terms. Conflict of interests may arise, and if this gets out of control initial idealism can turn to indifference or resentment. At that point the unwitting birds and mammals can suffer hardship or death if their erstwhile benefactors stop feeding them or try to get rid of them.

Some parts of this chapter deal with sensitive subjects. Cats, for example, are beloved pets, but are thoroughly hated by some folks because they eat birds. And what should be done if you're faced with having to destroy an animal?

I'm not suggesting that "problem" animals are uniquely a bird-feeders' headache. People who wouldn't dream of throwing a seed to a bird still have to confront raccoons, squirrels, and cats. But those of us who feed birds adopt a special relationship to wildlife and in good conscience must deal with animal problems humanely and with the animals' interests, as well as our own, in mind. I therefore felt that people would appreciate a discussion that emphasized prevention but didn't mince words when it came to discussing cures.

No-limit Demands

One downside of feeding arises from the fact that all animals, the desirable and the not-so-desirable, are programmed to survive by taking maximum advantage of resources when they have the chance. Therefore they have no built-in limits to their demands on your hospitality. In human terms they may seem plain greedy.

Not that this isn't an easily managed appetite. The demands of the vast majority of species are easily met simply by ensuring that there is a continuing supply of the right kinds of feed, accessible in the right places. No matter how insatiable their appetites, a half-dozen chickadees, a nuthatch or two, and a family of jays are not going to strain your patience or your

39

budget. Their presence is not likely to be anything but a pleasure, their goings-on an amusing diversion.

That state of tranquil stability can change quickly if you are abruptly blessed with a big flock of Evening Grosbeaks. These happy wanderers have big appetites and love to gang up on your feeder in noisy scrambles. If you have a small feeder and elect to leave it at that, these cheerful birds will likely move on, possibly to someone who has a bigger table. From time to time a few may drop in as they do the rounds of neighborhood feeders.

But if you choose to play the major host by setting up a big table, you had better be ready to serve up a lot of seeds. It would be thoughtful as well to put up several hanging feeders to give your faithful little chickadees and nuthatches a chance if they are crowded off the main feeder by the jostling finches.

What you'll have is more of everything: more feeders to fill and keep clear of snow and droppings, more window washing if you have a window shelf, more uninvited cats, and more seed husks to clean up in spring. None of this is a problem if you feel you're still in control and that the rewards of having more birds to entertain and divert you more than offset the extra effort.

Some authors claim that sunflower husks are plant-growth inhibitors. I find that the grass under my feeders, whether I rake up or not, seems to thrive all right. But if you're concerned, rake them up, and don't add them to the compost heap.

Bird Problems

Window Pain   A real problem for many feeding station keepers is birds colliding with windows. If birds can see through the house, as they will if adjacent walls have large windows, they may attempt to fly through the transparent corner. Closing one set of drapes will correct this situation. In my view, however, the main cause of collisions is a deadly mirror effect; birds see their world reflected in the glass and attempt to fly into it. Pulling the drapes in this case will have no effect whatever.

Some windows, even large ones, rarely cause collisions; others, even small ones, are real killers. If you have one of these, and you feed birds, you are conscience-bound to immediately do what you can to minimize the casualties. The hastiest fix is to cut the reflecting effect of the glass by smearing or spraying the outside of it with something to create a visible film. This may look messy, but will give you time to devise something more satisfactory.

Paper Hawks   Among the touted correctives are silhouettes or cutouts of birds of prey that can be mounted on the glass. I have never tried these; some who have say they work, others say they are useless. I have also heard that sticking a round piece of bright red paper in the middle of the window, on the outside, will work. If one doesn't, maybe a scattering of them would.

The only sure method is to put some kind of obstruction between the birds and the glass. Nylon or twine fish net stretched over the outside will do; beware of nets so small-meshed and fine that birds might entangle themselves. A friend attached boards along the bottom and top of a problem window. In each, spaced about 3 in (8 cm) apart, were small nails. She strung grocery string back and forth between the boards, creating vertical lines, like the strings of a harp, over the entire window. This stopped the birds and was only a minor intrusion on her view.

Rescue and Recovery   Birds that stun themselves against windows should be picked up right away; some cats are very quick to connect the thump of bird on glass with an easy grab. Put the bird into a small box or paper bag, closed but with provision for air, and leave it in a quiet place. In a few moments you may hear it scrabbling about. Leave the box closed, take it outside, and give the convalescent a chance to fly. If nightfall comes while the bird is recovering, leave it alone until morning, then liberate it.

Most window rescues proceed in this way; the bird is stunned and badly shaken, but with time in a warm place, recovers. Injured birds unable to fly after a decent period of recovery might be nursed back to health if they can be persuaded to eat. Fruit- and seed-eaters are easy to provide for; a generous cage, water, and patience could have the desired effect.

Woodpeckers   Now and then woodpeckers proceed to drill holes in a building or to hammer on parts of it at dawn, for reasons that completely baffle and annoy the owner. All woodpeckers drill, and most drum, although the most enthusiastic drummers seem to be Downy and Hairy woodpeckers.

The drumming is a super-fast rapping on surfaces that resonate well. It is a courting ritual, the preliminaries beginning in late winter. Spoiling the drummer's access to his instrument can be done by draping it loosely with netting or some heavy fabric. Or you might muffle it with scraps of carpet. Putting up hardware cloth with spacers to keep it an inch clear of the surface may be sufficient foil. These deterrents can be tacked temporarily in place until the birds find other drums or the silly season ends. Sufferers who have simply persisted in scaring off the birds when they begin their drumming report that this works. As a diversion, one might put up a piece of thin plywood some distance from the house and hope that this will give the birds an alternative.

Another form of damage is drilling, in some cases a full-sized hole obviously intended as a nest. In a shed or outbuilding this may be acceptable, but it is not usually considered tolerable when done on a house. Again, scaring off the birds or covering the hole with metal or screen will eventually discourage them. What they really need is a nest tree, a dead-hearted aspen trunk, still fairly sound on the surface, 10 to 15 ft (3 to 5 m) high, 6 in (15 cm) in diameter at the top. Here, you might repeat an experiment conducted by Lawrence Kilham, medical scientist and amateur ornithologist of note. Unable to get to the woods one busy autumn, he collected a number of fallen tree trunks of various degrees of unsoundness and wired them upright to the posts in his backyard. To his delight, four Downy Woodpeckers soon called and began tapping up and down and around the new stubs. All eventually made roost holes.

It was apparently important that Dr. Kilham gave the downies a choice, so if you decide to repeat the experiment, don't be stingy with the imported "trees." And don't trim the branches off closely; some woodpeckers show a definite preference for locating holes under good-sized limbs.

Woodpecker drilling often has nothing to do with either sex or nesting, but consists of rows of punctures in plywood, cedar, or other wood siding. The birds are insect-hunting, probing into natural cavities or pre-existing insect tunnels in boards, or into gaps between the inner plies of plywood that resemble tunnels. They may actually be digging out flies, wasps, or tunneling insects that shelter in the gaps, gaining access through the edges of the plywood.

In some cases a good coat of paint abruptly stops the damage. If this doesn't fit in with the decorative scheme, however, a filler material of an unobtrusive color can be applied to any exposed ends of board or ply siding. This will effectively block both the insects' access points and the woodpeckers' reasons for poking holes.

A Gnawing Problem

Rats and Mice   Rodents of all kinds are enthusiastic about seeds, as any squirrel will be glad to demonstrate. But inadvertently attracting rats and mice is another matter. Hence, prevention, *strict* prevention, is the necessary course of action.

In the chapter on seeds I have stressed the importance of vermin-proof storage. The best vessels for me are metal garbage cans. Anything made of plastic can easily be chewed into by a determined rodent. Garbage cans with good, tight-fitting lids are also raccoon- and rain-proof and can be left outside.

In advance of each winter I do a patrol of the premises to check for burrows and gnawings. Tunnels under ground-level footings or slabs I doctor with a few mothballs and then fill with coarse crushed rock. I close off above-ground breaks or holes with sheet metal, a flattened tin can if the patch is out of sight or you're not proud, or both.

Having taken all reasonable measures to keep rodents from getting in where they don't belong, I set out small containers of rodent poison in crawl spaces and attics where it is securely out of reach of anything except a rodent that has dug or chewed its way in. I realize that this might include something cute, like a chipmunk, but I repeat that these lethal baits are set out *behind* my main perimeter of defenses; I have done all I can to keep them away from animals willing to stay on their side of the wall.

Before discussing this subject further, I should say that my system of preventive maintenance works; it has been several seasons since I have had problems with squirrels, and longer ago than I can easily recall when a mouse breached my outer perimeter of defenses. I cannot stress prevention enough, for the animals' sake as well as your own. But supposing . . .

Squirrels   It takes a dose of personal experience to appreciate what large rodents can do to a house from the inside, and how difficult it is to evict them once they're in. If squirrels are an example, the damage can be very upsetting, and there is also the nagging fear of their chewing through electrical wiring and starting a fire.

Sheeting over or boarding up entrance holes or stuffing them with steel wool laced with mothballs will simply result in more damage when the squirrel chews its way around them. Sooner or later most people come to the grim conclusion that there are only two possible solutions, death or deportation.

Poison (you never hear that word nowadays; one "controls" undesirable wildlife) may seem very severe. I am certainly not promoting its use, but if it's going to be considered as a means of ridding yourself of an unwelcome animal when other measures fail, then it should be handled knowingly. The only "rodenticide" available nowadays off the shelf is the anticoagulant first marketed as "warfarin." I have found that, although it is effective on rats and mice, it is of doubtful impact on squirrels. Firstly, it's usually grain-based, which is good mouse bait but not high on the squirrels' list of favorites. They'll be particularly uninterested if they've already stashed several thousand acorns in your belfry and you are laying on tasty sunflower seeds at the feeders. Secondly, even if they do take it, they appear to have to eat a great deal more of it to get a lethal dose.

One might try mixing peanut butter in with the poison. That mix must of course be kept strictly out of the way of pets and small children.

Cage Traps   But enough about deadly potions. Long ago I equipped myself with cage traps, one squirrel-sized. If you bait this with everything the squirrels seem to be eating, plus some peanut butter, and place it where they do most of their scurrying, you might make a catch. Be sure, of course, to check the trap at least a couple of times a day.

Now what? If you've caught a squirrel, particularly a red, it'll be battling frantically to get out. You owe it to the animal to make up your mind in advance what to do and to act promptly. First, cover the trap or put it into a box or dark garbage bag (leave the opening loose for air). This calms the captive down. Whatever your plans, first check the animal from underneath, particularly any time between March and the end of July. If it has a double row of swollen nipples, it is a nursing mother and you had better either apologize and turn her loose again or go in search of the nest and deal with the whole family. My own conscience would bid me turn it loose to finish its maternal duties rather than destroy a nestful of squirrel pups or be the agent of their death by starvation.

There is one slim hope of early solution to this particular dilemma. One spring some years ago I had a Red Squirrel nesting in a new workshop, and resolved to put up with the busy owner until I was sure there were no innocent dependants around. One afternoon I did a little bit of tinkering that involved hammering something into the wall of the shop near the nest. Within a half hour the mother squirrel was busy moving her brood. Gripping each pup by the skin of its belly, its body curled around her neck like a pink shrimp, she carried them to a hole in a nearby maple.

The lesson in this anecdote is that mothering squirrels may be very sensitive to unfamiliar disturbances, and the right kind of threatening din could cause them to relocate their litters to a quieter neighborhood.

Nonreturnables   If exile is an option it should be timed with sensitivity. Assuming no maternal complications, release time is between spring breakup and the end of September. This allows the deportee some chance of establishing itself and laying in a store of winter food. Later than this, its chances greatly diminish; dumping a squirrel into strange territory in winter is almost certainly condemning it to death by starvation and stress.

To ensure that your exile is nonreturnable, drive it well out into the country and liberate it near an extensive patch of likely-looking treed habitat. Taking squirrels a few blocks away, or even a couple of miles, probably means they will be back in your yard in a few hours.

If the time of year forbids conscionable relocation, and no other alternative is possible, the animal will have to be destroyed. In earlier years this was frequently accomplished by rigging a hose from the exhaust pipe of a car to a box with the animal in it and letting the car run for ten minutes or so. But the emission controls of today's cars render the exhaust gases less lethal and it takes an inhumanely long time.

Most people, given access to a veterinary clinic or a humane society center, would likely prefer to leave the "euthanizing" to the professionals. There is a fee, usually less if you take the carcass back and dispose of it.

However, if you must handle the unpleasant task yourself, my suggestion is to place the cage in a garbage bag with no punctures in it and spray in ether. It is easily available from automotive supply stores, in an aerosol can used for starting diesel motors in cold weather. Once the inside of the bag is thoroughly filled with the vapor (a couple of long bursts), seal it quickly with a twist-tie. The animal loses consciousness in a couple of minutes, sometimes almost immediately. Once it is down, repeat the process and then leave the bag sealed for a couple of hours.

Under no circumstances do this indoors. Ether is highly volatile and much more explosive than gasoline.

Rat Traps   The standard mouse, or "snap," trap is available in an oversized version for rats. When a mouse or rat is caught in a snap trap, it is usually stunned instantly and killed by the blow of the stiff wire bail. Theoretically, a rat trap should be big enough to kill Red Squirrels, since they are about the same size and conformation as rats.

However, they rarely work; one finds the trap sprung. The reason is that Red Squirrels, given enough maneuvering room, are too quick for the trap. They may get smashed on the head or the nose, but at the instant of contact are already recoiling and end up with an injury. For this reason, rat traps should not be used in an effort to trap Red Squirrels. As for grays, they are so much larger that I have doubts that a rat trap would do more than give an extremely painful blow to anything but a half-grown one.

Once rid of a problem squirrel, don't waste time before removing accessible nests and closing off all their access holes to the building. If you delay, you'll very likely find a replacement has moved in within a few days of the former resident's departure. As well as closing, sheeting, or screening over all holes, try to mask the scent of the previous squirrel. Put moth balls into the holes before closing them off, spray or wipe the area around the holes and the patch with something strong-smelling, or apply a fresh coat of paint.

Cats   Every autumn I get one or two stray cats around the house in the city. And at our country place, refugees from a cottage development a mile or so away show up about the time the leaves fall. How to tell a stray from a house pet? After the snow has been on the ground for a month in early winter, a cat's behavior and appearance are the giveaways. It can be seen on miserable days, rough-coated and humped-up in the cold, when house pets are comfortably indoors. A real stray will also tear into garbage bags and strew the contents around. It will pull down larger game, like rabbits. If you observe it carefully you will discover that it is living under or in a shed, a brush pile, or a heap of scrap lumber.

If you don't want to adopt it or feed it outdoors, ignoring it may be difficult. Aside from its preying on your birds, its deteriorating condition might be a sorry sight to watch. You may decide that a cage trap and either the vet clinic or the humane society are the best alternatives. You can of course put down a cat with ether, as described for squirrels.

Capturing such a cat is usually very easy; a bit of smelly grease or fish oil on a couple of paper towels will do for bait. Put the trap up off the ground, out of reach of skunks and the neighbor's beagle. A chagrined dog or raccoon can be released with no problems, but a skunk is another matter. They den up in the dead of winter, but in autumn or early spring they can be aprowl.

Frustrating the Felines   There is no way to make your premises or the birds cat-proof. But you *can* make it much more difficult for roving felines to prey on them at your feeders.

Here we are not talking hapless strays but well-fed pets hunting for sport rather than necessity. And since we're talking about peoples' cherished household pets, there is a definite limit to the kind of countermeasures you can take. But if you refer to the cat section of chapter 7, like me you may be convinced that it is worthwhile to take some time to cut down on cat predation around your feeders.

When assessing your bird-friendly setting, it helps to be able to think like a slinking cat with a greedy eye on your birds. As a cat, your objective would be to get as close as possible to a preoccupied bird, undetected, and to strike from cover. Waiting in ambush would achieve the same purpose. An experienced cat knows the value of patience and will crouch immobile for long periods in concealment. It obviously makes the hunting easier if there is a bush, scrap pile, or piece of yard furniture close to a feeder where birds, pursuing spilled seeds, habitually feed on the ground. In front of the hiding place there must be clear space for an unobstructed rush.

In setting up its ambush the cat may be unable to walk in under cover. This introduces a delay, but doesn't put the kibosh on the enterprise. The birds' initial alarm and flight at its approach will diminish if it crouches down and remains still, even if it's only partially concealed. As the minutes pass, some birds, more hungry perhaps, bolder, or just plain "bird-brained," will chance a quick flight to the feeders. When nothing happens, others follow, at first nervously, then with more confidence. Latecomers, seeing the busy activity, may not even notice the lurking danger.

Eventually, pinpointing a close-by target that is preoccupied with feeding and has its back turned, the cat makes its grab. Everything explodes as the birds burst away—all except one.

Futile Measures   Much as outraged bird lovers might fantasize about cat-bashing, setting booby-traps of the Sylvester-and-Tweety-Pie variety, or otherwise taking revenge, such plots are successful only in the imagination. Dashing outside, yelling "scat!", throwing things, or brandishing the garden hose spread only temporary alarm; the cats quickly learn contempt for such futile spluttering.

Escalating the conflict with traps and firearms is not only antisocial, dangerous, and potentially inhumane, it is expressly forbidden under the statutes of most towns and cities. Intense provocation notwithstanding, I say again we *are* talking about pets.

Ownership of a spirited dog of sufficient size to be intimidating is one way of keeping the environs clear of cats. A dog, even a boisterous one, doesn't seem to bother birds much once they realize it is not a potentially dangerous predator. However, a dog doesn't fit in with everyone's household lifestyle.

My own answer could be called Passive Obstruction. It is nonviolent, calls for a minimum of time and cash, and needs no tending. Done with sufficient ingenuity it can create a safe haven for birds in which all but the suicidally foolhardy can happily feed and flaunt themselves before the cats. It allows cat-owning bird lovers to liberate their pets in their own yards without worrying about fatal conflicts of interest around the feeders.

Over the Wire   First of all, get rid of any obvious ambush points that can be conveniently cleared away. For those that can't, the key is in the judicious placement of wire, using the same principle that governs the use of barbed wire entanglements by the military, which is to impede movement at key points.

This simply means putting up a wire screen around places of concealment and around the edges of shelf feeders. Let the cat lash its tail and drool under the junipers all it wants; a low perimeter of stucco or chicken wire around the bush totally robs it of a clear rush. The birds can of course clearly see through the wire, and if the cat has to break cover first and then jump over the wire at the start of its rush, they will have that split-second of warning they need to get away. The construction requirements are simple. The wire barrier need be only 18 to 24 in (45 to 60 cm) high, and it can be tacked or stapled at the ends to a couple of stakes driven into the ground or packed snow. Curving the wire around the hideout gives it more stability and minimizes the need for props.

Similarly, if you have a feeding shelf close to a hideout that you can't eliminate for some reason or other, like not wanting to dynamite the garage, you can frustrate the grab-over-the-edge business by installing a fringe of wire that sticks out around the sides of the shelf for 8 to 10 in (20 to 25 cm).

For those in whom cats arouse instant hostility, the level of cat frustration the wire treatment must generate should satisfy any reasonable thirst for vengeance and give harmless reign to the streak of diabolical genius latent in the psyche of even the most benign of bird lovers.

The most suitable, and least expensive, wire for my purposes has proven to be stucco wire. It comes in 4- and 4.5-ft (1.2- and 1.4-m) widths, with a 2-in- (5-cm-)square mesh, and you can buy it off the roll from building-supply retailers. It can be snipped to the desired shape with wire cutters or sturdy tinsnips. It stands up more stiffly than chicken wire (poultry screen), and thus doesn't need to be put in a frame or propped up. It is much neater than chicken wire; deployed around the ornamentals at the front of your house it tends less to give the place the look of an unfinished rabbit hutch.

A further advantage of stucco wire is that small birds can flit through it easily, larger ones like Blue Jays and doves can squeeze through it, and crows and pigeons are excluded.

CHAPTER 5

Those Fascinating Creatures

Very quickly, as you observe birds and read about them, you become aware that they are endowed with physical capabilities that go beyond the humble capacities of ourselves and indeed of most other mammals of our acquaintance. From the centrally heated side of our windows we see tiny birds that can feed and fly and move about on their side of the glass, where it's forty below, and in bare feet, even! We hear of pilots spotting geese, vultures, and other large birds cruising or soaring along at altitudes three times higher than the point where humans require supplementary oxygen.

And yet, when you pick up a bird or hit one with the windshield of your car, it seems vulnerably delicate, light, and fragile. Obviously, this is a very special kind of body. And since we're dealing with its ability to withstand our winters, it is appropriate to do a brief review of how it accomplishes this.

Physiology

Humans have envied the birds ever since we developed the wit to ponder the relative merits of walking and flying. Free, powered flight is the ultimate form of transportation, afloat in the cushion of air, free of the rough, entangling path and the pounding burden of gravity.

But there is a catch—indeed, several of them. The laws of physics limit your weight to a maximum of around forty-four pounds (twenty kilograms), found in the Great Bustard of Europe and Asia. On this continent the flying heavyweight is the Trumpeter Swan. Any heavier than these and you walk. Flying is also extremely expensive of energy, which in turn requires a high relative intake of both food and oxygen.

To minimize the penalties of flight, birds evolved eons ago for a combination of strength and lightness, beginning with the skeleton. The bird air frame is rigid, the backbone fused along most of its length into one member, the ribs braced against each other, the sternum a huge keel set in a supporting hull of light bone. The wing and leg bones are hollow, light, and supported inside by a latticework of supporting struts. They are part of the bird's respiratory system.

Supercharger Lungs   A bird's lungs are small, relative to those of comparably sized mammals. But they have phenomenal throughput, being connected to a system of air sacs and the hollow limb bones that permit a flow of air that is largely one-way. When a bird breathes under effort, each puff clears almost all the stale air out of the lungs. When a mammal gasps for breath, a certain percentage of each exhalation is left behind. In terms of performance, this means that birds can exert the considerable effort of flight, even at high altitudes, and maintain it, as they do in migration, for long periods.

A vivid demonstration of the relative respiratory ability of mammals and birds is cited in *Birds of Britain and Europe*. In the experiment, sparrows and mice were placed in a chamber where the air pressure was equivalent to that atop Mount Everest. The birds went on with their activities apparently unperturbed, while the mice were severely distressed and could only grope and stagger about.

To complement the capacity of the lungs, birds' hearts are relatively much larger than are those of mammals of similar size. And they operate at high-performance levels; even at rest a chickadee's heart beats four hundred times a minute, double that when it is active.

High Temperature   Metabolic processes work faster at higher temperatures, and birds have higher normal body temperatures than do mammals. As a farm lad, when farms were still a menagerie of various animals, I knew that hens, for a then-mysterious reason, could survive deep wounds that would have killed other animals from infection. The reason was that mammal-adapted bacteria can't survive in the birds' high body temperature, which hovers around 104°F (40°C) for a bird at rest. This is very close to the critical upper limit; above this, protein enzymes become unstable and begin to break down, and essential body functions go awry.

Very obviously, feathers are critical to the maintenance of stable body temperatures in our wintering birds. They are a double defense; the smooth, slick contour feathers, arranged shingle-fashion, are an efficient wind barrier. Beneath them lies a layer of insulating down, one of nature's most efficient ways of enclosing a small body in an envelope of warm air.

Fuel   Gathering the food to fuel this high-temperature, high-speed body is made possible by the very equipment that burns most of it, the wings. Birds have access to insects, their eggs, and their pupae in places few mammals can reach. This includes the outermost extremities of trees as well as their woody hearts; chickadees forage among the smallest twigs and branches of trees, woodpeckers drill beneath the bark. In the chickadees' case the pressure to be productive is intense; it is estimated that in winter their cousins, the titmice, must find a food item on the average of every two or three seconds in order to survive.

Winter Survival

A few winters ago in mid-February I was watching a White-throated Sparrow on my window feeder. White-throats are very unusual winter holdovers at my latitude, so I had been paying particularly close attention to him during the several weeks since his first appearance. He seemed to be dizzy; whenever he attempted to lift one foot into the warmth of his belly feathers, he teetered sideways drunkenly. It would have been a mildly comical performance, except on that bitterly cold day he was in the last throes of starvation. Too weak to feed, he finally fluttered away. I never saw him again.

Every winter, birds that normally migrate are either forced or choose to stick around. With luck—a combination of a mild winter, very good shelter, and an unusual source of plentiful food—holdovers might survive. But considering the behavioral and physiological adaptations that allow nonmigrants to live through the rigors of a subarctic winter, my unfortunate white-throat was undoubtedly more the rule than the exception.

Cold Tolerance   The most obvious reaction of birds to severe cold is to fluff up their body plumage and stay out of the wind. They may momentarily stand on one leg, pulling the other up into their belly feathers. Ground feeders like juncos and redpolls crouch low, from time to time squatting down to cover their legs and feet.

Low temperature of itself is a secondary problem, since birds are already equipped to fly about in frigid air, as they must do for extended stretches at high altitudes during migration. Winter-acclimatized goldfinches, Pine Siskins, and Purple Finches experimentally subjected to sustained temperatures of $-94°F$ ($-70°C$) went on with their usual activities apparently little stressed by the numbing cold. They maintained normal body temperature and function as long as they had sufficient food to maintain a critical level of body fat.

All who feed birds have no doubt marveled at why the wire-thin little legs and feet of small birds don't instantly freeze on bitter winter days when the mercury is at twenty below or lower. Part of the answer lies in the circulatory system feeding the legs. The arteries and veins pass close to each other in a heat-exchange network of capillaries where incoming veinous blood is warmed and outgoing arterial blood cooled. The result is that the legs and feet are maintained at just above freezing and very little heat is lost from them. The oily tissues of the fleshless feet and legs retain little residual moisture and resist freezing. Unlike human fingers, rendered uselessly numb when the nerves cannot function at even moderately lowered temperatures, the nerves in birds' feet retain their function at near-freezing temperatures.

Hoarding   For most birds the supply of winter food and, even more crucially, the amount of daylight in which to search for it are severely restricted compared to summer conditions. To use an extreme example, in arctic Fairbanks, Alaska, midwinter daylight can be as short as three and a quarter hours, and temperatures during the long nights regularly drop to forty below or lower. And yet Boreal Chickadees survive these conditions, with or without the help of Fairbanks bird feeders. In these conditions hoarding could be a crucial factor. At feeding stations many wintering birds will store surplus food.

Once they have stoked up, chickadees and nuthatches will spend much of every short winter day diligently stashing sunflower seeds, to the end that, by springtime, each probably has enough hidden away to feed at least twenty of its kind. Complementing the hoarding impulse is a good memory; chickadees have shown an accurate recall interval of up to eight months. Given unrestricted access to suet, crows, jays, and magpies usually start hauling away chunks of it, in great haste, before eating. They will keep at it until the supply is exhausted, a habit that has taught bird benefactors to offer suet in protective cages that limit the take to bite-sized pieces.

Cuddling Up   Further behavioral adaptations help solve the problem of the long, cold, foodless nights. Woodpeckers roost in tree holes excavated for the purpose. Chickadees habitually sleep together in holes, nuthatches less frequently, but twenty-nine White-breasted Nuthatches have been found in one tree cavity and twenty or more Brown Creepers in close huddles beneath slabs of loose bark. Redpolls may avail themselves of mouse holes or dig their own cavities in the snow.

Among House Sparrows, the more fortunate get into buildings, signs, and light fixtures with a built-in source of heat, while the less privileged wedge themselves into holes and crannies, perhaps utilizing last summer's nest for additional insulation. Ravens, sometimes in large numbers, roost in dense conifers.

Hibernation, which turns winter into one long night of deep torpor, was unconfirmed in birds until a Poor-will (*Phalaenoptilus nuttalli*) was found dormant in a rock crevice in the Colorado Desert of California in 1946. Others have since been discovered dormant, with body temperatures down from normal 106°F (41°C) to 64°F (17°C). Less pronounced torpor occurs in swifts, swallows, and hummingbirds, enabling them to cut energy expenditure during periods of food shortage.

The point of this example is that it is therefore not entirely surprising to discover that during cold winter nights roosting chickadees become torporous. Their body temperature drops by 13°F (7°C), and their respiration falls from ninety-five to sixty-five breaths per minute.

Big is Best   The smaller a creature is, the greater is its surface area relative to body mass, and the greater its problem of retaining heat. We demonstrate this ourselves when slim appendages like ears and fingers chill, even freeze, although the rest of the body is comfortably warm. Within warm-blooded species, northern animals tend to be larger-bodied and have smaller appendages than their southern counterparts. Confirming what has been codified as Bergmann's rule, the Hairy Woodpeckers of Alaska weigh over 4.2 oz (120 g), those of the subtropics 1.4 oz (40 g).

Over a minimum body size, and given adequate reserves of fat, sitting still may be more efficient than foraging. When a domestic hen simply stands up from resting, its energy consumption increases by 40 to 50 percent. In his *Watching Birds*, Roger Pasquier relates perhaps the most marked manifestation of the sit-and-save strategy short of outright hibernation: In Finland, Ringneck Pheasants are reported to roost in trees, immobile and insensitive to disturbance, for forty or more days at a stretch. This may not be as farfetched as it first appears; captive Golden Pheasants routinely brood their eggs for twenty-two days, taking no food or water and moving very little. Chickadees, too, may opt for the sit-and-save strategy, waiting out storms and extreme cold in their roosts rather than fighting a losing battle in which the energy costs of foraging exceed the returns.

All-important Fat   The key to cutting losses in this manner, and indeed to overall winter well-being, is an all-important reserve of body fat. The high-performance metabolism of birds enables them to alternately lay on, and burn off, significant percentages of their body weight in fat with each twenty-four-hour cycle. A House Sparrow going to roost may weigh .9 oz (25 g); 8 percent of this is fat that it can metabolize overnight to maintain itself.

Chickadees will raise their daily fat deposits by from 4 to 7 percent of their body weight of .35 to .42 oz (10 to 12 g) on a natural diet of dormant insects and weed seeds, up to 11.8 percent on black sunflower seeds. Under usual Upper Midwest winter conditions most of this store of fat will be depleted by morning, and the birds must quickly replenish it. This accounts for the flurry of intense dawn feeding familiar to station proprietors. There is a similar last-minute stoking-up at dusk.

The Midnight Snack   Our seed-eating winter finches have a supplementary method of surviving the night's long fast. They possess an esophageal diverticulum which, like the analogous chicken's crop, is used to store hastily gathered seeds. Redpolls will collect a load of birch seeds, then retire to a sheltered hideaway to regurgitate and husk the seeds. At night these and other finches go to roost with what amounts to a packed lunch, supplementing their fat reserves by snacking on their stored seeds.

Midwinter Nesting

A book on wintering birds may seem a strange place to find mention of nests at all. Actually, for those interested in birds in general, an appreciation of nests is a helpful avenue to understanding an important aspect of their adaptive strategies. And winter is a good time to take inventory of all those constructed above the snow line. Bare-stemmed weeds, bushes, and trees reveal nests otherwise concealed in summer by foliage. The nests themselves often carry tell-tale caps of snow that show up against the backdrop of frozen vegetation like scoops of ice cream. One can clip and collect these abandoned lodgings with a clear conscience because the builders have no further use for them.

Another aspect of nests—winter roosts—can also enrich one's appreciation for the adaptability of wintering species. Chickadees, nuthatches, and Downy and Hairy woodpeckers roost in tree holes. Tracking them to their nighttime bivouacs could be an entirely defensible way of postponing some tedious winter chore in favor of the pursuit of enlightenment.

One of the marvels of the winter bird world is the ability of crossbills and Gray Jays to nest in the harshest conditions. Crossbills have been found nesting every month of the year, the determinant being a supply of conifer seeds. Their winter nests are noticeably more bulky and well insulated than those of summer, the chinks between the fibers of the lining filled with punky powdered wood. Thus, the temperature under a brooding female can be as much as 100°F (60°C) warmer than the air temperature. For the first week the female broods the young, the male supplying food, a creamy soup of regurgitated seeds. Thereafter, both parents feed. The young, exposed to the cold, chill and grow torporous but revive quickly when the female resumes brooding.

Gray Jays commence nesting in late February or early March. The nest is invariably in a dense conifer of middling size located in a site exposed to the south and east. Most nests are precisely oriented where the strongest rays of the late winter sun will strike them. In preparation for their family, both birds will have stored food in caches well above ground where it won't be buried in the snow. It is suspected that they also store nesting materials. The food will be globbed together into balls by the birds' copious supply of sticky saliva, a substance that freezes but does not form a solid lump of ice.

I was reminded in a personal communication from C. Stuart Houston of Saskatoon, Saskatchewan, of a memorable photo in an early edition of the *Canadian Field Naturalist* that gave "double brooding" a double meaning. This picture showed a male Gray Jay sitting on top of his mate in their nest, presumably to help her keep warm in a spell of extremely low temperature.

By the time other birds have begun nesting, juvenile Gray Jays will be on the wing, following their parents and learning the art of snitching morsels from wolf kills and cadging handouts from cottagers and backcountry picnickers.

One of the more unusual adaptations to winter as it relates to nests is found amongst owls. Great Horned, Boreal, and Saw-whet owls are known to thaw out frozen prey by incubating it in their roost nests as they would a clutch of eggs.

A Meal of Ticks   A quite unusual source of winter food for Gray Jays was noted by Bill Walley of Dauphin, Manitoba, while doing work on these birds in Canada's Riding Mountain National Park. He observed several of them intently pursuing a moose, picking blood-gorged ticks from around the tail.

These moose ticks, or winter ticks (unrelated to "wood" ticks), can be present in numbers over one hundred thousand on severely infested animals, every one of which takes at least three blood meals. The torment can be judged by the fact that some moose scratch and rub themselves so much most of their hair is worn off by late winter. Small wonder many die from direct blood loss, stress, and exposure. Blood-engorged ticks would be a rich source of food for birds, and one might wonder if ravens, magpies, and others could be among those also taking advantage of the moose's misfortune.

CHAPTER 6

Knowing
Your Visitors

Getting Everything Organized

This chapter describes the individual species of winter birds and mammals that visit feeders in the Upper Midwest, and the families they belong to. To make better sense out of the write-ups it will be helpful to summarize how science organizes and names animals.

Taxonomy   The study of classifying living things is called taxonomy. Under its direction all life is arranged into two huge family trees, one for the plant kingdom, one for the animal. All relationships in each "tree" are determined on the basis of recognizable differences and similarities in structure, physiology, and (sometimes) behavior.

Part of bringing order out of chaos is to attach descriptive names to each member of each family tree. Virtually all plants and animals that come to people's attention have folk names. But this is really no help. There are the multitude of different languages, of course, and in each of these, local dialects and customs often give quite different names to the same species. For example, a "gopher," depending on where you are in North America, is either a ground squirrel, a turtle, or a snake.

A Swedish botanist, Karl von Linné, developed a naming system using words and roots from two languages that are no longer spoken. Thus, in one stroke, he avoided putting anyone's linguistic nose out of joint, and he tapped into the rich vocabularies of Latin and Greek. Linné himself is now universally known by the Latinized version of his name, Linnaeus.

Thanks to him, all plants and animals now have at least a two-word name. Species (the second name) are ranked into Genuses (the first name), which in turn are arranged into Families, these in turn into Orders, and so on. As well as being a universal label, the names try, but don't always succeed, at being descriptive. By custom, scientific names are printed in *italic* type face.

Confusianus ignoramus   The use of scientific names is often interpreted by nonacademic folk as a sign that someone is getting unnecessarily technical or is trying to intimidate them. Since this is not a technical book, the use of terminology not familiar to the average reader has been kept under control. However, there is economy and clarity to be gained by the judicious use of descriptive words specifically coined for biology. They need not constitute a barrier if, either in context or with definitions, their meanings are clear.

It is no accident that the bird families in almost all field guides are presented in more or less the same order, beginning with what is generally regarded as the earliest evolved (loons), and ending with the most recently evolved, usually finches. For my own guidance I arranged my species more or less as they appear in the major field guides, although these differ among themselves.

Family Write-ups   There turned out to be much more of interest about most birds and mammals than could be encompassed in the confining structure of the individual species write-ups. Therefore I incorporated the leftover neat bits into family write-ups. Where the subject and available material warranted it, I also wrote on subgroups, such as the crossbills, and even about individual species, like the juncos.

Species Write-ups   In this chapter each species is discussed under a standard set of subheads that cover its names, appearance, behavior, range, food, and nest. The wording is spare, since the purpose is to provide a brief sketch. The "Comment" subhead allows me some space to fill out that sketch with interesting details.

What's In a Name?   As already pointed out, I don't approach scientific names as a necessary evil, but as an opportunity to learn something from and, from time to time, to have a little fun with. Each species write-up begins with a thumbnail summary of the sources of both the common and the scientific names. For this I have drawn almost entirely on Ernest A. Choate's *The Dictionary of American Bird Names*, revised edition, with some help from *Webster's New World Dictionary*, second college edition.

Descriptions

The surface anatomy, or "topography," of birds has long since been mapped in detail. The appendages and each contour and pattern of the body and flight feathers have been

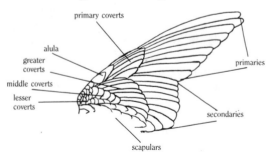

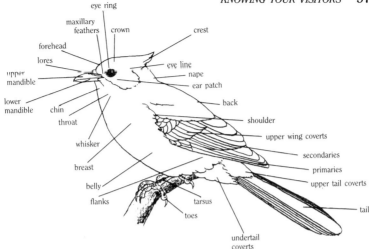

eye ring
maxillary feathers | crown
crest
forehead
lores
upper mandible
eye line
nape
ear patch
lower mandible
chin
throat
back
shoulder
upper wing coverts
whisker
secondaries
breast
primaries
belly
upper tail coverts
flanks
tarsus
toes
tail
undertail coverts

accorded names. The accompanying diagram identifies the major parts of a typical bird. Knowing these will aid in the enjoyment of this, and other, reference books and will also sharpen your ability to spot key field marks on birds at your feeders.

Range   Although this is a book about birds of the Upper Midwest, I felt that it would be more useful to deal with breeding ranges on a continental basis and, where appropriate, to be more regionally specific about wintering ranges.

Nests and Roosts   In chapter 5, "Those Fascinating Creatures," I discuss nests. Some incredibly well-adapted birds build nests, brood eggs, and feed and warm their fragile young through our worst winter weather. Most would agree that such heroic care-giving deserves more than passing mention. So, it was felt, do the nesting habits of the less heroic summer breeders, since their works remain in the frozen landscape, as potential objects of scrutiny, right through winter. Therefore, each write-up features a brief description of that species's nest and preferred location. For those birds that actually nest in winter, I describe the eggs.

References   Each species write-up concludes with a list of page references in four of the major field guides, plus Janssen's *Birds in Minnesota*. All are the latest editions, as of mid-1991. The color illustrations in the major guides will provide a complementary reference to Peter Sawatzky's black-and-white interpretations in this book. Following is the key to the reference abbreviations:

A   *The Audubon Society Field Guide to North American Birds,* Eastern Region
BM   Janssen, *Birds in Minnesota*
GO   Golden Guide, *Birds of North America*
NG   National Geographic, *Field Guide to the Birds of North America*
P   Peterson, *A Field Guide to the Birds,* Eastern and Central North America

Grouse, Partridges, Pheasants
Family Phasianidae

This family is a member of the larger order, the *Galliformes*, which includes the chickenlike, scratching, ground-living birds found the world over. Collectively they are often referred to as "game" birds due to their most commonly being regarded as objects of sport hunting, or "upland game" birds as distinct from hunted waterfowl. *Galliformes* is from the Latin *gallina*, "a hen," and *Phasianidae* is from the Greek *phasianos*, "a pheasant." Some five thousand years ago the Red Jungle Fowl of India was domesticated and became the farmyard chicken in its many varieties. The qualities that made it valuable then were its high reproductive rate, flocking habit, and the tastiness of its meat. It was also easy to keep, scatching through manure and litter for waste grain, picking shoots and leaves, and chasing insects around the dooryard. And it was conveniently nonmigratory.

The high reproductive rate meant large clutches of eggs, a trait that could be exploited with a little management. If you systematically stole the hen's eggs as she laid them, preventing her from accumulating a clutch large enough to trigger her brooding mode, the confused bird just kept on producing. Wild Gray Partridges will occasionally fill nests with more than twenty eggs, and if captives are subjected to nestbox larceny, will overproduce heroically. If you know where to shop you can buy tins of diminutive quail eggs.

Would Rather Walk   Given a choice, most members of this group prefer to keep their feet on the ground. Their wings have, in fact, been described as getaway devices held in reserve to escape predators that can't be hidden from or outrun. Our native grouse, however, do routinely use their wings as feeding aids when they flap a few feet up to browse on tree buds.

The grouse-type wing is short, broad, and rounded, and has to be flailed at a high speed to achieve flight. Liftoff, particularly for heavier species like turkeys and pheasants, is straight up in a burst of thrashing wings that gets the bird from zero to flat-out in a couple of seconds. The buffeting of this blastoff is often augmented by a simultaneous cackling or other vocal racket. The object is to startle the unsuspecting, to get out of reach, fast, before a predator can collect its shattered composure and pounce. Or shoot.

Once airborne and at cruising speed, the bird sets its wings stiffly and glides, usually settling a short distance away.

"White" or "Dark"   The huge breast muscles that power this explosive burst of energy are the "white meat" of the dinner table. Powerful as they are, they can exert themselves for only short periods because they contain fewer blood vessels, less oxygen-storing myoglobin, and are made up of coarser fiber bundles than "dark" meat. The breast muscles of migratory birds need to be able to work over long periods of time and are richly supplied with blood vessels and myoglobin, and are made of finer fibers. You can see, from the contrasting color of the muscle groups, where evolution has put the emphasis: On a duck the breast meat is "dark," on a chicken or grouse, it's the leg.

I have read that if you were able to pursue a pheasant or grouse closely enough to force it to repeatedly fly, that after four or five takeoffs the bird's flight muscles would be exhausted and you could simply pick it up. Between running shoe and roasting pan another factor could intervene, however. Even a wing-weary grouse or partridge can probably still turn on some brisk footwork, and a pheasant in a real hurry can do about eighteen miles per hour.

Snowshoe or Shovel? A clue to the adaptive background of some members of this family can be seen in their footwear. Grouse have furlike leggings down to their toes, and in winter the toes grow combs of stiff bristles along each side. Neither pheasants nor partridges have these accessories.

The toe bristles are assumed to be an adaptive "snowshoe," giving the wearers better "float" on soft snow. It has also been observed that the toenails grow longer, probably for the same reason. This is no doubt true. But there is another possibility that I haven't seen suggested yet, and that is increased digging facility in soft snow.

As most readers of nature lore know, grouse and ptarmigan sleep in winter under the snow, often plunging in from flight. They burrow along horizontally for a foot or more, plugging the entrance hole and creating a snug, insulated pocket for the night. In the morning they usually burst through the roof into flight.

How they actually dig through the soft, yielding snow is an interesting question. It is probably with a combination of beak and footwork. But scooping the loose stuff back behind them would have to be done with the feet. For this, those toe fringes would help a lot, since without them, moving loose snow would be a bit like trying to shovel sand with a fork.

An important factor in native grouse's winter survival is their ability to switch to tree buds or conifer needles as food. Seton in his *The Birds of Manitoba* mentions Sharp-tailed Grouse he shot toward the end of the winter with a large gap in their beaks behind the tip where both mandibles had been worn down, presumably from plucking aspen and willow buds.

The Imports Trying to do nature one better by introducing exotic species has come to be recognized by even casual nature watchers as bad management. Three streetbirds, that matched set of environmental calamities—the starling, the sparrow, and the nuisance pigeon—are constant reminders of previous folly.

Thankfully, relatively few introduced birds have become successful in North America. And among those that have made it in the Upper Midwest are two that were deliberately brought in to provide sporting targets in place of native species wiped out by a combination of the gun, the axe, and the plough. These are the Ring-necked Pheasant and the Gray Partridge. To a much lesser extent the Chukar Partridge has also become established, with remnant populations hanging on here and there in the region, a permanent, scattered population surviving in parts of Montana.

Whether or not their overall contribution to the environment is beneficial, it is difficult now to find fault with the presence of these hardy and beautiful imports. In distribution and numbers the Gray Partridge and Ring-necked Pheasant are more plentiful than the native Northern Bobwhite in most parts of the Upper Midwest. The gray seems especially able to survive in areas of intensive agriculture where native game birds have little chance of making it, and where "clean" farming practices make it difficult for the pheasant. Winters take a heavy toll, but the survivors' high egg producing ability helps restore the losses. So also may double-parenting; only the male gray helps his mate tend their brood.

Bygone Strawstacks   For the gorgeous Ring-necked Pheasant, northern midcontinental winters are an even tougher test than for the Gray Partridge. It started out rather well. Older style farming, with brushy gullies and weedy fence rows dividing the stubble fields and strawstacks, seemed to suit the ringneck. But the post–World War II combine harvester did it in over much of its newly won territory. The strawstack, where the waste grain and weed seeds of an entire field used to be concentrated, disappeared. The bulldozer took care of the gullies and fence rows.

Now, over much of its Upper Midwest range where it is still plentiful enough to be a significant gamebird, the ringneck is a winter ward of the public. Wildlife management agencies, sympathetic farmers, and sportsmen's clubs shovel grain out to keep it alive until forgiving spring comes 'round again. Very often it also becomes a guest of rural and small-town bird feeders.

Gray Partridge *(Perdix perdix)*

Pheasant family. Also "Hungarian Partridge" or "Hun"; "partridge," says Webster, arises from Middle English *partriche*, a direct descendant of the

Latin and Greek *perdix*, which in turn is probably akin to *perdesthai*, "to break wind" (whence "fart"), from whirring sound made as birds burst into flight; term incorrectly but widely applied also to Ruffed Grouse; *Perdix* from Latin and Greek, "a partridge."

Description   Chunky, squat, short-tailed, smaller than native grouse, larger than bobwhite; gray on chest and neck, flanks barred in rusty brown; males have a brown, rough U-shaped patch on belly; cheeks, throat, and outer tail feathers plain rust-brown; upper parts pattern of gray and browns, with light feather edgings and fine lines.

Behavior   Social; feeds, flushes, and flies in close flock; strictly a ground bird of open country; family "covey" sleeps huddled in a circle, tails inward, presumably for a fast getaway if alarmed; in winter they dig open craters through snow in fields, ditches, and weed patches to scratch on the ground for seeds and green bits, and apparently also sleep in these; call is a harsh, rasping "krrrr-ik," heard particularly in spring; also cackle when they flush.

Range   Nonmigratory; has been released widely; best established from Mississippi west through Dakotas and Montana; in southeast Wisconsin and extreme southeast Michigan.

Food   Seeds, green leaves, shoots, rose hips; growing chicks are insectivorous and may be starved out if agricultural insecticides are widely used; attracted to feeding stations by spilled seeds and by screenings or grain offered on the ground.

Nest   Very well-hidden cup scratched in ground, lined with grasses; in crops, fence rows, tall grass, and edges of low shrubbery.

Comment   The most successful and widespread introductions in North America took place in Canada around 1908 in southern Alberta, followed by successful stockings in Saskatchewan and Manitoba. These were shortly followed by releases in North Dakota, where the birds also flourished. Releases in Iowa established rapidly and by 1915 spread naturally into southern Minnesota. The first hunting season in Minnesota was in 1939. Very sensitive to agricultural practices, they were abundant in the '50s and '60s in areas where they have now vanished. The loss of field-edge habitat, clearing of weedy ditches, and early-season mowing of hay (which destroys nests) are among the factors contributing to their disappearance.

Winter is hard on them, especially when it brings ice storms. But they make up for losses with huge clutches, the largest in the bird world with an average of fifteen to sixteen eggs. The female doesn't start brooding until the clutch is complete, so during the laying period, which may be up to three weeks, she covers the eggs-in-waiting with grass and leaves. The male takes no part in brooding, but when the chicks arrive he helps tend them, bringing up the rear of his numerous brood, ready to fight or feign a broken wing to lead a predator away.

REF: A–496; BM–105; GO–92; NG–220; P–148

Ring-necked Pheasant *(Phasianus colchicus)*

Pheasant family. Sometime "Chinese" pheasant; "Pheasant" is from Greek *phaisianos*, "a pheasant," referring to the River Phasis flowing into the Black Sea in the ancient country of Colchis which is now part of the Georgian Republic of the USSR, and at the mouth of which these birds were especially numerous; *colchicus* is Latinized "of Colchis"; taxonomy has thus given us a double locality name.

Description   Chicken-sized; males resplendent in brilliant copper-maroon and gold with parts of body bearing beautifully contrasting base colors and varying patterns of spots, teardrops, bars, and checks; head iridescent green with small "ear" tufts; eyes set in red face patches; may have white ring around neck; long pointed tail; spurs on lower legs; females smaller, in subdued brown camouflage pattern, tails proportionately shorter.

Behavior   Social, females and grown young may be escorted by territorial male; ranges in grainland, ditches, irrigated fields, and pastures; a swift runner; when flushed bursts straight up on thrashing wings, cackling; scratches through snow cover for seeds and green pickings in winter, may scrounge in farmyards and feed-lots, sometimes in considerable numbers; males' call in spring is a raucus two-note crow followed by rapid flurry of wing beats.

Range   Widely and unevenly distributed throughout entire region except absent in northern Minnesota, Wisconsin, and Michigan; presence often depends on local restocking and winter feeding programs.

Food   Omnivorous; seeds, grain, green leaves, shoots, and buds; insects, small vertebrates; will feed on carrion in times of scarcity; at feeders will pick up spilled seeds of all kinds and can be attracted with screenings, corn, grain, and baked goods.

Nest   Depression in the ground lined with leaves or grass; in tall ground cover, fence rows, under bushes, and along bluff edges.

Comment   Pheasants were brought to Britain by the Normans not long after 1066 where they rapidly became a favorite of the hunter and the gourmet. Many attempted introductions into North America failed until 1881 when the American Consul-General in Shanghai sent thirty birds to Oregon. The twenty-six that survived the trip were released in the Willamette Valley. Beginning around 1905 there were numerous releases through the Upper Midwest, and hunting seasons were routine in the '40s and '50s, South Dakota being a premiere destination for hunters.

However, in many regions where it prospered for a few years following initial introductions, its numbers diminished for reasons not apparently due to habitat or weather changes. Even in England, where it has been ranging free for nine centuries in a relatively mild climate, its numbers dwindle very quickly, and it vanishes altogether in many areas if restocking efforts lapse.

REF: A–497; BM–106; GO–92; NG–222; P–144

Spruce Grouse *(Dendragapus canadensis)*

Grouse family. Also "fool hen" because its trust in camouflage and immobility, sometimes in plain view, make it seem suicidally tame; *Dendragapus* is from Greek *dendron*, "a tree," and *agape*, "love," i.e., tree-loving from habit of roosting and feeding in trees; in older guides generic name is *Canachites*, from Greek *kanacheo* meaning "to make a noise, or crow."

Description   Large, plump, chickenlike bird; male forehead, cheeks, throat, and upper breast black, edged in white; in display, red "eyebrow" combs raised; center of lower breast black; sides of breast and abdomen heavily checked in black and white; tail dark with light brown terminal band; legs feathered to toes; females checked, flecked, and barred with pattern of black, brown, and cream, told from female ruffed by shorter tail, lack of crest hackle, and absence of ruffs.

Behavior   Very quiet and secretive; sometimes "freeze" in exposed places, such as trees, and can be closely approached; males buffet wings, hoot, rattle wing feathers, and take short, erratic, noisy flights as part of courtship display; in winter, roost in plunge holes beneath snow.

Range   Nonmigratory; very much a bird of boreal forest, hence limited to northeast Minnesota and extreme northern Wisconsin and Michigan.

Food   Buds, shoots, leaves, flowers, berries, insects in summer, conifer needles in winter; rarely attracted to feeders, but may visit yards to dine on tips of ornamental evergreens, and while there sample seeds.

Nest   A shallow scrape lined with leaves and some feathers, usually close to a rock, tree, or small shrub that offers some concealment.

Comment   Spruce Grouse are routinely classed as rare or scarce, in spite of the presence of suitable habitat. A plausible reason is that most surveying is done near roads or human settlements where hunting is a factor and the bird's inherent response of sitting still to escape detection makes it the first and easiest target for roving plinkers. One of the bird's adaptations to its boreal environment is its ability to survive in winter almost exclusively on the needles of spruce, fir, and pine. To handle this diet of tough, dry fare its digestive tract increases markedly in size. The constant ingestion of aromatic needles imparts to the flesh of the bird a very strong taste of turpentine.
REF: A–675; BM–107; GO–86; NG–210; P–146

Ruffed Grouse *(Bonasa umbellus)*

Grouse family. Also known as "bush" or "birch" partridge; "Ruffed" from dark ruff of erectile feathers on sides of neck; "Grouse" from French *griais,* "gray," descriptive of several kinds of partridges; *Bonasa* is from Latin *bonasum*, "aurocks" (wild ox), or "drumming," as voice of male grouse suggests bellowing bull; *umbellus* is from Latin for "sunshade" (umbrella), referring to shape of ruffs when erect.

Description   Larger and longer-legged than pigeon; large tail banded in black with especially obvious subterminal band, tips of feathers light tan; hackles on crown may be raised into ragged crest; dark or coppery ruff on sides of neck, raised if bird is excited; camouflage plumage a complicated pattern of flecks, bars, and edging in black, dark brown, rustred; two color phases present in all populations, some birds being an overall rusty brown, some grayish; legs feathered; female slightly smaller than male, tail shorter with two central feathers lacking the black subterminal band, neck ruffs are less prominent; buff line through eye; winter bird has fringe of stiff bristles on sides of toes.

Behavior   Relies on concealment and camouflage to avoid detection; if disturbed but not flushed, first giveaway is urgent peeping and slight rustling of leaves as it high-steps cautiously away; alternately, it might await your close approach and burst almost from underfoot, sailing swiftly away to re-alight a short distance off; male drums from low vantage points in cover, starting with hesitant, muffled "whups" that accelerate to staccato roll; drumming heaviest in spring, with secondary busy time in fall, but can be heard during much of year except for coldest part of winter; outside of growing season often seen stepping and flapping about in bushes and trees nipping buds and catkins; roosts in tunnels under snow, locations of these marked in spring by small piles of pale, macaroni-shaped droppings.

Range   Nonmigratory; throughout forested portions of region, northeast Minnesota, most of Wisconsin and Michigan, western edge of Montana, and disjunct wooded enclaves such as the Black Hills.

Food   Adults vegetarian, taking shoots, leaves, buds, petals, berries, and seeds; young insectivorous; at feeder takes sunflower seeds, screenings, and cracked or whole grain.

Nest   Bowl scraped at foot of tree or stump, near log or clump; lined with leaves and some feathers; departs as soon as last-hatched young are up and active.

Comment   "I don't think that thing'll fly even if he does get it started!" My wry friend was not the first to be reminded of somebody's trying to start a motor. In her charming book *Wings of the North*, Candace Savage says that if you walk softly into the woods of an early spring morning and thump your hands on the ground in a reasonable imitation of the grouse's signature drumroll, you'll get a reply. In autumn the young of the year seem to be overcome by an urge to disperse and under its spell fly into utility wires, fences, windows, and vehicles, often with fatal results.

Along with other northern species, most notably the varying hare, Ruffed Grouse are subject to a ten-year population cycle. During the lows one rarely hears or sees a grouse, but during the highs they seem to be everywhere.

Judging from the frequent scatterings of feathers one finds on the snow in winter woodlands, this grouse must be an important food source for owls, hawks, and, where they occur, lynx, marten, and fisher.

REF: A–630; BM–108; GO–86; NG–210; P–144

Sharp-tailed Grouse *(Tympanuchus phasianellus)*

Grouse family. Formerly, sometimes locally "prairie chicken," in confusion with Greater and Lesser Prairie Chicken; *Tympanuchus* is from Greek *tympanon*, "a drum," and *nucha*, "neck," from inflatable neck pouches of males that emit gutteral sound during courtship dances; *phasianellus* is from Greek *phasianos*, "a pheasant," plus Latin *ellus* for "little"; in older guides generic name is *Pedioecetes*, from Greek *pedion*, "a plain" and *oiketes*, "inhabiting."

Description   Plump, compact, chickenlike bird with short, pointed tail; no obvious field marks at a distance, but underparts beautifully "scaled" with pattern of V-marks; central quills of tail are brown with black bars, short outer feathers are white; in flight, belly, underwings, and tail coverts noticeably pale; courting male displays small, purplish neck pouches and yellow eyebrow combs; legs feathered; toes in winter edged with stiff fringes.

Behavior   Very sociable, rarely seen as single; more tendency to fly than most grouse, using short bursts of rapid wing beats with body rocking somewhat erratically from side to side, alternating with long glides on down-curved wings; bird often emits a low, gutteral "kuk-kuk-kuk-kuk" on takeoff, and with each subsequent spurt, more or less in time with wing beats; in spring courting males gather into groups to display to females; in winter, roost in plunge holes in snow, and may be seen morning and evening scrambling about in trees, plucking buds.

Range   At times erratically migratory; scattered irregularly through western plains area of region, and in northeast Minnesota, northern Wisconsin, Michigan's Upper Peninsula; favors crop or grassland adjacent to brush or open woods.

Food   Leaves, buds, flowers, berries, rose hips, waste grain in summer, and tree buds, especially aspen, in winter; takes screenings, grain, and mixed seed from ground at feeders if it overcomes wariness of human dwellings.

Nest   Cup on ground lined with grasses, in concealing grass, forbs, or low shrubbery.

Comment   For the nature photographer willing to seek them out, a "lek," or group, of courting male grouse is the ideal subject. They are very steadfast to their dancing ground, or court, returning year after year, often in spite of significant disturbance. Thus, a blind can be set up ahead of time a discreet distance from the court and if desired moved a little closer each day as the birds become accustomed to it. Most courts are conveniently located on open rises, so the view is unobstructed and the blind can be positioned to take best advantage of the dramatic light of the rising sun. One should be in place about an hour before sunrise, which in May means rising early. But you will witness an ancient ritual performed and perfected through countless other sunrises. You will see the orange light and the primitive intensity of their dance transform these plain birds into creatures of beauty and mystery.

REF: A–493; BM–111; GO–86; NG–214; P–146

Pigeons
Family Columbidae

There are fifteen species of pigeons occurring in the U.S., in the Upper Midwest represented by Mourning Doves and feral domestic pigeons. The difference between doves and pigeons is only one of size, the smaller by custom called doves, the larger, pigeons.

Referring to motley flocks of street pigeons as "Rock Doves," as some writers and many birders do, has always struck me as a bit precious. They are human-dependent ferals in North America, quite removed in their habits from the ancestral wild Rock Dove that still nests on cliffs from the Atlantic coasts of Europe south to North Africa and east to China. Since around 4500 B.C. when stock from the gorges and sea cliffs around the Mediterranean were domesticated, over three hundred breeds have been developed, some for meat, some to satisfy a fancy for the exotic or bizarre, some for racing. Our street pigeons are the freelance descendants of a mixture of these that were either liberated or flew the coop. They would in time revert to the ancestral type except for ongoing recruitment of domestics that keep the gene pool stirred up. In my view these are "pigeons."

Pigeon "Milk"   Many birds regurgitate to feed the young; pigeons, flamingos, and Emperor Penguins are unique in the production of special "milk." In pigeons, a few days before their two eggs hatch, the lining of each parent's crop swells and forms thick folds, tripling its bulk. The surface layer of cells sloughs off continuously to form a thick semifluid similar to cottage cheese. Hatchlings are fed exclusively on it until they are about half-grown, and then it is increasingly supplemented with regurgitated seeds.

They thrive mightily on this ration; a day-old nestling is twice its hatching weight, and for several days thereafter gains 38 percent every twenty-four hours. In about a month it reaches adult weight. Pure "milk" is about 15 percent protein, 8 percent fat, 1 to 2 percent mineral, with several vitamins. Poultry chicks fed a ration supplemented with it were over 30 percent heavier at the end of the test than comparables on regular feed.

Pigeons make up for two-egg clutches by more or less non-stop nesting. Under optimum conditions they may begin a new clutch before the previous hatch has fledged.

The flying ability and "homing" instinct of pigeons has long been exploited by humans for practical purposes and for sport. They have been used to carry messages in times of emergency and war. In Manitoba carrier pigeons played an important role in forest-fire fighting during the 1930s, displaced only by the advent of two-way radios.

In the sporting world, thousands of carefully bred birds are pampered and trained for racing every year. Champions, with flight muscles that constitute over 00 percent of their body weight, cover distances of 020 miles at average speeds of 45 to 50 MPH. Pigeons are said to be the favored prey of Peregrine Falcons, particularly for those that have taken to nesting in cities where little other good-sized prey is available. But, notwithstanding the dazzling speed it achieves in a hunting dive, considered opinion is that a peregrine would be hard-pressed to overtake and capture a healthy pigeon in level pursuit.

Supersenses   Explanations for the astonishing ability of pigeons to find their way home over long distances begin with the fact that the cliffs where ancestral birds nested, often along ocean coasts, could be far from inland fields and prairies where they foraged for seeds. A commuting lifestyle was thus demanded of the birds which in turn developed the ability to fly accurately over long distances in all kinds of weather.

To affect this capability they combine several senses. One is smell that appears to help them identify home territory. An awesome hearing range allows them to detect infra-sounds as low as 0.05 Hz, about one cycle every ten seconds. These are sounds made by storms, winds flowing over mountains, and surf. Ultra-low frequency sounds travel through the atmosphere for hundreds of miles, giving the birds a sound fix on geographic features far beyond visual limits. They have extraordinary visual memory; in experiments using several hundred color slides of landscapes, they could recall months later which ones could be responded to to provide a food reward. They can see ultraviolet light and detect changes in light polarization which would make them able to pinpoint the sun's location on overcast days. They are highly sensitive to changes in atmospheric pressure and are attuned to ground-borne vibrations.

These exquisite sensory gifts are shared in varying degrees by other birds. But what a rich world of signals and sensations our humble street nuisance lives in, a world far beyond the dull senses of its human critics.

Rock Dove *(Columba livia)*

Pigeon family. Most commonly "pigeon"; "rock" from wild stock's nesting on cliffs; "pigeon" is from Old French *pijon,* "a young bird," and from Latin *pipio,* "to peep" or "squab"; Latin *columba,* "a dove," *livia* from Latin *lividus* means "bluish."

Description Crow-sized; plump, with small, high-crowned head; short, pinkish legs; vari-colored, but tending to gray body, wings, and tail, with darker iridescent head and neck; tail usually with dark bar at end.

Behavior Social, ground feeding in flocks, often on roads; gait a hurried walk, head bobbing in time; steady, strong wing beats, glides with wings cocked at very high angle; wings clap sharply together over body on takeoff; courting males bow, coo, strut, turn animatedly before female; coo a soft, throaty, chortling "bucket-a-gooo."

Range Nonmigratory; found throughout Upper Midwest where humans, deliberately or otherwise, provide food and nest sites.

Food Seeds; buds, leaves, and shoots in season; garbage; at feeder takes grain, peanuts, baked scraps, and popcorn.

Nest Shallow saucer of straw, twigs; on ledge in or on building or under bridge, casually colonial where facilities permit; two or three nestings per year, may even attempt winter nesting if shelter is adequate.

Comment Pigeons in winter are primarily grain eaters, much preferring it served on the ground or on wide, flat shelves. But they will obligingly gobble anything, as generations of city park regulars have found, to the delight of themselves and the birds. Dropping-smeared buildings and park statuary are testimony to their messiness. But for an apartment-balcony station well above reach of other birds, pigeons might be the only clients.

REF: A–543; BM–169; GO–166; NG–224; P–180

Mourning Dove *(Zenaida macroura)*

Pigeon family. "Mourning" from sad-sounding call; "dove" assumed to be from Anglo-Saxon *dufon*, "to dive," from birds' swift flight; *Zenaida* after wife of Prince Charles Bonaparte who, after uncle Napoleon's setback at Waterloo, moved to U.S. where he is credited as founder of systematic ornithology; *macroura* is from Greek *macros*, "long" and *oura*, "tail."

Description   Trim pigeon shape; noticeably larger than robin; short-legged; slight iridescence to neck feathers; central tail feathers long and pointed, marginal tail feathers flared in flight to show white ends; overall color shades of soft beige, tan, light smokey brown with hint of blush on breast; dark "ear spot" on sides of head, black flecks on wings.

Behavior   Obviously a pigeon; often perches on utility wires, otherwise feeds on ground; in pairs during breeding season, gathers in small flocks at other times; wings whistle in flight, especially on takeoff; flight straight and swift on steady wing beats; voice a measured series of ventriloquistic, hollow "coos," the first ending in a short rise in tone, the other two or three a monotone.

Range   Migratory; Upper Midwest straddles limits of northern wintering area, i.e., frequent-to-regular winterer in southern half of Minnesota, South Dakota, Wisconsin, and Michigan; overwintering trend increasing, possibly due to bird feeders.

Food   Seeds; at feeder or on ground beneath it, most seeds, cracked corn, and grain; all pigeons drink by submerging bill in water and sucking it up rather than dabbling bill and raising head to let water run down as other birds do.

Nest   A flat, flimsy, sometimes see-through arrangement of twigs, up to 50 ft (15 m) up, but usually between 10 to 25 ft (3 to 7.5 m); may use abandoned nest of robin, catbird, or grackle as base for their stick platform; prefers thick cover, as in heavy shrub, evergreen, or vine tangle; prefers open woodland; rare host of cowbird.

Comment   Doves are symbols of peace and love, the expression "billing and cooing" arising from the courting and grooming activities of paired couples. In fact, doves are very aggressive birds; mating-season fights between males are fierce, drawn-out, sometimes bloody conflicts.

Almost every commentator has a go at doves' slovenly housing standards, wondering out loud how such a precarious tray can hold eggs and young long enough for brooding. Candace Savage, as she often does, says it best in *Wings of the North:* "The birds often turn lovey-dovey during nest-building as well, since every straw that the male brings to his mate may stimulate a new round of endearments. The finished nest is what you'd expect from a pair of love-blurred minds. . . ."

The sneers of critics to the contrary, the nests work very well for the purposes intended, which is to raise young. Doves are diligent, all-season parents, in the milder parts of the Upper Midwest bringing off as many as four clutches. Like pigeons, they feed their broods, usually a pair, on rich "pigeon milk." A game bird in much of the U.S., the annual kill runs around fifty million, far more than the casualty list inflicted on all species of waterfowl in the name of sport.

REF: A–542; BM–170; GO–166; NG–226; P–180

Woodpeckers
Family Picidae

Worldwide there are 210 woodpecker species, twenty breeding in North America, nine occurring in the Upper Midwest. They represent a highly successful group, having evolved to exploit, virtually unchallenged, the rich food buried in the bark and wood of the earth's abundant forest habitat.

Others have made creditable attempts to imitate woodpeckers, not surprisingly two of them members of the limitlessly ingenious finch family. The Maui Parrotbill chews into branches with its stout lower mandible, seeking insects. The Akiapolaau, another Hawaiian, chips into soft wood with its heavy lower mandible while holding out of the way its curved upper mandible which it will later bring into play as a probe for the insects its gouging exposes. But none of these have mastered the wood-chipper's trade as thoroughly as the woodpecker.

A number of specialized adaptations combine in woodpeckers to enable them to excavate efficiently into hard wood. It isn't enough to have a straight, hard, chisel-shaped bill and strong neck muscles. In the course of a day's activity a busy bird might peck eight to ten thousand times, whacking a hard surface with sufficient energy to generate, in the case of the Red-headed Woodpecker, 10 G's of force on the rebound from each blow. Under such a merciless hammering a normal skull would shatter apart and the brains turn to bloody slop. But the woodpecker skull is strong, heavily reinforced, and bound about with unusually heavy muscles. The mountings of the bill are set with some components that slide enough to absorb and dissipate impact shock; the brain is packed snugly into its bony housing and protected with both pneumatic and hydraulic cushions. The delicate eyes are similarly shielded.

This chopping implement is mounted on a body supported solidly on a tripod arrangement—two sturdy clamps, the feet; and a brace, the stiff tail quills. Thus bracketed, the woodpecker maintains a secure but relaxed stance. This is obviously an important consideration; anyone who has watched a woodpecker at work notices that its torso bobs slightly back and forth in time with its head, adding speed and force to each stroke of the bill.

A Versatile Tongue The capabilities of the chiseling beak are admirably complemented by the extensible, probing tongue. It is mounted on a remarkable apparatus, a stiff but flexible probe of bone, muscle, and cartilage. This divides at the back of the mouth and, supported by the forked hyoid bone, lies in a sheath that curls around the back of each side of the skull, over the top of the head, and is anchored near the nostrils. In most woodpeckers this elongated organ enables the tongue to be stuck out from three to five times the length of the bill. Extended, it resembles the tongue of a garter snake, whiplike and quick. But instead of being forked, the tip is fitted with a horny point carrying rows of backward-pointing barbs—a miniature harpoon. As tongues tend to be, it is richly supplied with nerves and the ability to taste.

If you add a layer of sticky, lubricating saliva to this sensitive, highly flexible probe, you have a food-finding and -gathering instrument that allows access to a menu few other insect-eaters can reach. The fact that most of our woodpeckers have no need to migrate is evidence of their year-round ability to exploit a nourishing and abundant food source. The migrating exceptions are the Red-headed Woodpecker, the Yellow-bellied Sapsucker, and the Northern (used to be "Yellow-shafted" or "Red-shafted") Flicker.

The spectacular Pileated Woodpecker uses its bill to hatchet gaping holes through the outer walls of carpenter ants' treetrunk fortresses and into their inner galleries. Alarmed by the breach, the ants swarm to their colony's defense, unwittingly playing into the invader's scheme. They are lapped up by the hundreds on the darting, gummy tongue. The size of the pileated, as big as a crow, is testimony to its ability to exploit the nourishing abundance of carpenter ants in the mature forests it inhabits.

A Big Investment   Chopping wood is hard work. Not surprisingly, woodpeckers are known to have prodigious appetites. The Green Woodpecker of Europe needs about two thousand lawn and meadow ants per day; the large European Black Woodpecker puts away nine hundred bark beetles or one thousand ants at a single meal.

Drilling a hole into solid wood and excavating a spacious cavity in the heart of a tree, as most woodpeckers do in preparation for nesting, demands a heavy investment of time and energy. For the larger ones some ten thousand chips have to be chopped out and dumped. Depending on the species, nest preparation can occupy from ten to twenty-eight days. The reward for all this effort is a secure home, well off the ground, where the young are protected from most predators and from the elements.

There is a further positive tradeoff; cavity nesters can afford more time to raise their securely sheltered broods. From hatching to nest-leaving, a young Downy Woodpecker takes three weeks, a Hairy Woodpecker a relatively leisurely four. But for most small birds in open nests the required strategy is to rush their young through the hazardous prefledging period as quickly as possible. Young robins are off and crash-landing on the lawn in two weeks, and most warblers are out of the nest in from eight to ten days. This accelerated pace generally means you can afford fewer young— too many mouths to feed would slow down the process.

Woodpeckers may or may not reuse last year's nest hole; most in fact do not, preferring to chip out a new one. Wintering Downy and Hairy woodpeckers also excavate separate roosting holes. The result is a good number of used tree cavities that, with minimum renovations, can be used by all manner of tenants. Depending on the size of the original builders, swallows, bluebirds, chickadees, squirrels, small owls, Wood Ducks, and others are the most frequent beneficiaries. Most of the above, in fact, cannot breed unless they have access to suitable tree cavities. There is another, less obvious spinoff effect; by providing more shelter for Saw-whet, Screech, and Boreal owls, as well as dens for Pine Martens, woodpeckers indirectly effect populations of these predators' prey species, particularly small rodents.

There is at least one documented downside to living in a hole with no back exit, and that is, once a predator attacks, it's much more difficult for a brooding parent to escape. Among titmice, evidence suggests that 20 percent of brooding females get caught by nest predators.

Singing is a proclamation of a bird's being, a claim to territory, an invitation to mate, a threat to a rival. Lacking the voice for it, at least for the kind of noises we humans arbitrarily declare to be "song," woodpeckers advertise themselves and their intentions by drumming. Hammering on a resonating hollow trunk, dead limb, sheet of plywood, or a piece of sheet metal is a song in the generic sense of the word, although it is anything but melodious, particularly if played on your metal chimney at daybreak, morning after morning.

Signs of this tympanic exuberance begin showing up in early February if you happen to be neighbor to a pair of courting Downy or Hairy woodpeckers. Later, when they begin nesting, they will drum at each other in debate over potential locations. Whatever the reason, their staccato bursts enliven the frosty silence of a late winter's day, or most emphatically punctuate the chorus of bird song of an echoing spring sunrise.

Red-bellied Woodpecker *(Melanerpes carolinus)*

Woodpecker family. A small, pinkish stain on the lower belly, seldom visible in the field, gave bird its name; vernacular name "zebraback" describes boldly striped back, "red-necked" would have acknowledged the bright red hindneck of both sexes which extends in the male over the crown; old folk names included "chad," "shamshack," "ramshack"; *melanerpes* is from Greek *melas*, "black" and *herpes*, "a creeper"; *carolinus* is Latinized "of Carolina"; in older guides *Centurus c.*, from Greek *kentron*, "a prickle," from bird's stiff-pointed tail feathers, and *aura*, "tail."

Description   Robin-sized, as is Hairy Woodpecker; bold horizontal black-and-white striping on back and wings; hindneck of both sexes poppy red, in male extended to cover top of head; eye prominent; plain, light tan-gray on side of head, throat, breast, and belly; lower belly may have pinkish wash; in flight white rump and wing patches flash prominently.

Behavior   Favors open woodlands, quite at home in dooryard trees; elaborate courtship and nest-selection rituals between mated birds accompanied by much calling, drumming, counter-tapping, and posturing; both parents brood eggs, tapping and calling ceremony accompanying each shift change; hopeful males with no mates will call persistently well into summer; very tame; hoards food; call a rolling "churrr," "chiv-chiv," some sounds resembling Northern Flicker.

Range   Partially migratory from northern edges of range; spreading north and west from original range in southeast U.S.; thinly distributed in Red River Valley, in varying numbers in southeast Minnesota, southeast South Dakota, southern half of Wisconsin and Michigan, and throughout most of Iowa.

Food   Insect larvae, ants, berries, and nuts; may scrounge litter from garbage cans and parking lots; readily comes to feeders for suet, peanut butter, and a variety of seeds.

Nest   In live or dead tree, snag, pole, 5 to 70 ft (1.5 to 21 m) up; hole diameter from 1.75 to 2.25 in (4.4 to 5.7 cm); will readily use bird house; a frequent victim of starling preemption.

Comment   Bluebirds, woodpeckers, chickadees, small owls, and others have been hit hard by the loss of old-growth forest. The shabby bark and moldering bowels of old and dead trees are nurseries for a great selection of tasty, nutritious insects and their larvae. The punky knotholes and heartwood of old trees are necessary for many birds that dig, or use second-hand, cavities for nesting and shelter.

But foresters, arbiters of assertive woodland management, have no time for venerability, labeling such trees "over-mature." Any tree with the effrontery to appear on its way to a dignified natural death is condemned as "decadent."

Yard-proud householders across the land have adopted these prejudices unquestioningly, diligently trimming, cutting, and clearing any tree not fit for the cover of a garden magazine. Those who also favor birds then wonder why certain desirable species never show up at their feeders. Over time, they could remedy the shortage by simply leaving the axe and chain saw in the tool shed.

If they want faster results, they could emulate author and ornithologist Lawrence Kilham, who wired trunks of dead trees and windfalls upright to fence posts around his yard in Maryland and was rewarded by the prompt appearance of Downy Woodpeckers that went to work making themselves a number of snug roosting cavities.

REF: A–645; BM–193; GO–196; NG–264; P–190

Downy Woodpecker *(Picoides pubescens)*

Woodpecker family. Downy seems no fluffier than its larger look-alike, the Hairy Woodpecker, seems hairy; *picus* is Latin for "a woodpecker," *oides* is Greek compounded from *o*, "the" and *eidos*, "similar"; *pubescens* Latin for "downy," as in fine hairs of puberty; in older guides now-outdated generic name is *Dendrocopus*, from Greek *dendron*, "a tree" and *kopis*, "a dagger."

Description Bold black-and-white pattern on head, back, wings, and tail; white stripe on back; belly is all white; male has small red bar on back of head; told from almost identical Hairy Woodpecker by smaller size and proportionally smaller bill; in life often doubtful who is who until two can be compared close together; diagnostic black spots on white outer tail feathers of downy (absent on hairy) may be indistinct or not visible.

Behavior Typical feeding and perching posture straight up on vertical surface, clinging with the feet, propped on the stiff, pointed tail feathers; gleaner of tree trunks and branches with females tending to work lower trunk and large branches, male upper trunk and smaller branches; pert, inquisitive, friendly bird around feeders, sometimes beating even chickadees to newly offered foods; call is a short, sharp "kyik" or shrill rattle descending in pitch at end.

Range Nonmigratory; in mixed, deciduous, all-aged woodlands, burnt-overs; common throughout Upper Midwest.

Food Largely insectivorous; loves suet and meat scraps, especially when it can pick them off big, raw bones; likes sunflower seeds.

Nest In winter each bird drills its own roosting nest in dead or decay-softened trunks; entrance hole perfectly round, 1.25 in (3.2 cm) in diameter, from 3 to 50 ft (1 to 15 m) up; occasionally uses nest boxes for temporary shelter.

Comment Why Downy Woodpecker males forage in the upper levels of trees and their mates the lower has been explained variously. Some dismiss it as mere male dominance, others attribute it to a provident parceling out of foraging resources and point to the slightly longer tongue of the male as suggestive of division of the sexes at mealtime. Whatever; both search randomly for dormant insects and pupae in and under the bark of trees, sometimes flaking off the bark, sometimes drilling into the insect's refuge and spearing it with the pointed, barbed end of the tongue. Once condemned as injurious to trees, downies and other woodpeckers, with the possible exception of the sapsuckers, are now tolerantly regarded as important controls on insects whose interests conflict with ours.

The mere presence of trees is no assurance that woodpeckers will be there. Downies require mixed-age woodlands, including a decent complement of the soft-hearted seniors that forestry types snear at and label "decadent."

REF: A–643; BM–195; GO–200; NG–270; P–192

Hairy Woodpecker *(Picoides villosus)*

Woodpecker family. "Hairy" puzzlingly undescriptive name for bird with so many other distinguishing features; *picus* is Latin for "a woodpecker," Greek *oides* compounded from *o*, "the" and *eidos*, "like" (similar); *villosus* is Latin for "hairy"; in older guides the now outdated generic name is *Dendrocopos*, from Greek *dendron*, "a tree," and *kopis*, "a dagger."

Description Robin-sized; oversized version of Downy Woodpecker; head, back, and wings patterned in sharply contrasting white on black; belly and outer tail feathers all white; adult male has small red flash on back of head; bill proportionally heavier and longer than downy's.

Behavior Typical woodpecker affinity for perching and feeding on vertical surfaces, especially tree trunks and suet cages; more wary than Downy Woodpecker, usually not as numerous where both share feeding site; in spring drums rapid fire on resonant surface as part of territorial/courting ritual; call is a sharp, abrupt "kyeek" along with a rapid, strident rattle resembling kingfisher's; during strongly powered flight, as in takeoff or sharp turn, wings make pronounced "whuck-whuck-whuck" noise, possibly a controllable sound used as alarm signal.

Range Nonmigratory; north to the limits of tree line, throughout most woodlands; throughout Upper Midwest where woodlands, parks and well-treed yards furnish adequate habitat.

Food Insectivorous, especially where prey are found in or on trees; at feeder very fond of suet and, secondarily, sunflower seeds.

Nest   Generally in live, firm wood, seeming to favor aspens; hole oblong, 2 to 2.5 in (5 to 6 cm) long by 1.25 to 1.5 in (3 to 4 cm) wide.

Comment   Woodpeckers tap sharply to test the resonance of wood, very likely to detect the hollow tunnels of insects. The sudden concussions might also startle hidden insects into moving and giving away their presence to the keen ears of the bird, upon which it drills in to make a capture with its probing, barb-tipped tongue. Exterior siding sometimes excites the excavating reflex in downies and hairies who respond to spaces in plywood by punching out the covering plies, or who drill holes in plastic or other coverings to check the hollow spaces behind them. This habit explains to frustrated householders a behavior they might otherwise mistake for willful property damage.

REF: A–643; BM–195; GO–200; NG–270; P–192

Three-toed Woodpecker *(Picoides tridactylus)*

Woodpecker family. Until recently, still in some guides as "Northern (or American) Three-toed"; *picus* is Latin for "a woodpecker," Greek *oides* compounded from *o*, "the" and *eidos*, "similar"; Greek *trias*, "three" and *daktylos*, "toe" combine to form descriptive *tridactylus*.

Description   The only other three-toed woodpecker is the closely related black-backed; three-toed is slightly smaller, but still noticeably larger than Downy Woodpecker; adult male has yellow patch on crown, dark crown of adult female may have light flecking; back, sides, wing primaries, and marginal tail feathers thickly barred in black and white, although density of barring is variable; prominent white stripes, one from back of eye down side of neck, other a "whisker" beginning at corner of mouth; wing coverts and central tail feathers black; chin, throat, and belly are white.

Behavior   Like larger cousin the black-backed, three-toed has reputation for being rather tame and trusting and shares preference for dense growths of mature conifers growing on low, marshy ground; favors stands of fire-killed and/or drowned trees; calls are sharp "kyik" and harsh rattle, very similar to, but softer than, the black-backed's.

Range Nonmigratory, although occasional winter irruptions may take it far south of breeding range; from coast to coast, throughout boreal forest; a rare occurrance anywhere in Upper Midwest, most likely to appear in extreme north of Great Lakes states.

Food Insects, principally those found in and under bark of dead, aged trees; at feeders takes readily to suet and may develop liking for sunflower seeds.

Nest Low hole, 5 to 12 ft (1.5 to 3.7 m) up in old or dead conifer; lower edge chiseled to bevel to provide easier access; allowing for "step," hole is 1.75 in (4.4 cm) wide by 2 in (5.1 cm) high, but into tree narrows to circular 1.5 in (3.8 cm) diameter.

Comment The Three-toed Woodpecker is circumpolar in distribution, unlike the black-backed which is exclusively North American. It feeds by drilling small round holes in bark or wood and harpooning exposed insects or grubs with its barb-tipped tongue. Nowhere throughout its extensive range is it a common bird, usually even less frequently encountered than the black-backed.

REF: A–683; BM–195; GO–200; NG–270; P–192

Black-backed Woodpecker *(Picoides arcticus)*

Woodpecker family. Common names have included "Arctic Three-toed," "Black-backed Three-toed"; *Picoides* compounded from Latin *picus*, "a woodpecker," and Greek *oides* compounded from *o*, "the" and *eidos*, "like" (similar); *arcticus* is self-evidently "northern."

Description Robin-sized, about same as Hairy Woodpecker; only other woodpecker with three toes is aptly named Three-toed Woodpecker, all rest having four; back, most of wings, central tail feathers, much of neck, and head black; sides and wing ends thickly barred; belly, throat, chin and dash below eye white; adult male has yellow patch on top of head, female's crown all black; told from three-toed by black back, otherwise difficult to see difference; to complicate matters, a very few Hairy Woodpeckers sport yellow crown patch instead of usual red!

Behavior Typical woodpecker posture, upright on vertical surface; scaler, rather than driller, flakes off patches of loose bark in search of prey; can be unusually tame, especially around nest; calls are a single, sharp "kik," and a harsh scolding rattle; in courting season, pairs stage staccato drumming duets.

Range Nonmigratory; coniferous and mixwood forests in northeast extremity of region; favors burnt-over conifer forests with tracts of standing dead trees and old-growth spruce forest in and around low-lying, boggy

terrain; occasional winter wanderer, appearing unexpectedly at feeders far out of usual range, then moving on.

Food   Scales bark off standing, fire-killed trees for insects, spiders, and grubs; readily takes to suet at feeders.

Nest   Usually low, from 2 to 15 ft (0.6 to 4.6 m) up in dead snag, post, or, if in live tree, usually one with dead heart; hole 1.5 in (3.8 cm) high by 1.75 in (4.4 cm) wide with pronounced bevel to lower rim forming a kind of step.

Comment   Not especially evident where it occurs, partly because its black upper body and barred flanks are excellent camouflage against the fire-blackened tree trunks it usually frequents. Its preferred haunts, lowland spruce near bog or muskeg, with its full complement of mosquitos, isn't preferred as a rule by humans, so this bird isn't often encountered by people. It is rare enough everywhere in the Upper Midwest, along with the three-toed, to cause a flurry of excitement when it shows up, as it now and then does, at a winter feeder.

REF: A–683; BM–196; GO–200; NG–270; P–192

Northern Flicker *(Colaptes auratus)*

Woodpecker family. Until recently also Common Flicker; previously "Yellow-shafted" (*C. auratus*), "Red-shafted" (*C. cafer*), or "Gilded" (*C. chrysoides*); folk names have (and do) include "high-hole," "high-holder," "clape," "pigeon woodpecker," "yellow-hammer," "yarrup," "hairy wicket," "wake-up," "yawker bird," "walk-up," "ant-bird," among many others; "flicker" from Anglo Saxon *flicerian*, "fluttering of birds," although word also highly echoic of bird's call; *Colaptes* is from Greek *kolapto*, "to peck with the bill, chisel"; *auratus* is from Latin "golden," referring to undersides of wings and tail.

Description   Larger than robin; short-legged, solid; in flight shows bright yellow underwings, boldly speckled undersides, bright white rump; bold black bid across top of breast; long, strong, slightly down-curved bill; both sexes with horizontal red dash on back of head; crown and neck gray; throat and sides of head tan; back and wings light brown with black barring; male only has black "moustache" from corner of mouth back under eye.

Behavior   Strong, markedly undulating flight, several rapid beats on up-swoop, wings folded for down-swoop; upright woodpecker stance in trees, but spends much time on open, grassy ground, hopping awkwardly about searching for ants; drums during mating season, sometimes on buildings; courting couples go through elaborate "dance" duet on tree limbs, flaring wings and tails, bobbing, and moving heads in circles; noisy calls a staccato, strident "yuk-yuk-yuk-yuk," a more deliberate "wicker, wicker, wicker," or a single, loud "kleee-yer."

Range   Migratory; breeds throughout region; habitat is open woodland, parkland, pastures, suburban yards, and parks; borderline between western "Red-shafted" and eastern "Yellow-shafted" in Dakotas and eastern Montana; winters irregularly in southern Montana, southern extreme of North Dakota, southern half of Minnesota, Wisconsin, and Michigan (not Upper Peninsula); regular winterer in Iowa.

Food   Ants, mostly from ground; in season fruit, nuts, and seeds; suet, peanut butter, and perhaps sunflower seeds at feeders.

Nest   Prefers to excavate hole in tree or snag with punky heartwood, thus favoring poplars; also uses utility poles, fence posts, buildings, natural tree cavities, or nest boxes; known to use holes in bank or cliff; excavated hole 2 in (5 cm) in diameter, from 20 in to 65 ft (.5 to 20 m) up; old tree holes important to other birds and small mammals; starlings frequently evict flickers.

Comment   Writers of this and previous generations have made special note that the flicker is "a bit of an oddball" or "a rebel in the family ranks" among woodpeckers. Worldwide it is one of only three that are true migrators, the others being the Yellow-bellied Sapsucker and the wryneck of Eurasia, the least woodpeckerlike member of the clan. The red-headed moves south from the northern parts of its range, but only far enough to find a living. Over most of its range it stays put, stashing acorns and other nuts in tree cavities to tide it over the winter.

The flickers until recently were listed as three species, but these have been "lumped" into one, renamed the Northern Flicker. What are now designated as three races have, except for the underwing colors that gave them their names, very similar plumage patterns except that the "Yellow-shafted" has a crescent of bright red encircling the back of its head; the "Red-shafted" and "Gilded" don't.

The really important plumage difference is sex-related; all males, otherwise identical to the females, have a colored "moustache." The Yellow-shafted's is black and the others' red. In the name of science, a deceptive "moustache" was painted on a mated female flicker. Her erstwhile lifelong mate promptly attacked her and drove her away. Interestingly, where the races meet and interbreed, the essential moustache may come out red on one side, black on the other. Except to sometimes befuddled bird watchers, it doesn't seem to matter.

REF: A–546; BM–198; GO–194; NG–264; P–190

Pileated Woodpecker *(Dryocopus pileatus)*

Woodpecker family. "Pileated" from specific name which is from Latin *pileum*, "a cap," refers to bird's prominent crest; formerly "cock-of-the-woods," or "logcock," red crest resembling rooster's comb; *Dryocopus* compounded from Greek *drys*, "a tree" and *kopis*, "a dagger."

Description   Crow-sized; except for extirpated Ivory-billed Woodpecker, is continent's largest woodpecker by far; with wings folded is predominantly black except for white stripe on each side of the long neck and side of face; white chin and narrow white eyebrow stripe; both sexes have conspicuous red crest, male's being larger, and he has red "moustache"; in flight, white lining on underside of wings flashes prominently.

Behavior   First clue to presence is often large, vertically oblong holes freshly chipped out of trunks of trees, snags, frequently close to ground; litter of chips especially obvious in snow; very wary except where it has had a chance to become habituated to people in protected areas such as national, or large urban, parks; on quiet days in mature woodland loud, irregular whacking noise of this bird at work usually first active sign of its presence; call loud, strident succession of "kyak-kyak-kyak-kyak"s often increasing in volume, similar to flicker with sound turned up.

Range   Nonmigratory; generally limited to substantial tracts of mature deciduous and boreal forest removed from human activity, but also found in parks and agricultural areas where there are tall trees, especially near water; throughout Upper Midwest east of Minnesota River Valley, eastern two-thirds of Iowa, down from Manitoba in Red River Valley, extreme western Montana.

Food   Insects, especially carpenter ants which it regurgitates to feed its nestlings; occasionally visits feeders for suet, said to also take nuts, meat scraps, and hamburger.

Nest   Hole usually 30 to 50 ft (9 to 15 m) up in large tree; entrance 3 to 3.5 in (8 to 9 cm) wide, somewhat longer.

Comment   Carpenter ants are the pileated's major food, swept up with the long, sticky tongue from the deep holes the bird excavates into the ants' galleries inside infested trees. Often the first outward sign an observer might have that a big, apparently sound tree is harboring ants is a pileated's fresh, gaping hole near the base of it. Pileateds eat hugely; the stomach of an adult was found by an enquiring biologist to contain 2,500 ants. In response to early settlement and logging, populations plummeted, to the point where the species was thought to be threatened. But numbers recovered, and may be increasing, due both to the birds' latent ability to adapt to cutover forest habitat and to lessened persecution, principally indiscriminate shooting.

REF: A–646; BM–198; GO–194; NG–274; P–188

Horned Lark *(Eremophila alpestris)*

Lark family. "Lark" from Anglo-Saxon *lawerce* which became Middle English *laverke* or *larke,* all of which mean "a lark." *Eremophila* is from Greek *eremos,* "lonely," and *phileo,* "to love," hence "loving solitude"; *alpestris* is Latin for "alpine."

Description   Somewhat larger and longer-tailed than House Sparrow; patterns of plumage among several recognized races similar, but color can vary; dominant race (prairie) has yellow throat over slightly crescented dark patch on upper breast; dark whisker broadening to cheek patch outlined in white; white bands over eyes meet over bill to form partial headband; bordering top of headband is another narrow, dark band circling front and sides of crown, ends terminating in small, dark "horns"; upper body has subdued patterns of browns; breast and belly off-white; underside of tail black; rear claw very long, slightly curved.

Behavior   Social in winter; flocks forage in cultivated fields, grazed pastures, airports, beaches, and roadsides; avoids stubble or anything with even short level of growth above ground; often roves with Snow Buntings; scuttles along very close to the ground, running (not hopping); courting male spirals high, to 800 feet, singing a high-pitched cascade of tinkling notes, then folds his wings and plunges back to earth.

Range   Migratory; circumpolar; in North America breeds from highest arctic islands to Central America, wherever there are expanses of bare, open ground; winters in all of Upper Midwest except forested areas of northeast.

Food   Insects; may scratch in earth for seeds in winter; has been known to approach feeders to try crushed crackers and crumbs; will gather where chaff or screenings are scattered on snow in open.

Nest   Small hollow on ground in shelter of plant tuft or stone; shallow cup of coarse grass, stems, and leaves, lined with fine grasses; outer side built up with pebbles, clods, and droppings to form a "patio" or terrace; very skillfully hidden, extremely difficult to find.

Comment   The Horned Lark is the bird, usually seen alongside the road in loose flocks, that reminds us that winter is coming to an end, even though conditions of the moment may deny it. It is also one of the earliest nesters; late snowstorms often destroy the first clutches. Although we associate it with melting snow and the north, it is equally at home on the hot Mexican tablelands as on the wind-scoured northern plains.

   This bird is a highly unlikely feeder visitor. Scattering screenings in areas where they are already known to feed, such as a road or railroad right-of-way, beach, or large parking lot could attract them in large numbers and hold them there as long as the seeds are offered.

REF: A–538; BM–209; GO–218; NG–294; P–200

Crow Family
Family Corvidae

Crows—the corvids—and their allies are an avian success story. Everywhere they are a testament to the benefits of being generalists with a repertoire of behavioral options they can play according to the conditions of the moment. In other words, they are adaptable.

By hedging on their options they have not acquired the power and speed of the flashy raptors, the specialized physiology of the divers and swimmers, nor indeed any obvious trait that makes them anything but oversized songbirds. Even the bulky raven faces his harsh world in the highest Arctic on dickeybird feet innocent of destructive capacity. Its bill is large and businesslike, but more a handyman's tool than a specialized instrument.

If there is one thing they can claim as special, it's their intelligence. There is no absolute way of measuring this attribute in humans, and not even a reliable approximation of any scale to rate one species of animal against another. But in comparison to other birds reacting to similar situations, the crow and its kin do seem to be "smarter."

In the corvid family, crows and ravens have been regarded as the most highly evolved. It is an assumption supported by their perceived relative intelligence, their ability to learn quickly and to remember, and their unusual degree of adaptability in a very wide range of habitats. Convincingly, they possess the highest brain-to-body weight ratio of any bird.

The popular literature repeats a seaside anecdote on how herring gulls and crows both attempt to feed on mussels. Neither is strong enough to smash the shells, nor pry them open with its beak. Both have learned to fly aloft with a mussel and crack it by dropping it. With the gulls, it is a hit-and-miss operation since often as not they bomb them fruitlessly onto soft mud. But the crows have learned to drop them onto the rocks.

Tufts, in *Birds of Nova Scotia*, reports nest-building ravens' pulling wool from the rumps of resting sheep.

Corvid intelligence isn't the lovable smarts of, for example, the porpoise. It is a defiant craftiness with a bent for larceny that humans usually find irritating and at times unsettling. Branded as pests of agriculture and of wildlife, they have been persecuted relentlessly. They simply respond to the plots against them by becoming more skillfully evasive. Crows are noted for their uncanny ability to sense the presence of a concealed gun, and to spot the difference between a shotgun and a similar-shaped cane.

Country Bird Moves Uptown   Throughout their range in North America several species of corvids, initially swept aside by the impact of settlement, have learned to capitalize on the changes humans have wrought. In any northern mining or lumbering town ravens are bold as street pigeons, often hanging about the downtown business sections in such numbers as to be regarded as nuisances. In Thompson, Manitoba, the city's emblematic bird is referred to, with mixed affection, as the "Thompson Turkey," a tribute to its size. Squadrons of them ensure that the contents of any garbage cans left open will soon be strewn about. Auto insurance claims are occasionally paid to repair dents caused by ravens dropping bones or frozen globs of refuse onto cars from on high.

In Calgary and Edmonton magpies are creating major controversy because they have become such obvious nuisances. Aside from their evident clever opportunism, these birds may reflect a fact of city life now long past. At one time retired farmers, the sworn enemy of the magpie, took their shotguns to town with them and without a second thought blasted away at any magpie or crow that crossed their path. Nowadays civic authority takes a dim view of gunplay within city limits, allowing the magpies to chalk off a one-time serious hazard.

The easterly states of the Upper Midwest have, from time to time, seen winter "invasions" of magpies, approximately one each decade. These are on record (Janssen) as coming from the southwest in the 1920s and 1930s, from the northwest since the 1940s. Given the apparent easterly movement of these birds, there may be a time in the not-too-distant future when cities in the eastern region of the Upper Midwest may have to deal with the civic displeasure that an oversupply of magpies is now stirring up farther northwest.

Not to be outdone, over the last few decades the crow has "gone urban," moving into suburbs where nesting sites and food are plentiful and where it enjoys the inadvertant protection from its natural predators that the presence of its new human neighbors affords.

"Good" and "Bad"   In nature there is an endless interplay of actions that can be misinterpreted according to human values as either "good" or "bad," even for activities that don't relate to human interests. These biases obscure the real roles of the species they affect, and in the case of the "bad" animals, make them targets of unwarranted persecution.

Unhappily, crows, magpies, and ravens, and, to a lesser degree, the jays are branded as "bad." All corvids will congregate around dead animals to feed on the rotting flesh, a habit finicky humans find ghoulish. Other emotions intervene; all corvids are nest predators, feeding on the eggs and nestlings of other birds. On a purely emotional level this is abhorrent; bird lovers feel pity for the bereaved parents, hunters fume over the loss of "their" game birds.

The answer for genuinely interested nature watchers is to learn more about the survival imperatives of the animals around them, to let real knowledge supplant prejudice and emotion. The important thing to keep in mind is that in nature there is no altruism and no vindictiveness, only the unbreakable rules of survival and reproduction.

Predators as Prey   It may help in overcoming our judgmental prejudices to realize that the scoundrel crow family is as much accountable to the laws of survival as any wild thing. In the game of eat-or-be-eaten, the corvids themselves, especially the young, provide food for larger predators.

I was reminded of this one early June day in 1987 in Canada's Riding Mountain National Park where I worked as an interpreter. A raucous din drew my attention to a Red Squirrel scrambling along the top of a fence with a Blue Jay in hot pursuit. The squirrel was carrying a large but unfledged nestling, obviously the property of the bird. The jays' nest was close by, with two nestlings in it the same size as the one borne by the squirrel. By the end of the following day the remaining two nestlings had vanished.

In the spring of 1989 at Riding Mountain, the garden staff discovered the headless carcass of a fully fledged young raven on the ground a few feet from the nest. Evidence suggested the killer was a Great Horned Owl which, at that time of year, likely had a nest of its own young to feed.

The crow family tends to be rather long-lived. A raven in captivity lasted for twenty-nine years, and wild Blue Jays have survived to fifteen. This of itself does not suggest a high IQ, but it is an advantage permitting both the time, in youth, to learn, and an extended adulthood in which to apply the accumulated experience.

Finally, for what it's worth as a measure of their intelligence, this family boasts the only native North American birds that can be taught to imitate human speech. Starlings share this talent but they aren't native birds.

Along with some species of gulls, the crow family has the most varied diet of any birds. They eat grain, green shoots from gardens, berries, dried fruit, carrion, eggs and nestlings, small terrestrial animals, insects, fish, and all manner of human refuse, and will hoard surplus food. Interestingly, *pica*, the Latin word for "magpie," is also a medical term describing an unusual craving for unnatural things, such as a child that eats dirt or paint.

Hoarding and migrating are responses to life in an environment where food resources are unreliable or vanish altogether as in our midcontinental winters. Of this family represented here, only the crow is a true migrant; the rest have adapted well enough to tough it out with occasional foraging migrations when conditions in their home territories are unusually stressful.

Gray Jay *(Perisoreus canadensis)*

Crow family. Used to be "Canada Jay"; lackluster "gray" title also replaces "Whiskey-jack," woodsy English version of Algonquian/Cree *wiskatjan;*

interesting to note that European writers syllabize call of Siberian Jay as "whisk-ee"; *Perisoreus* is Greek for "to heap up," i.e., to store up, hoard; *canadensis* is Latinized "of Canada."

Description   Off-white face and forehead shading softly into smokey gray accentuate the overall soft, puffy look; back of head, neck, and indistinct stripe encircling eye are gray to gray-brown; no crest; back, wings, and tail soft gray, underside lighter gray; bill of modest proportions; long tail.

Behavior   Actions deliberate, unhurried; flight often a smooth, suspended, descending glide; accomplished mooch, training picnickers to share food by approaching them with an air of poised expectancy, not above helping itself with well-timed grab if passive appeal doesn't work, hence the alternate bush name "camp robber"; compulsive food hoarder; call is a clear, descending "quee-oo" whistle; other sounds include typical jay repertoire of squawks, chortles, and imitations.

Range   Nonmigratory, but subject to occasional irruptive appearances out of normal haunts; breeds from tundra tree line south through boreal and montane forest; in forested Montana, extreme north of Great Lakes states, not in intervening plains and farmlands.

Food   Omnivorous; fruit, seeds, meat, insects, and carrion; in north quick to scavenge at wolf kills; at feeder takes suet, larger seeds, and table scraps.

Nest   Large, thick-walled; well lined with fine grasses, bark shreds, feathers, hair, fur, and spider and insect coccoon webbing; usually 3 to 10 ft (1 to 3 m) from snow surface, but occasionally much higher; usually close to trunk of small to midsized conifer in open woods, almost always on sunlit side; eggs very pale greenish splattered with olive and paler gray, especially at large end.

Comment   Gray Jays have elaborated on food-caching to a degree that allows them not only to survive our subarctic winter, but also to begin nesting well before it ends. Oversized salivary glands secrete copious amounts of sticky saliva that is used to glob fragments of food together and secure it to conifer twigs, bark niches, and other elevated hideaways that won't be covered with snow. Dried, the saliva is water resistant and apparently doesn't freeze solidly, permitting easier use in subzero temperatures.

REF: A–699; BM–214; GO–224; NG–302; P–208

Blue Jay *(Cyanocitta cristata)*

Crow family. "Jay" is rooted in the Latin *gaius*, "a jay"; may also be echoic of the call; *Cyanos* is Greek "blue," *kitta* "a jay"; *cristata* is Latin for "crested."

Description   Bigger than robin; gorgeous medley in blues; bright azure patterned with black bars and white patches on wings and long fan-shaped tail; back and crest uniform purplish blue; face patterned with a gray-bordered black eye-stripe extended downward into a narrow ribbon forming a circlet over the upper breast; breast and belly smokey gray, undertail white; crest elegant, jaunty; bill long, dagger-shaped.

Behavior   Movements graceful, attitude alert, wary; almost always in company, probably family; hurriedly gobbles food to carry away in throat pouch to storage places; size permits it to dominate feeders; highly vocal, with repertoire of squawks, whistles, chortles, and trills to add to its standard, rasping "ja-a-a-ay" call; usually noisy and visible, it grows secretive and silent during its own nesting season.

Range   Non-to-casually migratory; inhabits mixed and deciduous woodland, parks and suburbs; replaced in more northern habitat by Gray Jay; absent in region only from western Montana.

Food   Omnivorous; opportunistically predacious on songbird eggs and nestlings; sometime scavenger on carrion such as road kills; takes and stashes in quantity most feeder offerings except smallest seeds; buries acorns.

Nest   Rather loose, shallow platform of coarse twigs; cup lined with rootlets, bark, shreds of plastic, paper, rags, and feathers.

Comment   In a famous incident a captive Blue Jay tore pieces of newspaper from the bottom of its cage and fished with them for food pellets otherwise beyond its reach. It is a talented mimic of other birds, especially the Red-tailed Hawk, and of odd sounds like the squeaking of a rusty clothesline pulley. Although justifiably suspicious of humans on first acquaintance, it can be conditioned to trustfulness with food and patience. "Tame" Blue Jays can become bold, entertaining scrounges of hand-held goodies.

It is suggested that its taste for songbird eggs and nestlings stems from its own need for calcium during the female's egg-developing stage, and that supplying oyster shell or chopped-up egg-shell will diminish its drive to pilfer nests. Nice thought; bears verification.

REF: A–552; BM–215; GO–222; NG–302; P–208

Black-billed Magpie *(Pica pica)*

Crow family. "Black-billed" as distinct from "Yellow-billed" of California; sometimes "American" Magpie; "Magpie" has two roots, "mag" from the pet version of "Margaret" (although connection is a mystery), "pie" possibly from same root as "piebald," an animal with a patchwork of contrasting colors, or from Middle English *pie*, "magpie"; Latin *pica*, "a magpie."

Description   Pigeon-sized, slim; very long-tailed, strikingly beautiful; contrasting black-and-white body pattern; tail and wings iridescent blue-green-bronze; in flight, outer wing primaries flash white and horseshoe-shaped white mark on back is very evident.

Behavior   All movements graceful, flowing, particularly when springing about among branches; level flight on measured wing beats, almost languid, wings stroking the air; travels in small, loose groups; congregates around garbage dumps, road kills; call is a strident, rasping "yek-yek-yek," repeated rapidly or in a single, drawn-out, ascending "yaaag?"; usually very wary and alert.

Range   Nonmigratory; circumpolar; in North America a western native, from Alaska south to New Mexico; not a bird of boreal habitat; breeds in west through western half of Dakotas, occasional fall and winter visitor into northwest Minnesota, very rare elsewhere out of breeding range.

Food   Omnivorous scavenger/predator; at feeders, hauls suet away in bulk chunks until it's all gone, a good reason for dispensing it in sturdy wire screen holders with half-inch or smaller mesh.

Nest   Unmistakable; huge, loosely interlaced structure of twigs, often thorns, up to 3 ft (1 m) in height woven around a cupped nest of mud and fibers, completely enclosed except for one or more side entrances; in small tree or large bush, from 6 to 16 ft (2 to 5 m) up; takes forty to fifty days to build.

Comment   This is the same as the Eurasian species notorious as a noisy scold and thief. It is a western bird, possibly driven from the Plains originally by loss of bison and/or subsequent settlement. But it has reclaimed its former domain and is spreading steadily southeastward. Its legendary wariness is a response to persecution for its purported depredations on game-bird eggs and for pecking at wounds and warble fly sores on the backs of cattle. Sometimes it deepens these wounds enough to injure or kill the animals which unaccountably seem not to be troubled by the probing bills in their live flesh. In its turn, the magpie is prey to the wintering goshawk and Great Horned Owl, at a time when other game is scarce.

REF: A–717; BM–216; GO–224; NG–304; P–208

American Crow *(Corvus brachyrhynchos)*

Crow family. Sometimes "common" crow; Anglo Saxon *crawe*, "crow" imitative of call; *corvus* is Latin for "a crow"; Greek *brachys* is "short" and *rhynchos* "beak" because crow's beak is shorter than a raven's.

Description   All black; told from raven by considerably smaller size, relatively smaller bill, lack of hackle feathers at throat, and square tail (raven's is fan-shaped); best indicator is voice—the raven's a variety of croaks, the crow's a basic "caw."

Behavior   Not usually alone, out of breeding season may rove and roost in very large flocks; wary, alert, and sharp-eyed; flight on steady wingbeats

with little gliding unless circling or coming in for a landing; forages on ground in cultivated fields, roadsides, and garbage dumps; scavenges dead animals; voice a loud, harsh "caw," may be very noisy especially around nest when young are begging from old birds and when a group is "mobbing" an owl or hawk.

Range   Migratory; breeds throughout Canada and U.S. except Yukon, Alaska, and driest southwest desert; doesn't winter widely in North Dakota and northern Minnesota, but may hold over in small numbers where there is an abundant, reliable source of food.

Food   Totally omnivorous, taking seeds, fruit, insects, carrion, buds and shoots, eggs, and nestlings; at feeder suet, seeds, corn, and grain.

Nest   Large bundle of coarse twigs, usually well up in major crotch on trunk or branch, obvious from a distance when tree is leafless; bowl made of shredded bark, grasses, and vine stems, lined with moss, grass, fur, and feathers; most frequent used-nest-of-choice by Great Horned Owls, which don't make their own.

Comment   Vilified as bandits, nest-robbers, and destructive pests, crows have nevertheless worked their way into our language; as in "eat crow," "straight as the crow flies," "crow's feet," etc. If the average person were asked to name four birds, one of them would almost certainly be the crow.

Very likely that person could also do a fair impression of a crow. And although that hoarse "caw" is the only call we associate with this plentiful bird, it is nevertheless employed with great eloquence. To a listening human its inflection, duration, frequency, pitch, volume, and tone can clearly communicate fear, alarm, suspicion, curiosity, anger, hunger, and "come hither." As to its clever adaptability, American clergyman and lecturer Henry Ward Beecher summed up the crow in a trenchant comparison: "If men wore feathers and wings, very few of them would be clever enough to be crows."

REF: A–565; BM–218; GO–226; NG–306; P–206

Common Raven *(Corvus corax)*

Crow family. Sometimes "Northern" Raven; "Raven" is from Anglo Saxon *hraefn*, for "raven"; *Corvus* is Latin for "crow," *corax* is Greek for "a raven," akin to *krazo*, "croak."

Description   All black; distinguished from crow by larger size, relatively more massive bill, shaggy throat feathers, wedged tail (crow's is squared off), and voice; equivalent of crow "caw" is a grating, gutteral, resonant croak.

Behavior   Usually seen in pairs or small family groups, except at food sources like garbage dumps where it may congregate by the dozens; more inclined than crow to circle aloft and soar, and frequently indulges in rolling, tumbling, diving aerial games; voice has highly variable repertoire of throaty honks, squawks, and an unexpectedly musical, bell-like "tok"; fur traders called it "barking crow"; vulturelike in ability to detect carrion and kills.

Range   Year-round from highest arctic islands throughout northern continental mainland and far to southwest in forests and mountains; breeds in extreme northeast Minnesota and Wisconsin; scattered winter visitor elsewhere in northern parts of Upper Midwest.

Food   Everything; "kills rabbits and birds" says a British field guide; in northern Minnesota close relationship in winter to timber wolves, following packs to feed on kills and wolf droppings.

Nest   Begin spectacular courtship aerobatics around end of March; nest is large mass of sticks and twigs on cliff ledges or in trees (usually large conifers); may build new nest on top of last year's.

Comment   On a number of occasions I have noted that most ravens approaching a scrap of food in the snow for the first time go through an elaborate routine. Surveillance comes first, from varying angles and elevations. The ground approach proceeds by hesitant stages and nervous retreats, ever nearer until the bird is close enough to stretch forward, stab and recoil, and pause. Slightly reassured it repeatedly jabs, bounds back, springs up on flapping wings until the prize is finally snatched and yanked back or flipped overhead. I call it the "trap dance," and assume it has been acquired from generations of ancestors that learned to rob the still-ubiquitous, baited leghold trap without falling into the deadly snapping jaws.

REF: A–716; BM–218; GO–226; NG–306; P–206

Titmice

Family Paridae

The short form for "titmouse" causes North Americans to flinch. But "tit" in this case is from the Norse *tittre*, a general term for anything small or little. Perhaps via the Vikings and their well-known practice of dropping in to stay, the word became Middle English *tit*, meaning "small." "Mouse" is a case of linguistic mistaken identity, for it has nothing to do with mice, arising instead from the Anglo Saxon *mase* or *mose*, a term for small birds. It would be a quibble rendered hopeless by time and long custom to suggest that the plural should really be "titmouses."

Titmice are a widespread family of forty-six species, ten of them in North America, inhabiting a wide variety of habitats from subarctic to tropical. They missed only Australia, New Zealand, and South America.

Although in some cases separated by great chunks of geography, the family resemblance between our chickadees and several species of Eurasian tits is obvious; the Marsh, Somber, and Willow tits could pass at first glance as Black-capped Chickadees, the Siberian as a boreal. The latter in fact shares the Boreal Chickadee's territory in central Alaska and the neighboring Northwest Territories. Their dissimilar voices would likely be the first giveaway, although the Marsh Tit's call is described as including a "chikka-dee-dee-dee" along with a sneeze-like "pitchoo" and a nasal "chay."

The best-known titmouse in North America is the spritely little tufted, occupying the eastern and southeastern U.S. and down into eastern Mexico. Since the turn of the century it has slowly spread north and west from its original range. One might think that its similarity to the hardy, adaptable chickadee would have made its spread into new territory an easy expansion, particularly when one considers the whirlwind invasion of the House Sparrow and the starling. Its conquest should have been helped a great deal by its compatibility to bird feeders.

But to those who would welcome this spritely little acrobat to their territory, its coming has been disappointingly slow.

Competition in the Family   The chickadee itself may be one of the inhibitors. Both are cavity nesters; the chickadee excavates its own, the titmouse doesn't, which puts it into competition for used lodgings with, among others, the starling. The more self-reliant chickadee rarely uses birdhouses, the titmouse frequently does. Both take advantage of feeders, but the titmouse's natural feeding pattern upon the onset of winter is to switch from insects to tree mast, especially acorns and beechnuts. The chickadee's seasonal switch is to mixed fare of insect dormants and eggs, and weed seeds.

This difference might affect relative survival rates. Insects, in their multitudes of species, are likely to be plentifully available in one form or another every year. And weeds, as gardeners will testify, have yet to suffer a total crop failure. But one or two species of trees are vulnerable to drought, frost, and insect attack, and in some years both will fail to bear a crop. Hence the chickadee's winter diet is better buffered than the titmouse's against the vagaries of weather and pestilences.

In suburbs, towns, farms, and adjoining parklands and forests, the versatile chickadees often forage in the company of nuthatches, woodpeckers, titmice, and siskins. There is no doubt an advantage here for someone; perhaps the food search of one species uncovers sources for another, perhaps with more eyes on the alert there is better security against predators. Given the chickadees' opportunistic ways, one wouldn't be surprised if they turned out to be the ones that profited most from these integrated outings.

Snakeskin Deterrent   On the subject of nesting, there is an interesting relationship between snakes and Tufted Titmice. Where they can get them, the birds habitually weave discarded snake skins into their nests. This is a habit shared by the Great Crested Flycatcher, another cavity nester. The flycatcher occasionally even allows part of the skin to dangle outside the nest entrance.

The arguable point is whether the skin is selectively used to scare off would-be nest robbers, or is simply another handy item of nesting material. Many birds, including titmice, routinely use strips of plastic in their nests, material that looks and feels a lot like discarded snake skin. For the choice to be deliberate, both the titmouse and the robbers have to recognize the skin for what it is, and the robbers have to associate it with danger. I'm not aware if other small birds add skins to their nests. If they don't, the case for the choice of skins as a selective predator deterrent is stronger.

There is a further link between snakes and the titmouse family. Brooding females, when threatened on the nest, will open their mouths, hiss loudly, and move their heads back and forth in a manner clearly imitative of a snake's threat gestures. As pointed out elsewhere, there is a significantly higher loss to predators of brooding females among some species of cavity nesters than among open nesters. Cornered in a dark hole with no way out, a convincing snake impersonation by the trapped occupant just might cause a predator to hesitate long enough to allow a last-chance opening for escape.

High Ingenuity Quotient   All members of the family share the trusting nature and the bold, inquisitive behavior that make our chickadees such favorites at feeders. No doubt the urge to examine anything new that comes to their attention is an adaptation to a harsh environment where opportunism in the search for food can mean the difference between life and starvation.

Ingenuity and a certain inventive bent are characteristics of the entire titmouse clan. An experimenter in Britain discovered that tits learned to retrieve a bit of food on the end of a long string tied to a perch. The birds would haul in with their beaks, clamp the loose loop under one foot, and haul in again until the food was reeled in. They could handle up to two feet of line.

In his book *A Complete Guide to Bird Feeding,* John V. Dennis recounts this experiment but notes that in his own efforts to duplicate it, his Carolina Chickadees and Tufted Titmice simply fluttered directly to the food, grabbed the string, and hung there with both feet while they scooped the prize.

One wonders if Mr. Dennis made things too easy for his subjects by providing string thick enough to cling to. Perhaps the use of monofilament fishline or thread would prevent that overly ingenious business of going directly to the end of the string. It would be a more searching test of our North American titmice, and more reassuring to their fans if they passed it.

Black-capped Chickadee *(Parus atricapillus)*

Titmouse family. "Chickadee" imitates call, although "chickadee-dee-dee" would be more accurate; *Parus* is Latin for "titmouse," *ater* is Latin for "black," *capillus* is Latin for "hair of the head."

Description   Very small, active, with tiny bill; body plumage soft and fluffy; crown, back of neck, throat and bib black; cheeks and sides of neck white; back gray-beige; wings and tail slate gray with edges of feathers lightly frosted; flanks tinged with buff; belly off-white; sexes identical.

Behavior   Acrobatic, hyperactive, excitable, vocal; undeterred by cold weather; usually first "customers" at new feeder; feed by fluttering hurriedly to feeder, selecting seed, and flying off; crack sunflower seeds by clutching them tightly against perch with one foot, hammering them open with beak; in winter travel in family groups; famous "chicka-dee-dee" call augmented in late winter with clear, slow "seeeee-fee-bee" whistle very much like song of White-throated Sparrow, emphasis on second syllable; also soft twitter.

Range   Nonmigratory; common coast-to-coast, from tree line south; throughout Upper Midwest.

Food   Insectivorous by preference, scouring winter twigs and bark for eggs, pupae, and dormant adults, but supplementing this with weed seeds; in the wild picks scraps from remains of predator kills; at feeder keen on sunflower seeds, nuts, peanut butter, and suet, much of which it stashes away.

Nest   Nests, and shelters in winter, in tree holes cleaned out of punky knotholes; in winter adults huddle together; can sometimes be tricked into using nest box if it is first filled with sawdust.

Comment   These beady-eyed charmers have done more than any other bird to convert indifferent householders into dedicated feeders. Their unquenchable, bubbly good nature is often the only evidence of life on bitterly cold winter days. The light tap-tapping from the edge of the shelf is familiar to those with windowsill feeders, indicating that a chickadee is hammering open a sunflower seed. Clean around feeders, unlike finches and House Sparrows, they don't congregate on platforms in a squabbling, defecating bunch. Compulsively inquisitive and trusting, they are the easiest of birds to tame, learning quickly to take seeds out of hand, then to search clothing, lips, and ears for hidden tidbits.

At certain places and times the normally stay-at-home chickadee takes off in fall migration. Janssen notes that heavy concentrations of the birds have been observed along the Minnesota shore of Lake Superior, at which times hundreds of birds could be seen on peak days between mid-September and mid-October. There were particularly obvious "invasions" in 1959 and 1968.

REF: A–657; BM–220; GO–228; NG–310; P–210

Boreal Chickadee *(Parus hudsonicus)*

Titmouse family. "Boreal" means "of the north," "chickadee" imitates its call; *Parus* is Latin for "titmouse" and *hudsonicus* "of Hudson Bay."

Description   Identical in size and plumage pattern to black-capped at first glance; chin and throat black, but cap dark brown; flanks ruddier; overall color tends to beige rather than gray.

Behavior   Shares acrobatic, fluttery energy of Black-capped Chickadee, but less trusting, more subdued; often forages with black-capped, nuthatches, and smaller woodpeckers; call definitely a chickadee's but thinner, wheezy "sik-a-day-day," drawled out, like slow black-capped with laryngitis.

Range   Nonmigratory, but occasional winter nomad south of usual range through boreal forest and southern tundra; unlike black-capped not usually found far from coniferous woodlands; present in northeast Minnesota, Wisconsin, and extreme northwest Montana which it shares with Mountain Chickadee.

Food   Omnivorous; winter gleaner of small branches and twigs for dormant insects, larvae, eggs, and scraps from predator kills; comes less readily to feeders than black-capped; once there, shares its cousin's delight with sunflower seeds, suet, and peanut butter.

Nest   Hole cleared out in decayed stub of conifer or birch, often quite low, almost never higher than 10 ft (3 m); prefers swampier, more enclosed habitat than black-capped.

Comment   Both the Black-capped and the Boreal Chickadees are at home throughout most of Canada's vast boreal forests, but the boreal extends its range farther north into the tundra. It breeds in the Upper Midwest thanks only to the presence of a slice of the Canadian Shield that dips down along the western Great Lakes shores.

Some guides suggest the boreal is less visible than the black-capped due to its preference for foraging in the interiors of dense spruce trees, coming less readily to the tips of branches. This habit and its more remote range combine to make the boreal much less well known, and to cause a minor flutter among bird feeders in the southern Upper Midwest when one shows up there.

REF: A–712; BM–220; GO–228; NG–312; P–210

Tufted Titmouse *(Parus bicolor)*

Titmouse family. Also "tufted tit," "crested tomtit," "peto bird"; "Tufted" from crest, finely fringed along rear edge when erect; *Parus* is from Latin for "a titmouse" and *bicolor* from *bi* ("two") and *color* because rust tint to flanks gives underparts a two-tone look, in contrast to Plain Titmouse.

Description   Sparrow-sized, slightly larger than chickadee; mouse gray upper body, lighter below; prominent dark eye; high, pointed crest; rust-colored flanks; small dark patch over base of bill.

Behavior   Much like chickadee, quick-moving, acrobatic, but slightly less inquisitive and trusting; usually travels in small family groups in fall and winter; may keep company with chickadees, nuthatches, creepers, and smaller woodpeckers when foraging; comes very readily to feeders; tucks sunflower seeds between toes on perch and chips them open with bill; call is a whistled pair of slurred notes, accent on first, "peetoe-peetoe-peetoe-peetoe" repeated over and over; alarm call a harsh, scolding "chaay, chaay."

Range   Nonmigratory; eastern and southeastern U.S.; occupies southern half of Michigan, Wisconsin, and extreme southeastern Minnesota; near northern limits of range found in localized pockets of habitat; prefers damp woodlands, open mixed and deciduous forest, orchards, and well-treed parks and suburbs.

Food   Insects; switches to nuts, seeds, and dry berries in winter; caches acorns and beechnuts; at feeder very keen on sunflower seeds and suet; said to be more partial to baked goods than chickadee.

Nest   Natural cavity or woodpecker hole, occasionally birdhouse; hole well filled with leaves, moss, bark shreds, grass, shreds of plastic, paper, and discarded snake skin when available; cup padded with hair, fur, and bits of string; from 20 in to 90 ft (.5 to 27 m) high.

Comment   It has been suggested that without winter feeders the titmouse wouldn't have managed even the modest expansion of territory it has managed into the Upper Midwest. Perhaps further benevolence, and plenty of nest boxes, would tip the survival scale a little further in favor of the titmouse. A heartening precedent is already at hand in the widespread provision of nest boxes for Eastern Bluebirds. For titmice, boxes would offer both crucial winter shelter and secure summer nesting.

REF: A–658; BM–221; GO–230; NG–308; P–210

Nuthatches
Family Sittidae

In one of the many introductions to birding books that he has written over the years, Roger Tory Peterson attributed the base level of interest in birds to ". . . the White-breasted Nuthatch type of bird watcher who feeds birds on the shelf outside the kitchen window and goes no further afield."

I took this as a tribute to the bird, and to the fact that it is one of the most consistent of visitors to winter feeding stations, often the first one to acknowledge a newly placed offering. For many of us, the faithful nuthatch is second in our affections only to the irrepressibly cheerful chickadee.

Nuthatch "faithfulness" extends through their mutually held territory to each other, and is a year-round bond. The sentiments of their human hosts notwithstanding, this is simply a matter of their behaving in their own reproductive interests. Constancy may be a response to their need for ready-made tree holes to nest in.

Safe, secure holes in trees, particularly if you are in the second-hand market, are a scarce item. The absence of a suitable hole means that they cannot breed. It is therefore crucial for those who already have a territory, nest site included, to hang onto it. And they can maintain better security if they stay on their turf and have a mate to help run off pushy intruders.

"No Trespassing"   Nuthatches aren't noticeably quarrelsome at feeders. But confronting an aroused one is something one does not do lightly. The body language is eloquent. Wings and tail are raised and flared, exposing otherwise concealed patterns of white that are a warning flash that cannot escape notice. The stiletto bill and the beady eyes are directed at the enemy with no-nonsense intensity. The agitated body is cocked toward the adversary and rotated jerkily back and forth, like a mechanical toy. The threat is unmistakable.

I once watched two embattled birds confront both Gray and Red squirrels over possession of an old flicker hole in a poplar in my yard. It was the doughty birds that raised their brood that year—in that tree.

The European version of the Red-breasted Nuthatch adds to the security of its nest hole by plastering the entrance with mud until it is barely able to squeeze in. This serves to keep out larger preemptors, especially starlings. Our red-breasted smears spruce, pine, or fir gum around the entrance hole. This might be a behavioral relic from a Eurasian ancestor, since its purpose, and the use of sticky gum, is not so clear. The pungent gum might obscure the scent of the nest, its gooiness repel trespassers. One reference noted that a nuthatch itself was found dead in the entrance to its nest, stuck in the gum.

A further variant on this behavior is to be found in the White-breasted Nuthatch, which has been seen rubbing the bark near its nest hole with blister beetles or ants that secrete irritant chemicals when handled roughly. The strong-smelling and/or repellant vapors thus deposited could be a way of deterring nest-robbers like squirrels or of masquerading telltale scent.

In common with many overwintering birds, both of our nuthatch species store surplus food. A feeder with a generous supply of sunflower seeds can trigger a marathon of activity, as happened with a solitary male red-breasted that arrived at my city windowsill early one October. He made a collecting flight from the shelf to nearby oaks once every forty-five seconds on average for extended periods. He must have had hundreds and hundreds of seeds poked into the rough bark of the oaks. Then he abruptly vanished, never to reap the rewards of his labors. Whether his disappearance was a decision to resume his journey south or the intervention of a neighbor's cat, one can only guess.

There are twenty-one species of nuthatches throughout the world. They are unique in their ability to climb down trees (or rocks or walls) headfirst as easily as they can climb up. This survival "idea" of scanning surfaces for food from the top down rather than from the bottom up, as conventional climbers must do, gave some ancestral proto-nuthatch a slight edge over its relatives. The descendants fortunate enough to inherit the knack gradually created a race of their kind, finally a number of separate species. All of them occupied a niche that was to be had for the taking; a diligent crew of other seekers had, and still have, the from-the-bottom-up niche filled to capacity.

Refinements   Nuthatches share with a lot of other scanners and probers a white chin and/or breast. Reflections off this bright surface into shadowy cracks, holes, and undersides would throw useful light onto food items concealed in them.

If you look closely at a nuthatch fixed in place you will see that it has one leg out behind, on the "up" side, with the over-sized hind claw firmly hooked onto the surface. The other foot is placed well forward, i.e., down, for steadying support.

There are other refinements that the nuthatch brings to its trade. One of them has to be a highly developed skill at selecting cracks and notches that will hold a nut or seed in place solidly enough for the dextrous bill to hack apart. That dextrous bill, in the case of the Brown-headed Nuthatch of the southeast U.S., also uses bits of bark as a tool to pry up loose bark in its search for hidden insects. Nuthatches will also attempt to cover hidden seeds with bits of bark or shreds of lichen if available.

Of the four species of nuthatches found in North America, only one, the red-breasted of the boreal forests right across Canada and montane coniferous forests of the western U.S., is migratory. But even this species is an irregular nomad, in some winters part of the population electing to stay behind or to migrate only part way, thus wintering in southerly parts of the species's breeding range.

Unattached white-breasteds will also drift south during their first winter if the prospects in their natal surroundings aren't too good. It would be less easy to detect such a population shift since the breeding range of the white-breasted extends to the Gulf of Mexico and well down into Mexico. Who are the locals, who the wintering Northerners?

Red-breasted Nuthatch *(Sitta canadensis)*

Nuthatch family. "Nuthatch" comes from "nuthack," original name brought to Americas by English colonists; *Sitta* is from Greek *sitte*, "nuthatch"; *canadensis*, Latinized "of Canada," reflecting major range of bird.

Description Shares slate blue back, wings, tail of larger White-breasted Nuthatch; distinguished from it by smaller size and by narrow black line through the eye and white line above eye; breast, belly, flanks, thighs, and tail coverts pale rust to brick red, varying with individuals; sexes similar, but female's crown is dark gray, ruddy parts less pronounced.

Behavior Very similar to white-breasted, foraging head-down on tree bark; a busy, businesslike, but sometimes dithery feeder bird; diligent hoarder of larger seeds and suet; voice similar to white-breasted's but weaker and higher-pitched, a thin, nasal "yank-yank"; also makes a clear, soft note, "hit," very high, repeated several times.

Range Migratory, but some periodically winter in southern sectors of breeding range; found throughout boreal forest, but not to tree line; much more a denizen of coniferous forests than white-breasted; breeds in northeast Minnesota, northern Wisconsin and Michigan, and western Montana; also breeds in Black Hills; may in winter be found anywhere in Upper Midwest.

Food Natural summer food is insects and spiders; in winter insect dormants, eggs, and seeds of conifers; in the wild joins chickadees and its white-breasted cousins to forage and to pick tidbits from predator kills; at feeder a lover of sunflower seeds and suet.

Nest Either ready-made cavity in tree or one excavated in punky wood, hence height highly variable; occasionally uses nest boxes; entrance smeared with spruce or balsam fir gum; female reported to fly directly into hole, presumably to avoid contacting resin.

Comment The little red-breasted closely resembles the European Nuthatch, *Sitta europaea*, with which it shares the habit of plastering the rim of its nest hole. Observers note that by the end of the nesting season parent red-breasteds acquire a very tatty appearance from the resin stuck on their feathers.

REF: A–685; BM–221; GO–234; NG–314; P–212

White-breasted Nuthatch *(Sitta carolinensis)*

Seventeenth-century British colonists brought "nuthack" with them, descriptive of familiar European bird's habit of wedging nuts into cracks and hacking husks off with bill; with dialectic drift it became "nuthatch"; *Sitta* is from Greek *sitte*, "nuthatch"; *carolinensis*, "of Carolina," where first described.

Description   Sparrow-sized; large head, short neck, tail, and legs impart compact, torpedo shape; body slate blue; crown and back of neck black; wings mainly slate blue with indistinct lines and flecks of black and white; stubby tail slate, outer margins pattern of black and white; sides of face to above eye, neck, and breast off-white; thighs and under tail brick red; prominent dark eye set in white; bill slender, sharp, and slightly upturned; sexes similar, except female's head is gray.

Behavior   Perches, feeds, and forages head-down on vertical surfaces; stance squat, scans world with neck craned back; cracks nuts and large seeds by wedging them into crevices, whacking at them to chip off husks; winter call is flat, nasal note repeated urgently several times, best imitated by a falsetto "yaank" whilst holding nose.

Range   Nonmigratory; southern Canada is northern margin of range; occurrence governed by presence of mature deciduous woodland; throughout most of Upper Midwest, in Plains regions drawn to cities and towns with enough big trees to qualify as "woodlands."

Food   Searches tree trunks for insects and spiders in all stages; nuts, some berries, larger seeds; favorites at feeders are most large seeds, especially sunflowers, suet, peanuts, baked goods, and some kinds of table scraps; diligent hoarder, jamming seeds into cracks in bark; readily tries anything, often beating chickadees to check out new feeders.

Nest   In tree cavities, usually those ready-made by decay or woodpeckers; occasionally accepts boxes or uses cavities in buildings.

Comment   Nuthatches are the only birds able to move easily down vertical surfaces headfirst; even the tree-adapted woodpeckers hitch awkwardly backward when descending. Their trim shape, air of urgent busyness around feeders, bold plumage pattern, and upside-down orientation make them unmistakable. Confusion is only likely between it and the smaller red-breasted where they coexist.

REF: A–646; BM–223; GO–234; NG–314; P–212

Creepers
Family Certhiidae

The creepers are divided worldwide into three families. This one, the holarctic, has six species in two genera, only one of which is represented in North America. Our little Brown Creeper is circumpolar; in England it is called the Treecreeper. At one time all Brown Creepers were *Certhia familiaris*. This name now denotes the Eurasian bird and ours is now *C. americana*. In Ernest Thompson's (Seton) *The Birds of Manitoba*, published in 1891, the Brown Creeper is *Certhia familiaris americana*. Seton, like many a birder after him, classified this retiring little bird as "rare."

Bark Specialist   While many of our birds, especially the wintering species like chickadees and Downy and Hairy woodpeckers, are foragers in and under bark, the Brown Creeper is perhaps the most dependent of all birds on tree bark. It not only searches on it for food, but utilizes it for winter roosting and for nesting. Other cavity nesters may opportunistically use the shelter of a buckled slab of bark if nothing else is available, but the creeper will rarely use anything else.

Some writers note that if you nail a slab of bark to a tree by the ends, being careful to hump it outward in the middle to leave a decent space of several inches between it and the trunk, the Brown Creeper might use the contrived cranny as a winter roost, or even as a nest. I wonder if the sole of an old rubber boot, or some other suitable discard, would be an acceptable substitute for the bark providing it blended in fairly unobtrusively with the surface of the "host" tree.

As befits a bird that spends its active hours hitching itself ever upward, the creeper's feet are long-clawed and strong. It also shares with woodpeckers a tail equipped with strong, pointed hackles that serve as a brace while the feet are clamped into the bark. They very likely also snaggle into the surface, preventing backslide when the bird hitches upward, which it does by moving both feet simultaneously in a quick hop. Woodpeckers and nuthatches, in contrast, move their feet in sequence, in a very quick motion that seems like a hop, but is in fact a very quick step.

Closet Machismo   Surprising for one so timid and retiring, the male turns into an exhibitionist like the rest of us during courting time. He woos his prospective mate with a burst of song, described in Noble Proctor's *Song Birds* as "a wonderful, descending musical jumble of notes," a generous review of a talent most other critics classify as meager. Then this drab little elf turns athletic with a fast, spiral flight upward around the tree trunk he has selected for his display. The female may join in this flight, allowing herself to be pursued in the same dizzy spiral.

If, ultimately, she is sufficiently impressed, the two of them go to work building a nest behind his preselected slab of loose bark. He helps fetch the raw materials, she does the weaving; the project can take as little as six days, as long as a month. Nests are situated from 5 to 15 ft (1.5 to 4.6 m) up. Observers report that the nest tending is done with typical creeper reserve. Adults approach it the same way they do their foraging, landing below it, spiraling upward in those rapid, jerky little hitches until, with one quick hop, they just vanish behind their shield of bark.

Brown Creeper *(Certhia americana)*

Creeper family. "Creeper" comes from the way it moves close against the bark of trees as it forages; *Certhia* is from Latin *certhius*, "a creeper," and *americana* is Latinized "of America"; in older guides species name *familiaris*, Latin "homelike," hence friendly, now referring to Old World species.

Description   Very small, slim, with slender, down-curved bill, longish tail with stiff, pointed feathers flared slightly against the bark; upper plumage a camouflage pattern of buff spots, streaks, and lines on brown base; belly, breast, and chin white.

Behavior   Secretive, timid; constantly searches bark of larger trees by starting near the base, hitching upward in short, quick jumps in a spiral around trunk until it is well up, then flying quickly down to base of another tree, to begin again; favors mature trees, especially damp, mossy woodlands; call is a very high, thin "tsee."

Range   Partially migratory; in Upper Midwest breeds only in northeast and north regions of Great Lakes states, the Black Hills, and several other disjunct tracts of forested habitat, and in western Montana; winters in varying numbers throughout entire region.

Food   Close scanner of bark for insect eggs, pupae, and adults, using its sharp, decurved bill as a fine probe; rare visitor to feeders where it takes suet; may be coaxed to specific trees if bark is smeared with suet or peanut butter.

Nest   Unique in that it almost invariably nests behind or under loosened slabs of bark on recently dead trees; nest may be compressed considerably by confines of space and reveal shape of a sharply up-turned crescent when exposed; base of twigs, grass stems, and bark shreds often arranged to block off most access to the space beneath the bark; lining of fine bark threads, grass, root fibers, spider silk, mosses, and occasional feathers.

Comment   This little bird is professionally inconspicuous, dwelling in deep, shady woods by preference, hugging the bark of the trees it forages on, making little noise and no disturbance. It is fitting, then, that such a shy woodland recluse is usually listed as "rare" or "infrequent." Some observers allow, however, that its status may be more an apparent scarcity than a real one over much of its territory. One gathers that "keep looking" is the word.

Some station operators note that creepers seem to pay more attention to trees in the vicinity of feeders. The reason could be that they are gleaning fragments of seeds and fat left on the bark where other birds wiped their bills after feeding.

REF: A–647; BM–223; GO–234; NG–314; P–212

Kinglets
Family Muscicapidae, Subfamily Sylviinae

Latin *musca* means "a fly," *capere*, "to take," hence "flycatcher"; Latin *silva* is "a woods," *Sylviinae*, "of the woods."

It would take approximately one hundred Ruby-crowned Kinglets to make a pound. I have never had the unhappy task of weighing a dead one, but several references assure me that they run from just under four to 4.5 grams, the greater figure just equaling .16 ounces. The Golden-crowned Kinglet is even tinier, the smallest songbird in North America.

For most midwesterners, and even for those who live in mixed or spruce woodlands farther north and east, kinglets are not very obvious birds. In summer they favor a heavy cover of evergreens, often back among the muskeg and mosquitos where wayfaring humans don't venture. And even when the two do meet, the birds are so small, so busy and unobtrusive, and often so well up in mature spruce that they aren't noticed. Experienced birders say that the nests are so small and so well-camouflaged up near the roof of the spruce canopy that they defy detection.

Although they are members of the thrush family, only the ruby-crowned is noted as a singer, observers commenting that so small a creature could belt out so much volume. Many people who have heard a clear, vibrant song echoing over spruce woodlands, and have looked without results for the songster, have been treated to the "heard-but-not-seen" performance of the ruby-crowned. The golden-crowned, unlike its virtuoso cousin, has a weak, small voice that is easily lost to human ears in its dense evergreen habitat.

In winter, gathered in larger flocks and with fewer of the bigger, noisier and more colorful birds around to distract the eye, they are more noticeable. In infrequent years the ruby-crowned, the more strongly migratory of the two, will winter in small, scattered numbers in the southernmost parts of the Upper Midwest. The diminutive golden-crowned more frequently includes the Upper Midwest in its wintering grounds, especially where tracts of natural or plantation evergreens occur.

In such winters, given their habit of foraging in the mixed collections of chickadees, Downy and Hairy woodpeckers, and nuthatches that patrol the winter woodlands, they might follow these others to feeders. Only then is it possible to observe the details of their drab plumage, and to appreciate their downscaled proportions. Seen next to a kinglet, a chickadee looks positively hulking.

Golden-crowned Kinglet *(Regulus satrapa)*

Old World warbler, gnatcatcher, kinglet subfamily; in larger family that also includes thrushes; "Golden-crowned" from small dash of yellow on crown, "kinglet" meaning "little king"; *Regulus* is Latin for "little king," Greek *satrapa* means "a ruler," i.e., one who wears a golden crown; an example of taxonomists' maximizing single feature on otherwise undistinguished little bird.

Description   Tiny; olive green and grayish; short-tailed; delicate, fine-pointed bill; two-toned crown stripe, bright orange in center bordered by yellow edged in black, visible only at close range or when raised in display; sexes alike, but female has no orange in crown; off-white line over eye.

Behavior   Tirelessly flitting about, usually near tips of branches, often well up in conifers; so active, field marks other than diminutive size difficult to see; constantly flicks wings; often forages by hovering near twig tips; gleaner of smallest twigs and conifer needles; may forage in mixed parties of woodpeckers, chickadees, and nuthatches; call is a hurried, thin, high-pitched "tsee-tsee-tsee"; song is a very high, weak, rapid trill.

Range   Migratory; breeds in boreal and montane forests, hence in northeast Minnesota, Wisconsin, and Michigan's Upper Peninsula, and in western Montana; resident in Black Hills and other disjunct tracts of coniferous habitat; most likely to be seen during migration times.

Food   Insects, eggs, larvae, and pupae gleaned from twigs and needles; sap from sapsucker tap-holes; infrequent feeder visitor, then taking only suet and perhaps peanut butter.

Nest   A neat little suspended pouch cunningly hidden beneath foliage at tip of evergreen bough, often very high; well camouflaged with moss and lichen; feathers in lining set so tops will fold down over eggs when parent is away.

Comment   On the occasions when people can observe wintering kinglets, they can't help but be amazed that such small creatures can generate and hold enough warmth to survive. No doubt the physics of size and windchill *do* foredoom many of these undersized bundles of energy to a quick, shivering end. But heavy losses are quickly replaced; each female that survives to mate and nest can brood up to ten eggs the following summer, so many that they repose two-deep in her tiny nest, a fact that doesn't seem to curb her brooding success.

REF: A–704; BM–230; GO–252; NG–322; P–216

Thrushes
Family Muscicapidae, Subfamily Turdinae

The *Muscicapidae* family includes Old World warblers, kinglets, gnatcatchers, Old World flycatchers, and the thrushes and their allies. As well as the thrushes proper the subfamily *Turdinae* includes bluebirds, solitaires, and the familiar robin. In the genus *Turdus*, the true thrushes, there are over sixty species and they are found on every continent except

Australia. No other single genus of songbird is so widespread, and wherever they occur, there is at least one species that is a common yard and garden bird.

The niceties of bird nomenclature were not uppermost in the minds of English immigrants piling off the boats to tame seventeeth-century America. Thus, any bird with a reddish breast, or even a suggestion of ruddiness about it, was dubbed a "robin" after the familiar red-breasted bird of British fields and gardens. At one time the Eastern Bluebird was a "robin," the towhee was a "ground robin," the oriole was a "golden robin," the Cedar Waxwing a "Canadian robin."

The American Robin vies with the Red-winged Blackbird as the most common bird in North America, and with the House Sparrow as the most familiar. Unlike the sparrow, it is not a human-dependant street bird. It's just as much at home in the rainforests of the West Coast or the upper reaches of the boreal-tundra transition zone as it is dodging lawn sprinklers in suburbia. But people so associate it with the latter scene that their first reaction on encountering it in the wilderness is a surprised: "What is *our* robin doing away out here?"

"Cheer-up!"   The thrushes are noted for their great voices, and although the American Robin isn't rated as the greatest songster of them all, its dawn carol is one of the best-known and loved of nature's sounds. It isn't a continuous cascade of warbling, like the finches, but a series of clear, whistled phrases, separated by the briefest pauses. To some the clipped phrases sound like football signals and they have nicknamed the robin the "quarterback bird."

The main recital is the one that heralds the dawn, often well before the sun has even tinted the horizon. At the height of the concert season, in late April or early May when the males are consolidating territories in anticipation of the females' return, the singing can go on for most of the day. But when the intensity diminishes, dawn and dusk are the principal singing periods. It's as if the bird has timed his presentations to suit the workaday schedule of his human audience, seeing them off in the morning, accompanying their chores or backyard barbecues in the evening.

In *The Birds of Manitoba*, Seton commented on a variation in bird song that can be readily observed in robins since their singing is so loud and they sing from regular vantage points. At times a bird will abruptly begin singing in a muted, distant-sounding voice. Seton noted that a singing male, if made uneasy but not frightened off by something close at hand, would keep on singing, but with his bill shut. He said he had noted this habit in several other species.

Sex and Violence   Lust and fence-line disputes have been sources of bloodshed and legal fees among humans for as long as our history can recall. Put them together, and you have the potential for rivalry of awesome, or farcical, proportions.

Male robins compete with such frenzy in the territorial/mating game that at times they behave as if completely addled. In addition to wild low-level pursuits on the wing, accompanied by rapid "get! get! get!" shrieked at trespassers, male robins have worked themselves into frazzles attacking their own images in windows, windshields, hubcaps, and rear view mirrors. The cue to aggression being the ruddy breast of a male rival, they have tackled similar-colored socks, handkerchiefs, and other items on clothes lines, and ornaments and discarded toys on the lawn.

Domesticity   Although the female robin selects the site, builds the nest, and does all the brooding, the male nevertheless proves to be a dutiful helpmate, feeding the nestlings and assuming full babysitting chores when his mate builds a new nest and starts brooding a second clutch. The harassed male can then be seen scouring lawns for food with his brood dogging his heals, begging loudly when he pulls up an earthworm. These fledglings reveal their species's thrush ancestry; their breasts are dappled with brown spots on a washed-out background.

At this time there are a couple of things that can be done to give robins a hand. Keeping the family cat shut in while the baby robins get over the "stupid" stage of life may help at least one or two make it to early adolescence. It may also be a real help to nest building, if the weather is dry, to leave a pie plate of good stiff mud on or near the bird-bath, or to turn on the lawn sprinkler where it will create a muddy puddle.

Foraging robin pairs recently demonstrated that new knowledge about animal behavior doesn't have to come from costly expeditions to remote sites. By watching four pairs of robins working the lawns of a Kansas college campus, an observer discovered that they subdivided their territories roughly in half along an east-west axis when searching for food. The female always searched one half, the male the other. Such an arrangement would minimize competition between the two, avoid overlapping searches, and therefore enhance foraging efficiency.

In common with other thrushes, robins are omnivorous to a certain degree in that they freely switch from preying on invertebrates, principally earthworms, to gathering fruit and berries. They do not seem to be very interested in seeds. Their liking for fruit has frequently brought them to grief with farmers and orchardists trying to grow soft fruits and berries.

American Robin *(Turdus migratorius)*

Thrush family. "Robin" diminutive of "Robert" and of French origin; in England "redbreast" was original name, then "robin redbreast," then "redbreast" was dropped; *Turdus* is Latin for "a thrush," *migrator,* "wanderer."

Description Rather leggy, long-tailed bird; dark gray tail, back, and wings, darker head; brick red breast and belly; chin light with dark, vertical streaks; broken white eye-ring; lower belly and undertail coverts white; beak yellow; female same as male but paler.

Behavior Most commonly seen hunting worms on lawns, alternately tipping forward to scan the grass intently or standing erect when alert for danger; runs or hops; most wintering robins take to heavy bush where they seem to be much more elusive than their summer equivalents; song famous as harbinger of spring, a loud, clear, distinctly separated series of "cheery, cheery, cheer up, cheerily" phrases; call of alarm a sudden "cheep!" or rapidly repeated "get-get-get!"

Range Migratory; breeds from coast to coast, north to beyond the tree line; increasing winterer in easterly agricultural regions of Upper Midwest, less so on plains.

Food Mixture of insects, earthworms, and fruit; may be encouraged to feeders with raisins, berries, fresh or dried fruit, and shredded coconut; early spring migrants may be driven to feeders if late snowstorm blankets natural food sources.

Nest Substantial base of twigs, straws, and stems mortared from inside with heavy layer of mud formed into deep, round cup; inner lining of fine grasses; in fork of tree or solid branch, in tangle of vines, on ledge or beam about buildings; from 6 to 30 ft (2 to 10 m) above ground.

Comment   I read that in times of drought if nest-building female robins can't find a source of mud they will pick up beakfuls of dirt and take them to water to mix their own. Failing even this, some will build entirely without benefit of mud.

Basically a bird of open forests and edges, it very likely benefited when logging and settlement changed forested areas to fields, pastures, and orchards, and when agriculture and settlement brought trees to the open plains. Whatever its historic niche, today's robin seems to have a foot firmly in two worlds, the back yard and the back woods. It's as if there were two species occupying the same region, one accustomed to living in close proximity to people and the other wild and remote.

REF: A–548; BM–242; GO–244; NG–330; P–220

Waxwings
Family Bombycillidae

There are only three species of true waxwings in the world. Two, the Cedar and Bohemian, occur in the Upper Midwest. Their closest relatives in North America are the Silky Flycatchers, a connection acknowledged in the waxwing family name: *Bombycillidae* is a compound of Greek and pseudo-Latin meaning "silk tail."

If you see one of these elegant birds in summer it is almost certainly a Cedar Waxwing. It will likely be perched on a prominent lookout from which it will launch aerial pursuits of flying insects. This easy-going fruit-eater turns out to be a very adept flycatcher, agile enough to capture even swift and maneuverable dragonflies.

The flycatching is a response to the needs of its new hatchlings. They require a starter diet high in protein, a demand fruit cannot fill. After a few days of the booster menu, fruit gradually replaces insects, and then in generous quantities. A parent waxwing transports berries in its crop; one was seen to disgorge thirty chokecherries at the nest, popping them one after another into the waiting gapes of its young.

While its first cousin the Cedar is hawking after insects over a pasture or pond, the Bohemian Waxwing is doing the same thing farther north, probably from the edge of a boreal bog.

In the fall, both migrate, the Cedar south to more benign winter holdings, the Bohemian south and east into what had been the summer range of the Cedar. A winter waxwing in the Upper Midwest could be either one, the Bohemian more likely to be found in the northern, forested areas, the Cedar to the south. But numbers vary greatly from season to season and in accordance with the availability of dried and/or frozen tree fruit.

Both birds travel widely; banding shows that Bohemian Waxwings banded in Saskatoon, Saskatchewan, came from breeding areas west of the Rockies. A Cedar Waxwing juvenile banded near Kingston, Ontario, on the north shore of Lake Ontario in August of 1980 was shot February 13, 1981, in Morelia, Mexico, 2,100 miles distant.

Avian Dandy   The waxwing's elegant figure, slightly more rotund in the Bohemian, is impeccable in sleek plumage that always looks as if the wearer is freshly groomed for a formal night out. The colors are tastefully subtle, shades of rich gray-brown melting into fawns with a suggestion of saffron. The few highlights—most noticeably the jaunty crest, complemented by a velvet black line through the eye, a natty bar of deep yellow at the end of the tail, and a tiny daub of red on the wing—accentuate the overall statement of restrained elegance.

About thirty years ago birders started noticing the occasional Cedar Waxwing with orange instead of yellow at the end of the tail. In the intervening years the incidence of orange-tipped waxwings has markedly increased. The most plausible explanation is that the color comes from the berries of ornamental yew which has come into fashionable use as a landscape plant over the last thirty years, and which is a favorite winter food of waxwings.

For all its nattiness, the waxwing personality is that of a gentle, easygoing wayfarer, fond of dining well in good company, as polite as he is handsome. In *Wings of the North* Candace Savage notes that the beguiling trustfulness of the bird is shown in accounts of their taking string from outstretched hands and of trying to pull hair from a person's head, all in the interests of collecting nesting materials.

The "Plume Trade"   Incredible though it seems to us now, at one time millions of songbirds, and others, were shot indiscriminately every year to supply feathers for women's hats. The brutality and waste of the "plume trade" outraged many, but the influence and money of the fashion industry frustrated all efforts to put a stop to it.

Then Frank Chapman, ornithologist for the American Museum of Natural History, staged an inspired protest that helped change the course of nature preservation in North America. He went birding on the streets of Manhattan, recording the feathers in women's hats. Prominent among the forty species he listed were Northern Flicker, Snow Bunting, Northern Bobwhite, and Common Tern. But the most frequent species identified was Cedar Waxwing, a bizarre tribute to their lustrous beauty. The sharp-eyed

Chapman noted only one Bohemian Waxwing plume in his fashion-parade inventory. There would undoubtedly have been more except that their remote breeding range kept them safe from the feather hunters' birdshot.

Nature-lovers of the day, spurred by Chapman's imaginative protest, launched an impassioned campaign appealing to the conscience of the fashionable to stop wearing feathers of wild birds. The plume and millinery industry fought back, claiming that eighty-three thousand American workers would be plunged into unemployment if the plume hunt were stopped. They dismissed the charges of cruelty and of the threatened extinction of certain species with a barrage of dubious assurances. The rhetoric of the times rings familiar to bystanders in today's controversy over the wild-fur fashion industry.

The bird preservationists eventually won out. Fashions changed, and the thousands of "threatened" workers were promptly put to work turning out featherless headgear. Birds such as Snowy Egrets slowly recovered from the brink of extinction.

Feathered Gourmands   Birds that feed on fruit trade quality for quantity, fruit being less nutritious than insects and most seeds, but often available in great abundance. Waxwings feeding of cotoneaster berries consume three times their weight of them every day. To process such bulk they have a short gut designed for fast through-put; passage from beak to the top of the car can take as little as sixteen minutes. This need to eat hugely has gained waxwings an undeserved reputation for gluttony. They are often seen gorging on fruit and then lolling about like overstuffed Christmas dinner guests.

Now and then this feeding pattern brings them to embarrassment when they encounter fall fruit that has fermented. Householders then report, in some alarm, that their ornamental crab is full of birds fluttering and falling about for all the world as if they were drunk, which indeed they are.

The "wax" that gives the birds their name is exuded from the tips of the feather shafts of the secondaries on the wings of both sexes. Its presence varies considerably, being nonexistent to sparse in young birds, most pronounced in breeding adults. Although it is an uncertain and obscure field mark, among the birds it may function as a badge of fitness and maturity.

Bohemian Waxwing *(Bombycilla garrulus)*

Waxwing family. Common name likely arising from vagabond "bohemian" winter wanderings, rather than with any link to west Czechoslovakia where they are only occasional visitors; "waxwing" from tips of secondary wing feathers which seem to have been dipped in red wax; formerly called "silk-tail"; Greek *bombyx* means "silk"; *cilla* is invention from Middle Latin mistakenly wrought to mean "tail"; *garrulus* is from Latin *garrula*, "chattering," waxwing's crest making it resemble the European Jay, *Garrulus glandarius.*

Description   Robin-sized; elegant, smooth plumage is subtle blends of soft grays and rich ochers; trim, sharp-tipped crest, narrow black mask through eyes, black chin; bill small and black; tiny cluster of waxy tips on wing secondaries difficult to spot; best told from smaller, more slender Cedar Waxwing by cinnamon undertail coverts, by white bar and flecking on dark wings, and by broader yellow band at end of tail.

Behavior   Always in busy flocks, especially in winter around fruit-bearing trees like Mountain Ash or ornamental crabapple; constant calling while feeding or in flight; tame; share habit with cedars of sitting in a close row on a branch passing a berry or bright object back and forth; call is a weak, trilling, slightly buzzy "tzeee."

Range   Circumpolar; breeds in boreal forest of western Canada, only occurs in Upper Midwest in extreme northwest Montana; irregular migrants in winter, wandering widely, visiting towns well planted with requisite fruit and berry trees.

Food Fruit-eater, optionally insectivorous and when feeding nestlings; might visit feeding stations to try frozen crabapples, apples, or berries, or raisins, prunes, or dates; best attractants are berry or fruit-bearing trees that hold fruit over winter.

Nest Usually in conifer on forest edge near clearing, lake, marsh; 5 to 20 ft (1.5 to 6 m) up; cup of conifer twigs, lichens and grass, lined with hair and down.

Comment It is easy to see why waxwings were once called "silky-tails." In their subdued way waxwings are the most elegant of birds, and there are those who hold that the bohemian, in spite of its slightly more rotund figure, is the more dapper of the two. Should a flock appear to feed on the frozen fruit of a nearby tree, get out the binoculars promptly and give their beauty, and their busy sociability, a long look. They travel far and wide in search of food, and once they have plucked every berry, will not be back again.

REF: A–711; BM–248; GO–258; NG–344; P–224

Cedar Waxwing *(Bombycilla cedrorum)*

Waxwing family. Has been called "cedar bird" from association with this tree, and "cherry bird" for its diet of fruit; like Bohemian, secondary wing feathers bear red tips resembling wax once used to seal envelopes; Greek *bombyx* means "silk" in reference to family link to silktails, *cilla* is Latin non-word in error thought to mean "tail."

Description Smaller than robin, slimmer than Bohemian; plumage silky, smooth; obvious crest sharp-pointed and backswept; color predominantly a blending of soft browns melting to fawns, beiges, and khaki; narrow satin black face mask elegantly lined in off-white, chin dark; belly and flanks pale yellow; undertail coverts white and unusually long, extending well toward end of tail; rump and base of tail gray; squared-off tail has wide, dark subterminal band, ends in bright yellow or saffron band; unlike Bohemian, darkish wings have no bars or yellow checkmarks; trill is a high, thin, rather metallic monotone.

Behavior   Sweeps about in fast-flying flocks, constantly calling; settles into fruit trees or berry bushes, feeding busily in an amiable, well-mannered scramble; may grab berries on the wing by hovering at bunches; may eat plucked berry by tossing it into the air and catching it; quite tame, especially when preoccupied with eating.

Range   Migratory; a North American species, breeding in a wide band across continent from coast to coast; nests throughout much of Upper Midwest in woodland habitat; winter wanderer, often in towns and suburbs where it seeks fruit and berries of ornamentals.

Food   Fruit, petals, and buds most of year; during nesting reverts to flycatcher ancestry to feed young for a few days before gradually switching to fruit; may come to feeders for raisins, frozen berries, and dried fruit.

Nest   In open woods, hedges, orchards, shelter belts; on horizontal limb well away from trunk, 6 to 20 ft (2 to 6 m) up; a bulky, loose base of twigs, weed stems, grass; cup of grass and plant fibers lined with rootlets, fine grasses, and plant down; might appear at first glance to be a clump of debris caught by chance in a cleft in a branch; occasionally nests sociably, close together in same or nearby trees.

Comment   Both our waxwings have inspired generations of observers to (dare I say it?) wax lyrical, not only on their beauty but about their charming manners. Together in an ornamental crabapple in winter or a bird bath in summer, they seem to be gracious about sharing space and waiting turns. Courting couples sit close together, passing a petal or berry back and forth, doing a sedate little side-step dance. Their devotion doesn't end with ritual; if one of a couple is killed, the survivor may call disconsolately for a couple of days.

Among birds that households have rescued and adopted, a disproportionate number seem to be waxwings. Their dietary needs of fruit are easily met and their placid nature allows them to accept their human benefactors without too much stress.

REF: A–558; BM–249; GO–258; NG–344; P–224

Shrikes

Family Laniidae

Many people who have never seen a shrike nevertheless know of the "butcher bird's" seemingly ghoulish habit of impaling the bodies of its victims on thorns and barbed wire. The skewered remains are thus supposed to be easier to dismember, since shrikes lack the powerful feet and sharp talons of full-scale raptors. A secure meat-hook makes it easier to pull larger prey apart, but is it crucial? Crows and magpies, likewise handicapped with dickeybird feet, nevertheless use them very effectively to hold down large food items while they tug at them. The shrike's feet are at least as heavy, proportionately, as a crow's.

The idea that shrikes are compensating for weak feet, and that hawthorn shrubs festooned with little carcasses represent a food cache or larder, are firmly rooted in popular nature lore. But it has been convincingly challenged by researchers in Israel. The June 1989 issue of *BBC Wildlife* recounted a study by Reuven Yosef and Berry Pinshow of the Ben-Gurion University of the Negev. They observed that if the collection of prey is a larder, it's a very poor one since it's obvious to every passing scavenger and pilferer. And while shrikes do employ thorns and barbs as meat hooks to dismember large prey, this may be more an incidental convenience than a necessity, since they also impale small, fragile items like crickets, and even inedible things such as snail shells.

Working with resident Great Gray Shrikes, the same *Lanius excubitor* we call the Northern Shrike, the two men have demonstrated convincingly that the impaling habit is actually courting behavior. It is demonstrated only by males, and the more conspicuous and well-stocked his display is, the better able a male is to attract a female. For a year Yosef and Pinshow manipulated the displays of males in a cluster of territories, consistently depleting some, augmenting others, leaving a control group untouched.

When returning migrant females sized up the prospective mates, the ones with the boosted caches were chosen first, pairing an average of a month earlier than males in the control group. Subsequent nesting success was also markedly improved. The unfortunates whose caches were cleaned out every week all failed to mate and abandoned their territories.

One persuasive conclusion from this is that a good cache advertises to cruising females that the displaying male is more able to obtain food, whether by better hunting skill, his ability to recognize and defend a superior territory, or both. Either way, he will not only be a better provider for his offspring, but will pass to them genes reinforcing these traits.

One-On-One   The Northern Shrike is one of the relatively few predators that kills prey, one-on-one, that is close to its own size, and whose weapons are not so obviously superior to those of its prey. They have better success with smaller birds, but will attack and kill larger species. They have been seen pursuing robins, and there are accounts of their killing Evening Grosbeaks. Whether they have the skill of predators such as wolves in singling out individuals that are more vulnerable than their flock-mates is not known.

It is postulated that the shrike relies in part on what would be the ultimate disguise, its resemblance to an unthreatening songbird. Thus masked it gets close enough to an unsuspecting victim to pounce or launch pursuit from close quarters. Certainly this innocuous cover, if it is one, doesn't fool all birds. On the infrequent times when a shrike has appeared at my feeder, the reaction of the regulars has been one of alarm and/or panic. Some observers, however, report that victims will sometimes remain as if mes-merized as a shrike makes its fatal approach.

Once the victim is overtaken and buffeted to the ground, the shrike hammers at its head with its heavy bill, employing an unusually strong set of neck muscles. Having buffetted the victim senseless, it can dislocate the neck or pierce the skull with a well-placed bite. It may then hang up the body, a skill that begins as an instinctive reaction. In *Bird Behaviour* it is reported that young Loggerhead Shrikes at twenty-two days of age start to hold food in their bills and to draw it along a perch in random fashion. If the food happens to catch on a twig or crotch the bird immediately concentrates on dragging it repeatedly over the obstacle. In this way it very quickly learns to direct its dragging action to the right places.

Northern Shrike *(Lanius excubitor)*

Shrike family. "Northern" as distinct from the Loggerhead Shrike, a more southerly occurring relative; "shrike" is from Anglo-Saxon *scric*, "a shrieker"; also "butcher bird" from habit of impaling or hanging prey on thorns or barbed wire; *Lanius* is from Latin for "a butcher," *excubitor*, "a sentinel."

Description   Robin-sized; black-masked, boldly patterned in off-white, gray, and black; belly, rump, and undertail coverts white; wings black with white patch and frosting at ends of longest flight feathers; fan-shaped tail black with white edges; crown, nape, and back smoke gray; large head; heavy, straight, dark bill with sharp, pronounced hook; breast of juvenile lightly lined, faint or absent in adult; sexes identical.

Behavior Perches quietly on high, exposed lookout; pumps tail upward; undulating flight on rapidly beating wings often low, ending in sharp swoop up to perch; may hover, kestrel-style, when hunting over grassy cover; chases small birds in pell-mell pursuit, occasionally around feeding stations; favorite hunting grounds on plains a dry slough with circle of willow; call is a harsh "shek" or "shak," song is an extended medley of warbles, whistles, and phrases from other birds' songs mixed with discordand notes.

Range Erratically migratory; a shrike in summer is almost certainly a loggerhead, in winter a northern; northern breeds in boreal forest north to tree line, seen in Upper Midwest only as winter visitor.

Food Predatory on small birds, mice, and large insects which it may capture on the wing; may take suet at feeding stations.

Nest Bulky, on foundation of twigs, cup lined with roots, hair, feathers; prefers dense conifers, height dependant on size of available trees; favors proximity of thorn-bearing shrubs.

Comment Shrikes rarely visit feeding stations for the usual purpose; rather, they are attracted by the concentration of other birds. When one does call it is an event fraught with potential for life-and-death drama at close quarters. Lacking size and the powerful clutching, piercing talons that are hawks' and owls' primary killing tools, the shrike kills in an often protracted struggle in which the prey is buffeted to the ground and bludgeoned on the head with the heavy bill. Once subdued the prey may be dispatched with a bite through the neck or back of the skull.

A detached view of predator-prey relationships is hard to sustain when one sees beloved birds assaulted so brutally. But the shrike, and its prey, are following the dictates of behavior millions of years in the evolving. And it is the shrike that, over the past decades, has suffered an alarming decrease in its range and numbers. Viewing it at work, first-hand, should be regarded as a rare look into life's reality, definitely *not* an emergency to be interrupted.

REF: A–514; BM–250; GO–260; NG–334; P–224

Starlings
Family Sturnidae

This is an Old World family of 103, 106, 111, or 130 species, depending on which authority you read. There are three in North America: the European Starling and two mynas. The Hill Myna is an escaped cage bird breeding near Homestead, Florida, and the Crested Myna was released in Vancouver, British Columbia, in 1895 and has spread only to nearby portions of Vancouver Island. Apparently its tropical habit of not incubating its eggs for extended periods during midday has inhibited its reproductive success.

No such laxity inhibits the European, or Common, Starling; it is a determined, opportunistic breeder. Apparently with little hesitation it will attack nesting birds as large as flickers and evict them from their holes. The little starlings it raises in the usurped premises are—wouldn't you know it—noted in their turn for being unusually hardy.

Shakespeare was inadvertently responsible for adding this ubiquitous nuisance to North America, although direct blame rests with a group called the American Acclimatization Society. Its self-appointed aim was to introduce to America every bird mentioned in Shakespeare's works. Regrettably, in *Henry IV* Hotspur proclaimed: "Nay, I'll have a starling shall be tought to speak nothing but 'Mortimer' . . ." Accordingly, the Acclimatization Society ordered up a few cagefuls and turned them loose in New York's Central Park on March 6, 1890. The initial eighty releasees were joined in April of 1891 by twenty pairs of reinforcements.

Surprisingly, there had actually been previous failed attempts to start the scourge. However earnestly we might now wish it, do-gooders of the time didn't recognize initial failures as the disguised blessings they were. As early as 1872, according to Tufts in *Birds of Nova Scotia*, there had been a release in Ohio, and others preceding the infamous March 6 release in Central Park.

Whirlwind Takeover   The plague incubated in New York for six years before breaking out to sweep the southern expanses of the continent, taking only a little more time to invade the environmentally harsher north. It first appeared in Minnesota, in Fillmore County, in 1929, but didn't rate as abundant until the 1940s. It had reached the west coast by around 1950. Like House Sparrows, starlings are largely dependent on humans for their well-being and wherever they settle do not nest much beyond the confines of towns and farmyards. Although common winter residents of the Upper Midwest, the majority migrates, congregating with grackles and blackbirds to forage widely in the marshes, shorelines, and agricultural lands of the southern U.S. The size of some of these integrated roosting flocks is mind-boggling, by credible estimate the largest numbering seventy million. Branches break under the weight of the clamorous horde, and the accumulation of droppings beneath the trees sterilizes the soil.

The starling musters the standard adaptive repertoire that helps successful invasive species thrive—hardiness, assertive opportunism, a high birth rate, absence of homeland pathogens, and adaptability. Except for the pathogens, these are attributes possessed by birds the starling has displaced. What might confer the critical competitive edge could be its unusual jaw musculature that permits a feeding technique called "gaping." A very few other songbirds possess this feature, and it is found in only several members of the starling family.

Logically, most creatures that grip or chew with their mouths have powerful biting muscles; those required to open the jaws are relatively weak. But the starling can separate its jaws forcefully. Pushed into your lawn, the bill is forced open. Simultaneously the eyes are rotated forward to provide binocular vision down the hole. This open-bill probing enables the bird to detect immobile as well as active prey. Most soil-dwelling invertebrates in the southern U.S. would be dormant in winter, and inactive, a food source starlings are better-equipped to exploit than other birds, and at a critical time of year.

There is a further, sex-differentiated refinement to the starling's winter feeding pattern. Males will flock to garbage dumps and feedlots where grain and other high-carbohydrate food is the most likely fare. But the females go their separate way to seek out insect dormants, grubs, and spiders, rich in protein, which is stored in the pectoral muscles in reserve for the demands of egg laying later on.

Booby-trapped Nests   Species of birds that breed in used cavities and old nests, either their own or others', save labor, time, and the uncertainties of relocating, but their offspring run the risk of inheriting a swarm of nest pathogens and parasites. Many such birds habitually add fresh sprigs of greenery to the nest during incubation and pre-fledging. It turns out that the plants selected for this, like yarrow, agrimony, cedar, and the like, have fumigant properties that inhibit bacterial and parasitic growth.

The cavity-nesting starlings follow this habit. And like other birds, they also keep the nest clean of droppings, or at least until the young begin to fledge. At that point they stop both housecleaning and adding fumigant greenery. Thereafter, to quote *The Birder's Handbook*, the nest hole becomes heavily fouled and resembles "a pest-ridden compost," swarming with lice and thousands of mites. Predictably, starling fledglings are hardy enough to tolerate such infestations. But what they leave behind is a biological "booby trap" fatal to the young of competing species that might reuse the nest.

Like the crow family, starlings have a reputation for "smarts." As cage birds they can be taught, as Shakespeare observed to our regret, to imitate human speech. In traps that securely confine other birds, starlings have been observed to take as little as two minutes to get out by lifting drop-doors or pulling hinged ones inward.

On a positive note, starlings probe out and eat the larvae and pupae of the Gypsy Moth and Japanese Beetle, introduced pests that most other birds do not prey on. It is also suggested that their probing bills pick up and spread the spores of insect-infecting diseases.

European Starling *(Sturnus vulgaris)*

Starling family. "Starling" is from Anglo-Saxon *staer*, "star," plus diminutive "ling," possibly from fanciful likening of flight silhouettes to stars; *Sturnus* is Latin for "a starling," *vulgaris*, "common."

Description   Robin-sized; chunky, short-tailed, darkly iridescent; delta-winged silhouette in flight due to straight-edged, sharply pointed wings; large head and long sharp bill; bill yellow from midwinter to early summer, brown otherwise; adult sexes identical except female eye has yellowish edge around iris; after late summer molt, body feathers light-tipped giving heavily speckled appearance which diminishes by spring as tips wear off.

Behavior   Social; outside of breeding season gathers in large flocks especially in migration and on wintering territory; struts about probing soft soils, pastures, and lawns; aggressive at feeders among themselves and against other species; noisy, voice is a series of whistles, squeaks, gurgles, chirps, and clicks in which it might imitate other birds.

Range   Largely migratory; throughout Upper Midwest, especially abundant around cities and irrigated farmland, but now nesting (Janssen) in wilderness like Boundary Waters Canoe Area; found in remote settlements like Churchill, Manitoba, west to southern Alaska.

Food   Omnivorous; probes soft soils and litter for insects, opening bill after insertion to expose hidden and/or immobile prey; winterers flock to garbage dumps and feedlots; at feeding stations takes most seeds, sunflowers last; likes table scraps and suet.

Nest   Cavity nester, including holes in buildings, signs, and light poles; preempts Purple Martin and bluebird houses if permitted; aggressively evicts flickers and woodpeckers from tree holes; nest is a collection of straw, weed stems, and trash with cup of fine plant fibers and feathers.

Comment   This abundant pest vies with co-immigrant House Sparrow for the title of bird we most love to hate. Pushy and preemptive at feeders, it is particularly hostile to woodpeckers which it seems consistently able to mob and vanquish. Migration from Upper Midwest varies, the northernmost populations more likely to move south for the winter than those of the south. But even in far northern locations a few stay the winter. You can make it awkward for them, and still provide for native species, by not scattering feed on the ground and by dispensing seeds in hanging feeders and suet in containers accessible only through the bottom.

REF: A–563; BM–252; GO–260; NG 346; P–256

Cardinals & Grosbeaks
Subfamily Cardinalinae

Of this small New World group, only three species are native to the Upper Midwest. The colorful Rose-breasted Grosbeak and Indigo Bunting are summer residents. Only the nonmigratory Northern Cardinal lives here year-round.

The name "grosbeak" has been applied as a handy descriptive name to several birds in different subfamilies, all of whom bear similar heavy-duty bills. The result has been slightly confusing; Evening and Pine grosbeaks aren't really grosbeaks, taxonomically, but are members of the Cardueline Finch subfamily. The cardinal is, however, a grosbeak, which is why, in most reference books and field guides, it is found nowhere near its fellow grosbeaks.

Northern Cardinal *(Cardinalis cardinalis)*

Grosbeak family. Sometimes "cardinal bird" and "cardinal grosbeak"; "Cardinal" is from Latin *cardinalis,* "important" or "chief," title of high ranking members of the Roman Catholic Church, who wear red robes and hats; some older guides list *Richmondena c.,* possibly from the name Richmond, Virginia.

Description Robin-sized; adult male all red except for jet black facial patch around bill, eye, and upper throat; long tail, and wings, darkened slightly due to grayish feather edges; prominent crest on both sexes; bill short and heavy; adult female grayish olive, wings and tail with dull red wash, crest reddish; bill of both sexes red or pink, brighter in male.

Behavior   Mated pairs on year-round territory; may visit feeders in family group; a bird of thickets, woodland edges and well-treed suburbs, male noted for ability to vanish into cover in spite of bright color, both sexes sing, sometimes on sunny winter days; call is a thin "tsip!" in alarm, or repeated "cue, cue, cue"; song is a rich, clear whistle, "what cheer! what cheer! purty, purty, purty," female's voice softer than male's; calmer and more deliberate at feeder than other grosbeaks.

Range   Nonmigratory; rare visitor in northern Minnesota, Wisconsin, and Michigan, regular breeder elsewhere in these states; breeds north to Fargo in North Dakota, in scattered areas of southeast South Dakota; common in Iowa.

Food   Seeds, fruit, buds, blossoms, and insects, frequently foraging on the ground; helps itself to sap and insects at sapsucker holes; at feeders takes variety of seeds, especially sunflower.

Nest   In thick shrub or small tree, from 3 to 20 ft (1 to 6 m), generally below 10 ft (3 m) up; base of loosely arranged twigs, stems, vines, grass, and shredded bark, lined with fine grass and hair.

Comment   This bird was closely associated with the Old South, its elegant beauty typifying the well-bred chivalry idealized as the mark of plantation life at the genteel level. Audubon himself was totally captivated, writing that "in richness of plumage, elegance of motion, and strength of song, [it] surpasses all its kindred in the United States."
    Notwithstanding its strong association south of the Mason-Dixon Line, the cardinal has been working its way slowly northward. Before the turn of the century it ventured into Minnesota, following the Mississippi, and by the 1930s was established from the Twin Cities southward and eastward. By the '60s it was established in several localities in South Dakota.
    The population's trend northward is no doubt abetted by the late summer and fall nomadism demonstrated by a small segment of the population in some years. This sometimes takes them far out of their normal range. In the winter of 1988 a pair showed up in the northern mining town of Thompson, Manitoba, five hundred miles north of the U.S.-Canadian border. Both froze to death before the winter was half over.

REF: A–578; BM–289; GO–308; NG–382; P–268

Sparrows
Subfamily Emberizinae

This group includes the buntings and their kin, the New World "sparrows." Employing the quotation marks acknowledges that our "sparrows" aren't really the same as the Old World birds they were (mistakenly, of course!) named after. Those of us who are slightly adrift about the kinships in this large group of songbirds are in good company; sparrows and "sparrows" have been, and remain, a source of controversy among taxonomists.

Our North American sparrows, unlike finches, are not as a group enthusiastic feeder attenders. Not counting the House Sparrow, there are five species that are commonly seen at feeders. These are the American Tree, White-throated, Song, Fox, and White-crowned sparrows.

Although economic justification is slowly diminishing as a dictate of our attitudes to wildlife, it still asserts a powerful influence. Exploitable species—game and furbearing animals—have traditionally dominated virtually all government agency interests, and, by virtue of the important role of government funding, most university research programs. Non-game species haven't existed in the world of wildlife management unless they interacted directly with the favored game animals or livestock. Their fate was usually to be dealt with as problems to be eliminated.

"875 Tons of Weed Seeds"   Historically, with no vested-interest lobby to coattail on, the champions of non-game species have battled ignorance, indifference, and exploitation with whatever initiatives came to mind, some good, some not so good. Having no obvious economic clout to back them, one ploy was to trumpet the "good" that some animals did for one sector or another of the economy. For species not so clearly virtuous, apologists for them have tried to spare them from persecution by arguing that the "good" they did exceeded the "bad."

Such "bottom line" rationalizing has produced some classic nonsense. Enter the humble Tree Sparrow.

Around the turn of the century a generally acknowledged expert on the subject determined that the average Tree Sparrow's intake was a quarter ounce of weed seeds per day. On this basis, presumably knowing how many Tree Sparrows there were at the time in Iowa, he confidently announced that these birds annually ate 875 tons of weed seeds, thus saving Iowa farmers the enormous trouble and expense that would otherwise have gone into eradicating the noxious weeds that would have sprouted save for the intervention of the sparrows. It sounded good, and it washed at the time.

No doubt such pleading had some effect in staying the hand of citizens who would otherwise have thoughtlessly shot a small bird or vandalized a nest. And the people who dredged up these statistics must be pardoned, even praised. The public of the day had no time for virtue that bore no earthly or heavenly reward, and the day of highminded ideas like preservation for its own sake were generations off. In that time and in that place anything in the way of a good word for our furred and feathered friends was a step toward enlightenment.

The surprise is that, shaky and outdated though the 875-ton "calculation" is, it shows up in current literature! It is quoted without reference to its time or to how technology has transformed Iowa, the farmers, and the birds' habitat almost beyond recognition from what they were back in 1910. It is now a fable, bankrupt of philosophical significance, statistically meaningless. It should be laid to rest. The Tree Sparrow, by simply being a Tree Sparrow, merits our unconditional protection and affection. It no longer should to be put to work to earn them.

American Tree Sparrow *(Spizella arborea)*

Bunting/New World sparrow family. Early English settlers named it after similiar, unrelated, red-capped European Tree Sparrow; has been called "Arctic Chipper" and "Canada Sparrow"; "sparrow" is from Anglo-Saxon *spearwa*, "sparrow"; *spizella* is from Latin *spiza*, "a finch," and *arborea*, "a tree."

Description Slightly larger than chickadee; fox-red crown, small chestnut patch on sides of breast at shoulder; only sparrow with a dark "stickpin" spot on plain breast; sides of head, neck, and breast light gray; brown wings have two irregular white bars; tail plain dusky with outer feathers edged in white; back heavily streaked with black, buff, and brown.

Behavior Travels in loose flocks in winter; busy ground feeder; constantly flashes light edges of outer tail feathers; feeding call is an icy, tinkling "tseewit," call note is a silvery, high "tseet"; often sings in winter, "sweet sweet sweet" followed by a series of fast warbled notes, last phrase dropped in pitch.

Range Migratory; tundra breeder, from north edge of boreal forest to arctic coast; rare winterer in northern Minnesota, most of North Dakota, common elsewhere in Upper Midwest.

Food   Weed seeds gleaned from field edges, meadows, and roadsides; readily comes to feeders for sunflower, millet, and other seeds.

Nest   On ground, against moss hummock or under woody shrub; rarely in low shrub; base of twigs, weed stems, rootlets, and shreds of moss and lichen, fully lined with feathers and hair.

Comment   The "winter chippy" is the sparrow most commonly seen and heard throughout its huge wintering range in the U.S. Its presence, and the fragile notes of its song, are a sure sign of winter. It is one of the most frequently observed feeder visitors, preferring the ground but moving readily to tables and shelves.

REF: A–522; BM–297; GO–338; NG–398; P–280

Juncos
Subfamily Emberizinae

In the northern parts of the Upper Midwest most of these pert little birds in formal attire migrate. But as you get farther south, more and more of them stick around for the winter. And, as with other casual migrators, some winters are different from others and the juncos may be totally absent or very abundant. In those winters when they pull their vanishing act, they make up for their absence by being one of the earliest returning spring migrants, and they often stick around for a month before moving on.

As in many species, junco migration is divided somewhat along age and sex lines. Females travel farther south than the males, but juveniles of both sexes remain farther north than adults. It is common for bird feeders to note that in spring juncos appear, usually before the snow has gone, stick around for a week or two, vanish altogether for a week or so, then reappear. What is actually happening is migration in two pulses, the males a week or two ahead of the females.

As mentioned in the species write-up, four regional color variations of juncos have been reassessed and found lacking sufficient differentiation to merit status as separate species. The only regional variant to retain its own species status is the Yellow-eyed Junco of Mexico and Central America.

Not all aspects of the changeover have been unanimously accepted by those whose opinions carry weight. In the most recent edition of his field guide to the birds of eastern North America, Peterson bids us call all juncos, except the Yellow-eyed, "Northern" Juncos.

Dark-eyed Junco *(Junco hyemalis)*

Sparrow family. Older guides list "Slate-colored Junco," "White-winged Junco," "Oregon Junco," "Gray-headed Junco," all now listed as color variants (races) of *hyemalis*, former species name for Slate-colored; Latin *juncus*, meaning "a rush," has no known connection to juncos, but Latin *hyemalis*, "winter," is linked to their appearing only in winter in south-temperate regions; "snowbird" frequently mentioned as alternate name.

Description   Sparrow-sized; most common race, Slate-colored; stubby, flesh-tinted bill shows up against dark face and breast; outermost tail feathers white, at rest almost completely hidden under central black feathers; male has unbroken slate gray on entire upper body; belly and two wing bars (when present) are white.

Behavior   Moderately social ground-foragers, but quick to follow other birds to table, shelf, or even hanging, feeders; may scuff down through light snow cover to reach bare ground; flicks white outer tail feathers from under centrals, especially just before takeoff, flashing them conspicuously in flight;

calls variously described as snappy "chip" or "dit"; soft twittering in flight; song a largely one-pitch trill, like Chipping Sparrow but more agreeable to some ears.

Range   Migratory, flying only far enough south to reach adequate forage; breeds throughout the boreal and adjoining mixed-wood forests from coast to coast; common winterer in varying numbers in Upper Midwest; white-winged race breeds in Black Hills.

Food   Insects during breeding season, seeds in winter; at stations will readily take to sunflower seeds, all small seeds, crumbs, and occasionally suet and peanut butter.

Nest   On ground, in open woodland, or forest edge; concealed in tree roots, under debris, rock, tussock, or occasionally in ferns or on rubbly slope; rarely in low shrub or conifer; small cup of bark shreds, stems, and light twigs, lined with fine grasses, rootlets, and hair; prefledged nestlings precociously active and able to scramble away from nest and hide if threatened.

Comment   The juncos that recently lost their species accreditation were lumped together because their differences, the lumpers assure us, are largely sartorial, and they freely interbreed where their ranges overlap. Nonetheless, it should remain a matter of excitement when a pink-flanked, brown-backed, black-caped "Oregon" Junco shows up amongst its all-slate fellows at a feeding station anywhere east of the Montana-Dakota borders.

REF: A–551; BM–314; GO–334; NG–402; P–266

Snow Bunting *(Plectrophenax nivalis)*

Bunting/sparrow subfamily. Popularly also "snowbird"; "Bunting" may be from Old English *buntyle*, the name of several ground-dwelling birds of western Europe; *Plectrophenax* is from Greek *plektron*, "something to strike with" or "a claw" (whence "plectrum," guitar pick); *phenax* is Greek "a cheat"; original generic name was *Plectophanes*, from Greek *phaino*, "to display," translating into something like "to show a claw," descriptive of very long hind claw; but *Plectophanes* was displaced, due to a taxonomic misadventure, with *Plectrophenax*, which means "something to strike a cheat with"; *nivalis* is Latin for "snow."

Description   House Sparrow-sized; in winter head, back, and rump light rusty brown, wings patterned in dark check marks; center of tail black, outer feathers white, edged in black; throat, breast, and belly white, with varying amounts of rusty wash; wing in flight white with dark end; bill small, conical, ocher in winter, black in breeding plumage; eye prominent; as spring nears, plumage wear in males transforms them into bright white except for bill, back, wingtips, and tail.

Behavior   Sociable; as flocks swoop, swirl in unison, they flash brightly as white of wings is exposed, then suddenly vanish; flocks feed on weed seeds in windswept fields, pastures, beaches, and roadsides, running low to the ground, occasionally jumping up to pluck weed seeds from higher stalks; calls are a clear, whistled "tew," a short, purring buzz, and a musical twitter in flight.

Range   Migratory; breeds in highest arctic islands and northernmost mainland; winters all through Upper Midwest except for heavily forested areas; gathers to forage in open fields, roadsides, and short-cropped pastures.

Food   In winter, weed seeds; can sometimes be attracted to chaff or screenings spread on the snow in exposed locations where birds are known to gather; very rare at feeders.

Nest   Tucked into crevices in cliffs, often well up; in rubble, rock piles, and other cracks and crannies; base of moss and grasses, lined with moss, hair, and feathers.

Comment   This is the real "snowbird" of windswept expanses, a migrant that shows up about the time snow-wary pensioners head for Florida. It stays out where the wind blows its hardest, oblivious to the cutting snow, sheltering at night on open ground behind tussocks of grass, rocks, or clods of earth in fields. It is often seen in deserted beach parking lots and on the wind-cleared shoulders of roads. It heads north again well before spring sunshine has lured the migrant pensioners back from the Sunshine State. It is interesting to note that a single Snow Bunting was recorded at the North Pole on April 24, 1979.

REF: A–530; BM–319; GO–344; NG–412; P–266

Finch Family
Family Fringillidae, Subfamily Carduelinae

Depending upon which reference one consults, and its date, the family *Fringillidae* totals over five hundred species, the largest in the bird world. Within this group are some 125 species (again writers differ) comprising the subfamily *Carduelinae*.

The contradictions arise because bird classification is a constantly evolving process that renders old references ever more obsolete. It generates debate and jobs within the ornithological establishment, and it's good for the field-guide business. But unless you are very sensitive to the scorn you might suffer by appearing afield with a guide that has two or three names out of date, don't rush off to the bookstore.

Finches are regarded, along with the corvids (jays and crows), as the most recently evolved birds, showing great adaptability and success at colonizing new territories and exploiting new niches. The finches of the Galapagos Islands helped Charles Darwin formulate his monumental theory of evolution. From a single species that somehow reached these remote islands evolved a variety of new species to fill the available niches.

One of the most famous of these is the Woodpecker Finch. Lacking the natural equipment to probe into holes for wood-boring grubs, this bird uses a twig or thorn held in its bill. It not only selects suitable probes, but trims and clips them, thus demonstrating both ingenuity of a high order and sophisticated tool use.

Finches are predominently seed-eaters, with stout bills, heavy skulls, and strong jaw muscles for cracking tough husks and crushing hard seeds. The Eurasian Hawfinch, with a bill even larger than that of our Evening Grosbeak, can exert a force of over ninety pounds, sufficient to crack olive pits.

Most finches have a crop for storing food and a powerful gizzard for grinding it up. Some feed their young exclusively on a milky porridge of regurgitated seeds, others may provide a mix of seeds and insects as a starter formula, switching exclusively to seeds as the nestlings develop.

Compulsive Songsters   A feature common to the carduelines is their singing ability. While most birds sing only in their nesting territories in the breeding season, carduelines sing wherever they happen to be, and at any time of year.

The serin of the Canary Islands, *Serinus canaria*, has been a domesticated cage pet from at least as early as the time of the Ancient Greeks. The variety that has brightened generations of homes from its wire cage was imported into Italy from the Canary Islands in the sixteenth century.

Easy to keep on a simple diet of seeds, it is now bred in an astonishing variety of plumage colors and patterns.

Its singing ability is legendary. In the early years of this century British fanciers taught a bullfinch to whistle "God Save the King." The bird invariably hesitated at the end of the third line, and if he paused a bit too long, a canary in the next room, that had picked up the melody on its own, would chime in and finish it for him.

The finches of our northern winters are famous throughout the continent (and the hemisphere for those that are circumpolar) for their erratic, usually massive winter migrations, or irruptions. The degree of irruptive behavior of these northern finches depends on the diet of each species. The American Goldfinch, the least "northern" of the lot, is also the most consistently migratory. It feeds primarily on the seeds of low-growing forbs, particularly dandelions and thistles. These either scatter upon ripening or are covered by snow in winter. Thus, with their northern food supply very likely to be buried, goldfinches fly south almost every winter.

By contrast, other wintering finches such as crossbills find their natural food higher up in spruce and pine trees well above the snow, and do not follow a set migratory pattern.

Feeding above the snow level is no guarantee of stability, however. Crossbills are the most irruptive northern finches. Years of superabundant spruce-cone crops alternate with years of sparse production over vast expanses of boreal forest. Crossbills have therefore evolved into foraging nomads, migrating west-east as well as south in search of productive tracts of evergreens. Finding them, they not only settle in to feed, but may commence nesting. They are on record as raising broods every month of the year throughout the Northern Hemisphere where conifer forests happen to have produced abundantly for that particular season.

Rosy (Gray-crowned) Finch *(Leucosticte arctoa)*

Finch family. *Leucosticte* is from Greek *leucos*, "white," and *sticte*, "varied"; *arctoa* is from Greek *arcto*, "north"; former name Gray-crowned is from Latin *tephrocotis*, from Greek *tephros*, "gray" and *kotis*, "back of head."

Description   Sparrow-sized; males rusty pink on rump and belly; darker wings pink with black and off-white lines; forehead black, back of head light gray; back, throat, and bib light brown; females brown with suggestion of dusky flecking and lighter patch and bar on wings; stubby bill yellowish with dark tip.

Behavior   Social, ground feeders, occasionally in company with juncos or other finches; prefers open country; "cheew" call similar to House Sparrow, song is a rich goldfinchlike warble.

Range   High mountains of west, south to California; in winter migrates to lower elevations, Rocky Mountain population into Montana foothills; rated "occasional" in extreme western Dakotas, rare "accidental" in Minnesota.

Food   Seeds of grasses and forbs; small and large seeds at feeders.

Nest   On sheltered rock ledges, in crevices, holes, and caves at high altitudes in montane tundra habitat; cup of grasses and mosses, with coarser stems, grasses, and rootlets towards inside, final lining of feathers, fur, and other fine materials.

Comment   These are high-mountain birds, nesting up among the rock slides and alongside the glaciers where pikas call and lupines wave. When they migrate it tends to be downhill, the most easterly into the foothills and, infrequently, well out onto the plains. "Islanded" into separate races by their broken habitat, their semi-isolation reinforced by restricted migration behavior, they have developed distinctive regional plumage patterns that at one time had them divided into separate species such as the brown-capped, black, gray-headed, and so on. These have now been lumped into a single species with the variants considered to be subspecies or races.

The Birder's Handbook says that males outnumber females by up to six-to-one throughout the year. If true, it poses some very interesting questions about how this comes about and what adaptive advantages it confers on the species.

REF: A(W)*–464; BM–331; G–318; NG–438; P(W)*–334
* Guides to western birds

Pine Grosbeak *(Pinicola enucleator)*

Finch family. *Pinicola* is from Latin "pine" and *colere,* "inhabit"; *enucleator* is Latin for "one who shells (out)," descriptive of the birds' habit of husking spruce cones.

Description   Chunky, robin-sized; short, dark, strongly curved bill; adult males dusky pink, may have patches and flecks of gray, with darkish line through eye; all have moderately long, dark, slightly forked tails; wings dark with two white bars; subadult males soft gray with crown and rump rusty rose; adult females gray with shading of olive to russet on crown and rump; larger than other pink finches (crossbills and purple), with relatively longer tail and no bold striping like Purple Finch.

Behavior   Sociable; flocks at feeders are often predominantly females and immatures; placid, sometimes very tame; call is a gentle, high-pitched "tew-tew-tew"; song is a brief, pleasant, unenergetic warble.

Range   Nomadically migratory; circumpolar in distribution; breed much farther north than Evening Grosbeaks, more inclined to overwinter in their breeding range but winter irregularly, in small flocks, in Upper Midwest; abundant during rare "invasions."

Food   Particularly fond of ash-tree seeds, but share with waxwings a liking for dried fruit and berries; feed on spruce seeds, periodic failures of this source accounting for their drift south in some winters; readily accept sunflower seeds at feeders.

Nest　Loose, bulky platform of twigs, fibers, and lichens; midheight in a conifer or birch, or low in juniper or underbrush.

Comment　"Ridiculously tame" is the phrase used for these easy-going birds in *The Birder's Handbook*. Tufts, in *Birds of Nova Scotia*, recalls days at the turn of the century when boys could hit them with snowballs and kill them with their slingshots. I have never encountered any so foolishly trusting, but around the feeder they are calm, unexcitable, exhibiting none of that busy finch energy typified by the Evening Grosbeaks.

Taylor, in *Wings Along the Winnipeg*, noted their feeding on lilac seeds. And in one winter he observed them foraging heavily in strips and patches of flax missed by the harvesters. Occasional reference is made to their evolution away from dependence on tree seeds to a diet of buds, fruits, and weed seeds, and that they are especially fond of crabapples. *Birds Around Us* says they relish cranberries, either canned or fresh. For several winters past I have therefore stored a bag of highbush cranberries in the deep freeze where they await the opportunity to test the postulated change of tastes of these lovely winter birds.

REF: A–414; BM–332; GO–316; NG–436; P–270

Purple Finch *(Carpodacus purpureus)*

Finch family. "Finch" is from Germanic *fink*, and Anglo-Saxon *finc*, but ultimate roots are possibly from Indo-European *pingo*, echoic of birds' calls; *Carpodacus* is from Greek *carpos* for "fruit" (i.e., seed), and *dacos* for "biting"; *purpureus* is Latin for "crimson," more descriptive of bird's color than misleading English "purple."

Description　"Like a sparrow dipped in raspberry juice" is Peterson's famous quip; color is brightest on head and rump, lighter on throat, breast, and flanks; dark ear patch on side of head, light eyebrow streak; dark brown wings checked and lined with subdued pattern, all with rose wash; tail dark, well notched; females and immatures heavily streaked on breast and back in browns and light beige; belly off-white; at first glance male could be mistaken for male Pine Grosbeak or crossbill.

Behavior   Sociable; flocks may be divided by sex and age, all-male or all-female-and-immatures; aggressive behavior at feeders intensified by crowding; flight fights have been observed in which grappling pairs thrash straight up for many yards and fall back to ground, still struggling desperately; calls a musical "churr-lee" and sharp "tink" in flight; song is a rapid, clearly enunciated, rich warble, ending with down-slurred "too-eee," delivered from tree-tops, occasionally also from flight with no loss of exuberant energy.

Range   Variably migratory; breeds in boreal forest and adjacent mixed woodlands; breeds in northeast and north-central Minnesota, northern Wisconsin, much of Michigan including Upper Peninsula; erratic winter nomad to areas south of breeding range and into eastern Dakotas.

Food   Primarily seeds; some tree buds and poplar catkins; insects and fruit in summer; sunflower seeds favorite feeder fare, but will eat other seeds, and suet, if "flowers" run out; will use high shelves; agile enough to use hanging feeders.

Nest   Well up in tall conifer if available, otherwise at variable heights in deciduous trees or shrubs; well-hidden cup of fine twigs, grasses, and rootlets selected to blend into surroundings.

Comment   In his *Joy of Birding* Chuck Bernstein notes that warblers don't really warble, that Purple Finches and goldfinches do. Among my warmest recollections of bird feeding at our cottage are bright late-winter days when the trees in the yard were thronging with these merry finches. About noon each day they would fill the sheltered valley with song.
    Recalling these idyllic interludes brings to mind an incident related by Seton in *The Birds of Manitoba*. On May 14, 1884, he "collected" a male Purple Finch. Shooting birds was then the standard method of verifying sightings, but it seemed a trifle ghoulish of him to go on and note that he blew it away "in full song." We can be thankful that the ready-made technology of modern cameras, binoculars, and field guides has made "collecting" largely unnecessary.

REF: A–696; BM–333; GO–316; NG–440; P–270

Crossbills
Subfamily Carduelinae

Carduelinae is rooted in another Latin word, *carduus*, "thistle," and it means "goldfinch." The cheery "thistlebird" is thus the flag-bearing species for the branch of the finch family that includes all the familiar native seed-eaters that are so welcome at winter feeding stations across the Upper Midwest.

Worldwide there are only four species of crossbills; our Red and White-winged crossbills range throughout the Northern Hemisphere and are joined in Eurasia by the Parrot Crossbill, *Loxia pytyopsittacus*, and in Scotland by what some writers believe to be a local race of the parrot, the Scottish Crossbill, *Loxia scotica*. All of them closely resemble each other and all are specialized to harvest the seeds of cone-bearing evergreens. Such differences as there are arise from further specialization according to which particular conifers a species is most closely associated with.

A Food Specialist   In spite of the obvious, vast abundance of cone-bearing trees in the subarctic reaches of the Northern Hemisphere, there are difficulties connected to a conifer-dependent existence. Conifers are reluctant, unreliable sources of very small seeds, housing them under tough scales in cones that open when it is in the tree's interests to release seeds to the wind. Cracking ripe but unopened cones is hard work, demanding special tools and skills.

The twisted beak of the crossbill is such a tool. As a fledgling it has a normal bill. But at four weeks the ends of the bill begin to twist sideways, one to the right, the other to the left. Which does which is varied, some birds being left-crossed, some right. The jawbones themselves are straight; it is only the horny outer sheaths that are crooked.

A Red Crossbill attacks a spruce cone by gripping it solidly with its powerful, oversized feet, perhaps first clipping the cone off for more convenient handling on the nearest steady perch. It inserts the tip of the upper mandible under a cone scale, bracing the lower mandible against the outside of the scale at the bottom. With special muscles it moves the jaws sideways in a lateral shearing action to pry the scale out, aiding this move with a twist of the head. This cracks the cone scale vertically. Holding it open, the bird inserts its large, muscular tongue equipped at the tip with a cartilagenous cutting edge and shears off the enclosed seed.

This shucking process is carried on with rapid, assembly-line efficiency. A flock of crossbills working through a grove of spruce create a sound like falling rain, what with the noise of the snapping scales and the shower of debris hitting the ground.

Among conifers, pines generally bear the hardest cones. The most extreme case is found in jackpines; anyone who has tried to force apart the hard, thick scales of an unopened cone discovers that it is built to stay resolutely clenched until time, or the heat of a forest fire, melts the cementing resin and it opens to release its imprisoned seeds. Spruce cones are large but the scales can be pried open, while the tamarack bears the smallest and least-armored cones.

The Parrot Crossbill of Eurasia is associated with pines and has the largest and heaviest bill, the tamarack-harvesting white-winged the lightest, with the red, reflecting its affinity for spruce, in between.

Feast-and-Famine   Another problem for conifer-dependent seed-eaters is the trees' irregular seed-bearing cycle. With no obvious, consistent connection to environmental causes, such as weather, they alternate a year of abundant cone production with several years of meager yield. The only consistencies seem to be that all the trees of a given species over great expanses of northland do it in rhythm, and the years of greatest plenty are followed by those of greatest impoverishment.

Nut-bearing trees follow a similar regime. Even cultivated ones retain their own agenda, frustrating orchardists' best efforts to optimize growing conditions and otherwise to beguile them into "forgetting" their imprinted capriciousness.

It has been postulated that the northern conifers use this mechanism to control the populations of animals that feed on their seeds. Unlike many plants, they don't have a system of traded benefits in which the plant provides food in exchange for pollination, seed dispersal, or some other inadvertent service. The cone-seed eaters, though noncarnivorous, are nevertheless predators, the seeds, their prey.

Operating in a system of evolutionary one-upmanship, each side has developed its own strategies. The trees alternately swamp the predators with so many seeds they can't possibly eat them all, and then cut production almost entirely to starve them out. Given the vast expanses over which this supposedly managed famine is wrought, it is for the numberless, unwitting seed-eaters a calamity of awesome proportions and incalculable misery. Red Squirrels instinctively hedge against this feast-and-famine regime by storing, in feast years, two winter's worth of spruce cones, as many as fifteen thousand.

Crossbills don't have this option. What they do have is the ability to nest whenever and wherever there is sufficient food. For, while conifers over great areas might synchronize their seeding schedule, it is not continentwide, nor is it coordinated between species. Thus, when the White Spruce of Labrador/Quebec abruptly fail, the regional Black Spruce or tamaracks might partially fill in. If they don't, perhaps the spruce of boreal Manitoba/Saskatchewan have produced a bumper crop.

This imposes a fly-or-die option in which the birds in huge numbers irrupt from their breeding grounds in an urgent search for food. Whether salvation is a matter of luck, or whether there are subtle clues that tell them where to look is not known. Whichever is the case, they sometimes show up in swarms, in places far removed from their normal haunts. Cameron B. Kepler, in *The Encyclopedia of Birds,* reports that from a batch of migrant birds banded in Switzerland, some were recorded the following fall and winter in southwest Europe, while others appeared in later years in the northern USSR, 2,500 miles from the banding site. The suggestion is that, however widely crossbills rove, they retain fidelity to a home range and may return there if they survive long enough.

Historic Invasions   If they find a land of plenty where several conifer species are producing bountifully, with cones ripening in sequential seasons, the opportunistic birds will keep on nesting as long as the food holds out, irrespective of the weather. Their ability to raise young in the bitterest of conditions was discussed in chapter 5 under "Midwinter Nesting."

Irruptions of crossbills have been so massive they have been written into history. In 1251 Matthew Paris wrote about the unusual birds that invaded England and devastated the apple crop. Chroniclers in Europe, Japan, and North America have noted the mysterious and sometimes destructive invasions of strange birds that abruptly appeared and then vanished, not to be seen again for generations.

When they show up at our feeders, they might demonstrate that, while they are highly specialized foragers, they haven't lost the adaptability that typifies the finch family. They can turn their bent bills to sunflower seeds, even suet. And in keeping with their exotic appearance, they often betray an exotic taste for highly unusual foods. Amused observers have watched them eating ashes, frozen dishwater, tea leaves, charcoal, bits of mortar, spots of frozen dog urine in the snow, and salt, especially salt. They frequently suffer heavy mortality on highways when they go after road salt. Perhaps these unpalatable substances help to counteract the sticky resin which they constantly encounter in their normal feeding.

Red Crossbill *(Loxia curvirostra)*

Finch family. "Crossbill" is descriptive of the seemingly misshapen beak; *Loxia* is from Greek *loxos* meaning "crooked," and *curvirostra* is Latin for "curved bill."

Description   House Sparrow-sized; ends of large bill crossed; tail short and notched; adult male dull red with sooty brown wings and tail; abdomen and undertail coverts gray; female olive-buff on back and head with close pattern of brown check marks; belly, undertail, and rump olive-yellow; wings and tail dark.

Behavior   Social, usually in flocks, chattering in flight; swarm through conifers like miniature parrots, climbing with bills and feet; grip cones with feet and expertly pry open the scales; at close quarters, as at a window feeder, further parrotlike behavior obvious in use of the large tongue to work kernels out of sunflower seeds; often very tame and easily approached; call is a repeated sharp "jit-jit-jit," song is a medley of vigorous canarylike warbles punctuated with clear "too-tee too-tee too-tee-tee" whistles.

Range   Circumpolar; nonmigratory; core habitat is northern and mountain coniferous forests, but wanders erratically within this range and occasionally far out of it, winter or summer; sometime visitor in great numbers anywhere through Upper Midwest where conifers can be found.

Food   Seeds of spruce, tamarack, fir, and pine; may also use elm seeds, and in times of starvation will eat fruit, including orchard apples; nestlings fed a porridge of regurgitated seeds and fluid; at feeder takes sunflowers, nutmeats, and cracked cereal grains.

Nest   In conifer at edge of woodland; usually high up, well concealed among twigs at end of branch; bulky base of twigs, built up with grasses, lichen, and bark shreds; lining of fine grass, hair, fur, and feathers; punky wood worked in as filler in winter nests; eggs are pale bluish white with purplish brown specks and scrawls near the large end; only female broods, fed by male.

Comment   One of the real delights of winter feeding is to have a flock of these unique northerners share space with you. If you happen to have a grove of spruce nearby, some of them might decide to settle in and raise a brood, as a pair did in the winter of '87/'88 at my station in Winnipeg. From late January through to early March the male and female regularly fed at my office window tray, an arm's length from my word processor. Whether they succeeded in raising any young I don't know, for none came to the feeder. They shared the close-by spruce with Blue Jays, and the neighborhood was prowled by the inevitable skulk of cats. I also wondered if sunflowers were an adequate substitute for the nestlings' natural diet of conifer seeds.

REF: A–696; BM–335; GO–322; NG–436; P–268

White-winged Crossbill *(Loxia leucoptera)*

Finch family. Wings are black, with two white bars, making the common British name "Two-barred" more descriptive; *Loxia* is from Greek *loxos*, "crooked," *leucoptera* from Greek *leucos*, "white," and *pteran*, "wing."

Description   House Sparrow-sized; ends of bill crossed; short tail notched; adult male dusky rose, eye darkly shadowed; wings black, with white tips on tertials and two bold white bars; female yellowish olive under lines of brown spots, with white bars on dark wings.

Behavior   Social, flocks chattering in flight; often very tame and trusting; parrotlike in climbing about conifer cones and twigs with bills and feet as they forage, and in use of large tongue husking sunflower seeds at feeders; call is a single, clear "peet" or a rapid, raspy "jeet-jeet-jeet" in flight; song is a sustained series of canarylike warbles and trills punctuated by harsh rattles.

Range   Irruptively migratory from home range in boreal and mountain evergreen forests in Northern Hemisphere; somewhat more northerly in Canadian breeding range than Red Crossbill; erratic winter visits determined by presence of sufficient numbers of suitable conifers.

Food   Seeds of conifers, especially tamarack; at feeder takes sunflower seeds, peanuts, cracked grains, and occasional suet.

Nest   Indistinguishable from that of Red Crossbill; bulky, base of twigs carrying cup of grasses, lichens, bark shreds, and leaves with lining of rootlets, lichen, punky wood, hair, and feathers; usually well up in conifer, on end of branch, well hidden; eggs pale bluish or greenish white spotted or splotched lightly with dark purple at large end; male feeds female during incubation and for first few days of brooding, his calling and hovering flight song is a clue to nest location; like Red Crossbill, nests at any time of year.

Comment   Both the Red and White-winged crossbills are noted as food specialists, their breeding governed by the abundance of conifer seeds, their irruptive migrations by scarcity of this wild crop. Observers note that the white-winged feeds on larch (tamarack) seeds, borne in a small cone of relatively flimsy construction compared to the much heavier spruce and pine cones favored by the red. Tools matching task, the white-winged's bill is noticeably less rugged than the red's.

REF: A–697; BM–336; GO–322; NG–436; P–268

Redpolls
Genus Carduelis

This genus includes goldfinches and siskins, members of the abundant finch family. *Carduelis* is Latin for "goldfinch."

Positive identification of Hoary Redpolls, even at the close quarters provided by feeders, is an uncertain business because the differences are subtle. The accepted method is to get out the binoculars and carefully scan individuals in a flock of Common Redpolls, since at Upper Midwest latitudes they prefer to lose themselves in crowds of their look-alike first cousins.

These two may be in for the same regrouping that recently befell the juncos in which four former species were demoted to the status of races and lumped together as a single species under a new common name. Hoary and Common redpolls are similar in all respects and interbreed where their ranges overlap. It may well be that in future field guides the hoary will be recognized only as a northern race of the common.

Like the other "northern" finches, redpolls are erratic migrants, appearing in huge flocks one winter, virtually absent the next. I recall that in the winter of '86/'87 a local farmer near our country place in southern Manitoba left part of a small field of sunflowers unharvested. By late winter redpolls swarmed like locusts over the ranks of frozen stalks.

Wherever, and in what numbers, they appear, they vanish in spring to nest in the far north. As an adaptive adjustment to these harsh surroundings, redpolls have been found better able to withstand cold temperatures than any other songbird yet studied.

In common with many other northern birds, redpolls often show remarkable tameness. There is at least one record of a birdbander able to pick them off her window feeder. It isn't that unusual to hear people tell of these bold little birds fluttering around them, landing on their heads and shoulders as they reload their feeders. This captivating tameness is often attributed to the birds' northern origins where they have no contact with humans and have therefore not learned to fear them. Another theory is that they are conditioned by the uncertain productivity of their environment to not allow caution to get between themselves and a meal when the chance presents itself.

When not availing themselves of the benevolence of feeding stations, redpolls search for roadside and wasteland weed beds, and for strips and corners of standing grain missed by the combine, especially flax and sunflowers.

They are also very fond of birch, which they harvest in three stages. They first flutter and climb about in the trees, swallowing some seeds, but knocking most of them out of the tiny cones onto the snow below. They then pick the seeds off the snow and store them in a bilobed pouch, the diverticulum or crop, about halfway down the throat. This done they fly to a sheltered spot, possibly their nighttime roost, regurgitate the seeds, shell them out and swallow them. It is an adaptive device, not unlike the cud-chewing of ruminant animals, to minimize the hazards of exposure during food-collecting by hastily storing it for further processing later in a safe hideaway.

Common and Hoary Redpoll
(Carduelis flammea) and *(Carduelis hornemanni)*

Finch family. "Redpoll" comes from color of cap or "poll," from Middle English *pol(le)*, "top of the head"; *Carduelis* is Latin for "goldfinch," *flammea* for "flame-colored" from pink wash on some parts of male plumage; *C. hornemanni*, Hoary Redpoll, named after J. W. Hornemann, Danish scientist; "hoary" refers to frosty appearance of plumage.

Description Chickadee-sized; both sexes have satiny, dark red forehead patch and black chin; back, rump, and flank heavily streaked with brown; two pale bars on brown wing; stubby, conical bill; tail sharply forked; males have pink wash on breast, often on rump; hoary is same but much paler, streaks on flanks and rump absent or faint.

Behavior Social, often in large twittering flocks; feeds on ground, weed heads or trees, often around grain elevators, seed plants; very tame, trusting; agile at hanging feeders, feisty with own or other species; flight very undulating, with rattling "chit-chit"; perch call a protracted "swee-eee-t"; song a series of trills and twitters.

Range Circumpolar; erratically migratory; breeds throughout northern boreal forest and tundra to (hoary) highest arctic islands, south to Hudson Bay Lowlands; fairly consistent winter visitor through Upper Midwest, sometimes in huge numbers.

Food Weed, birch, and alder seeds, insects when abundant; small seeds at feeding stations; quickly learns to husk sunflower seeds either on shelves or in hanging feeders.

Nest Small cup of fine twigs, grass, and plant stems, lined with plant down, feathers, and hair; in tree, low shrub, or on ground; often close together since birds are not territorial nesters; in Arctic old nests might be relined and used again; nest surroundings messy with droppings.

Comment   The erratic redpolls are one of the most welcome callers at Upper Midwest feeding stations. For station keepers much below the northern tier of states, the sight of a Hoary Redpoll in winter is a rare treat, and the farther south one goes, the higher it climbs on the list of "most-wanted" birds.

REF: A–578/9; BM–337/8; GO–318; NG–438; P–270

Pine Siskin *(Carduelis pinus)*

Finch family. "Siskin" is from same echoic root as Dutch *sidskin,* "a chirper," or Russian *chizh,* "siskin" or "small bird"; Latin *carduelis,* "a goldfinch," is from *carduus,* "thistle"; Latin *pinus,* "pine."

Description   Much smaller than House Sparrow; body and head buff with darker brown stripes; darker wings and tail; yellowish wash at base of tail; yellow on inner third of flight feathers barely noticeable except when in flight or when wings are raised in threat display; except between siskins, sexes indistinguishable; bill smaller and more pointed than other finches'.

Behavior   Very social, often in large flocks that swoop and swirl in swift synchrony, alternately bunching up and flaring apart; in spite of small size, reputed to be able to displace House Sparrows at feeder, using impressive raised-wing threat resembling that of nuthatch; call a raspy, rising "zweeee," a subdued "tit-a-tit," or loud "clee-it" chirp; song harsher version of goldfinch's melody.

Range   Migratory; nests erratically in forested northeast of Upper Midwest; very erratic winter visitor through entire region, varying from abundant to totally absent.

Food   In the wild, seeds of small cones such as alder, birch, and conifer, sharing goldfinch's liking for dandelion and thistle; in season insects and buds; at feeder takes most small seeds, quickly learns to crack sunflowers.

Nest   Adaptable, preferring conifer but will use shrubs and trees of any species, from 3 to 50 ft (1 to 15 m) high; large cup of twigs, fibers, and fine grass with lining of feathers, hair, and rootlets; often messy since adults stop disposing of feces after about nine days.

Comment   Notable, even among the nomadic northern finches, for its erratic ways, this scrappy little wanderer is a lively addition to the feeder crowd whenever it puts in an appearance. Almost always in a bunch, it tends to take over feeding stations when it appears, squaring off at much larger birds at the tray and pursuing them in the air. Although unable to bully Evening Grosbeaks, it feeds with them by dodging in and out, often picking up the bits dropped by the larger birds. Its sociability extends at times even to nesting in loose aggregations, foraging in flocks for the seeds it regurgitates for its nestlings.

REF: A–713; BM–339; GO–320; NG–434; P–272

American Goldfinch *(Carduelis tristis)*

Finch family. Yellow color and singing ability like cage canary, hence also "wild canary"; less commonly "thistle bird" due to liking for thistle seeds; *Carduelis* is Latin for "goldfinch," from root *carduus*, "thistle"; Latin *tristis*, "sad," is a singularly inappropriate label for this embodiment of cheerfulness; older guides give generic name *Spinus* from Greek *spinos*, "a linnet," British name of European cousin of our goldfinches.

Description   Smaller than House Sparrow; stubby tail and bill; winter males and females uniform brownish olive, sometimes yellowish wash on head and neck, one or two bars on dark wings; in early spring males acquire patches of yellow that spread as feather wear reveals summer body plumage of bright yellow with natty black cap, wings, and tail.

Behavior   Roves in flocks in winter and early summer; "bouncing" flight, wings flicked quickly for upward swoop, folded for downward, with rapid "per-chic-o-ree" or "potato chip" call with each "bounce";

song is a bubbly succession of sweet trills punctuated frequently by a rising "swee?" whistle.

Range   Migratory; breeds throughout Upper Midwest; usually migrates out of Montana, North Dakota, and northern Minnesota, but can be abundant there when it does winter over.

Food   Young fed on porridge of regurgitated seeds, with no "starter ration" of insects as provided by most other seed-eaters; heavily reliant on thistle and dandelion seeds; sunflower and smaller seeds at the feeder.

Nest   Latest regular nester of all our songbirds, commonly July and even August; small, deep cup in shrubbery, tall weeds, or low tree, usually near water or swampy area, in open setting; body of plant fibers, lined with plant down, including cattail and thistle, rim bound with spider and/or insect webbing; often woven tightly enough to hold water; nest and supports messy with droppings.

Comment   Our "wild canary" has a talent for mimickery that is apparently essential to his love life, for he bonds to his mate by learning the notes of her song and "playing them back" to her, the couple thus developing a shared, unique vocabulary.

I always have my feeders well stocked by the end of August. One reason is the hope that having seeds at hand when the thistles run out might just prompt the local goldfinches to switch to my feeders instead of flying south. There is considerable room for doubt that this would actually have much effect, but I feel better for trying.

REF: A–510; BM–340; GO–320; NG–434; P–272

Evening Grosbeak *(Coccothraustes vespertinus)*

Finch family. "Evening" assigned in 1823 by observer who first recorded them, one evening, northwest of Lake Superior; "grosbeak" is from French *gros,* "large," and *bec,* "beak"; *Coccothraustes* is from Greek *kokkos,* "kernel" and *thrauo,* "shatter," nicely describing feeding method; *vespertinus* is Latin for "evening."

Description   Chunky, robin-sized with stubby, heavy bill; males in bold pattern of black, white, and yellow that can't be mistaken for any other winter bird; females shaded gray-buff on head (darkest), back, breast, belly, and rump; wings and tail black with white marks; chalky white bill of both sexes peels in late winter to uncover light lime green breeding color.

Behavior   Sociable, in calling flocks of a half-dozen and up, often many more; crowds onto feeders with considerable jostling and threatening; tame when habituated to presence of feeder attendant; undulating flight; call is a clear, musical chirp; song is a robust, rambly warble.

Range   Erratically migratory; breeds in northern mixed forests in Great Lakes states of Upper Midwest, in Black Hills, and in the mountains of western Montana; winters in breeding range but frequently also wanders in considerable numbers into all or part of the region, and on southward.

Food   Large appetite for sunflower seeds at feeders; favored natural winter food the unshed, winged seeds of boxelder (maple); also feeds on leaked sap and buds of this tree; juniper berries; seeks out salt from treated roadways or livestock licks.

Nest   Shambly cup of twigs thinly interwoven with lichens and plant fibers; usually well up in tree, preferably conifer, close to trunk in crotch or well out on limb concealed in twigs.

Comment   Used to be called the Sociable Grosbeak; this or "wandering" or "western" would be more descriptive than the meaningless "Evening." It has been noted from the early eighteen hundreds as an irregular winter visitor throughout the east, sometimes appearing in great numbers in New England and down the east coast. Once breeding strictly in the West, it has rapidly shifted eastward. Its expansion is attributed to a combination of habitat changes brought about by settlement, the accompanying widespread planting of boxelder with their abundant winterfast seeds which the birds favor, plus winter bird feeding.
The fact that Evening Grosbeaks have the longest wings in proportion to their size of any of the other North American finches suggests they evolved in response to the benefits of long-distance flight. Certainly they range far; birds banded at Seven Sisters in eastern Manitoba have been reported from

Newport, Tennessee; Cedar Rapids, Iowa; Hale, Michigan; Owen, Wisconsin; Coulee City, Washington; and Bemidji, Minnesota. Conversely, birds banded at Wautoma, Wisconsin, and Elkins, West Virginia, have been recorded at Seven Sisters.

It has been suggested that what seem to be irregular, aimless wanderings are in fact a flexible itinerary of alternative paths that the birds follow in search of winter feed.

REF: A–384; BM–341; GO–310; NG–442; P–272

Weavers

Family Passeridae

Passeridae is derived from Latin *passer,* "sparrow." The same root gives us "Passeriformes," the name of the huge Order of songbirds that includes the un-sparrowlike, rarely musical, raven.

The passeridae are Old World sparrows, numbering 141 species native to Eurasia and North Africa. Of the two species imported to this continent, the Eurasian Tree Sparrow has not spread much beyond the environs of St. Louis, Missouri, where it was originally released in 1870. But the similar looking House Sparrow suffered no such limits to its preemptive, explosive colonization of North America.

Unlike many other species of exotic plants, insects, fish, birds, and mammals that have become ungovernable scourges, the House Sparrow was not set free by accident. Eight pairs were released in Brooklyn, New York, in 1852. These didn't take. Later the same year one hundred more were brought in and fifty were released. These also vanished. The fifty held in captivity over the winter of 1852/1853 were released in 1853 in Brooklyn's Greenwood Cemetery. They took, and the bird world's most successful introduction of a foreign species was unleashed.

Two Wrongs, No Right   Many reintroductions followed, some for the sentimental ties with homeland England that they represented, some due to the misguided assumption that inspired the initial release, which was to control the accidentally introduced canker worm. Two major potato growers in Nova Scotia imported a number from either New York or Massachusetts in 1856 or 1857, intending cheap elimination of potato beetles, another introduced pest.

Instead, the imports demonstrated with a vengeance that two wrongs rarely make a right. Their effect on the beetles was negligible; their unanticipated impact on many native species of songbirds was incalculably harmful.

Many other introductions of birds were attempted, and caged pets have repeatedly escaped. But North America, at least for birds, has not been the environmental pushover that the sparrow invasion suggests. Of one hundred species thus far introduced, only seven have been successful colonizers: House Sparrow, Starling, Rock Dove, Mute Swan, Ring-necked Pheasant, Chukar, and Gray Partridge. A few others have been able to establish themselves in restricted local habitats.

To their credit, not all our predecessors were motivated by self-interest or sentiment. Eminent bird biologist Elliot Coues vehemently opposed the House Sparrow, labeling it "public enemy number one." But his, and others', protests came too late. Westering pioneers, on trains, river boats, and covered wagons, had already carried along cagefuls of sparrows to be released at their destinations. They were introduced in the Twin Cities area in 1875 and were recorded breeding in 1877, and spread steadily through the state and westward, following railway lines from town to town. By 1894 they had reached Winnipeg, whether from the east or south up the Red River Valley isn't known. Moving ever northward, they showed up at Churchill, Manitoba, in 1930, and although twelve noted there in 1931 all froze to death that winter, the birds were soon successful permanent residents.

It is acknowledged that railroads accounted for many long-distance moves. Hang-abouts at elevators and stockyards, they were no doubt frequently shut into freight cars and shipped out.

The Perfect Partnership   During its peak in the second decade of this century, the sparrow was responsibly reckoned to be the most abundant bird in the U.S. In many areas it doubled the numbers of all other species combined. It flourished on the grains fed to domestic animals on countless small farms, and in villages where thrifty householders kept a cow and a small flock of chickens. But the draught horse was the sparrows' chief ally. Until after World War I it was the mainstay of public and private transportation in cities, and the principal source of farm power. Its droppings and spilled feed provided abundant and nutritious food, its barns furnished nest sites and shelter from winter's cold.

North America has not been the only witness to the whirlwind takeover of the House Sparrow. It was taken to Australia in 1863/1864 (for "aesthetic reasons"!); to New Zealand in a number of transplants from 1859 to 1871; to South Africa from 1890 to 1897. Other introductions saw it loosed in South America, the Falkland Islands, Mauritius, and Mozambique, all coincidental with the arrival of European colonizers. In all of these locations it spread rapidly, and in all it became a permanent resident at the expense of indigenous species. It now occupies two-thirds of the land surface of the earth.

This disliked bird has proven to be a master of adaptability in environments it shares with humans, a talent that has earned it a number of uncomplimentary names like "feathered rat," "avian cockroach," and "Woolco warbler." Shrilling at its world from an inner-city dumpster, it may be demonstrating that a strident voice is an advantage in an environment filled with traffic noise.

Ever the opportunist, it has learned to hunt insects at night under street lights. But the ultimate in adaptability was demonstrated by three that got into the Frickly Coal Mine in Yorkshire, England in the summer of 1975 and stayed 2,100 feet below the surface until the spring of 1978. Two of them nested and hatched three young, but they died.

"I'm With Him"   Away from people the bird has been notably unadaptable. It is rarely found far away from human habitation, and seems unable to hang on for long after farm homesteads are abandoned. A nest in a site more than several hundred yards from occupied buildings is unusual. Perhaps, in addition to food, it may well need the protection from predators that the close company of humankind affords. In a personal communication C. Stuart Houston of Saskatoon observed that the House Sparrow often builds a nest at the base of a hawk's nest, sometimes miles from the nearest farm. It gains the same kind of "I'm with him" protection from the hawk that it gets from humans.

Bird lovers might be grateful that the House Sparrow's impact on native species has been limited to those that can also tolerate closeness with us. Thus, the cheery House Wren, Eastern and Mountain bluebird, Cliff, Barn, and Tree swallow, and other desirables have been seen as the most-mourned losers to the quarrelsome import.

No doubt they were, and are. But the arrival of this brash exotic coincided with the beginning of the railroad age in North America and the consequent burgeoning of settlement. The wholesale habitat destruction that ensued guaranteed the dislocation of most wildlife. Given time, more native birds might have weathered the change and adapted to street and backyard life. But that niche was taken, even as the human immigrants arrived, by their avian tag-along, and the natives were put to a double disadvantage. In the self-forgiving way we have of shifting blame, the House Sparrow takes the rap for what was very much a human offense.

The only type of habitat that is not decreasing is human-altered habitat. This should have continued to favor House Sparrows in America. But they suffered a marked decline after World War I, a loss that paralleled the drop in horse populations. The downturn leveled out, but in many areas sparrow numbers continue a gradual fall. Farms are disappearing, and much livestock is concentrated in intensive-feeding factories. Most people are concentrated in cities. The sprawling new suburbs, with their tightly built houses, are not as compatible to the tough little sparrow as were the leafy back yards, gardens, ramshackle cowsheds, and garages of yesteryear.

House Sparrow *(Passer domesticus)*

Weaver Finch family. Also "English" Sparrow; *Passer* is Latin for "sparrow," *domesticus* for "house."

Description   Chunky, dingy, short-legged finch; back and wings brown streaked, breast plain dust gray; male has black chin and bib; cap and rump gray; gray-buff ear patch, band of brown from eye widening around back of neck; markings of winter male much subdued, clearest in early breeding season.

Behavior   Social, forages in small flocks, may congregate at night roosts in large numbers; prefers to feed on ground; rather heavy flier; noisy, squabbling occupant of streets, vacant lots, shopping malls, and barnyards; aggressive hang-about at feeders; voice a loud "chir-rup," often repeated monotonously; may gather in bush or tree at certain times of day where, for an extended time, all seem intent on out-shrilling each other.

Range   Nonmigratory; universally, and exclusively, where human settlement has extended, absent only in farthest north, and probably expanding there into frontier towns.

Food   Grain, weed seeds, edible human refuse, and insects; at feeders favors small seeds, breadcrumbs, cracked grain over sunflowers.

Nest   Hatful of dusty trash, straw, and feathers jammed into holes in eaves of buildings, in light standards, large signs, or birdhouses; often appropriates nests of Cliff Swallows; on rare instances builds large, domed ball of grass with side entrance, high in tree.

Comment   A feeder heavily streaked with droppings is the sign of a clientele of House Sparrows, although native finches can also be messy. Opportunism is this scrappy little bird's middle name. I have watched them on hot summer days diligently working service stations and campground parking lots, pulling insects out of the radiators and bug screens on newly arrived vehicles. No exception to the rule that undesirables must be prolific, the males begin competing for nest sites the autumn before the next breeding season, and pairs can be seen in March hauling nesting material about the eaves and into Purple Martin houses. This head start, abetted by an incubation period as short as ten days, allows double, often triple brooding, in the Upper Midwest.

REF: A–560; BM–342; GO–296; NG–432; P–262

CHAPTER 7

The Walk-in Trade

I have already referred frequently to some animals other than birds that routinely answer the call of your hospitality, for better or worse. In the annals of bird feeding in America some quite unusual beasts have joined the regulars at the table. These have included deer, elk, and moose; black bears and raccoons; porcupines, woodchucks, and all the ground squirrels; mice, voles, and shrews; weasels and mink, for suet and for the mice the seeds attracted; snakes, probably also for the mice; and oftener than one might suspect, coyotes which, it turns out, can develop quite a liking for "spits"!

I haven't heard, but wouldn't be at all surprised to hear, that stations in the far north have been visited by polar bears, caribou, and muskoxen.

The two animals that attract the most attention and comment, however, are cats and squirrels. A close runner-up in some locations is the raccoon, well-established urbanite that it has latterly become.

Because these mammals are so much a part of the feeder scene it is essential in my view to deal with them other than solely as nuisances to be discouraged or dispatched. They do, after all, have their own natural history, even though cats play theirs out as half-time pets, half-time predators.

Squirrels
Family Sciuridae

Sciuridae is Latinized "shade-tail," from Greek *skia*, "a shadow" and *oura*, "tail," from tree squirrels' summertime habit of stretching out on limbs with their tails over their backs to shade themselves from the sun.

This is quite the opposite to the problem that beset a Red Squirrel just outside my study window of a sunrise in mid-December not long ago. A west wind was rattling the sparse branches of my oak trees. In one of them the squirrel was curled into a tight ball, facing the sun, exposing his leeward quarters to the feeble rays. He was trying to muffle his windward side with his tail. But his sunbath wasn't going at all well; a few seconds on his branch was all he could manage before the tearing wind would whip his tail aside. He would hump impatiently, shake himself, race down the tree and then right back up to another windswept perch, to repeat the process.

If it were possible I would point out to him that the best basking to be had is in the lee of the gable of my woodshed where there is no wind and where the sun beams so strongly that the wood on the lean-to roof under the gable steams a bit, even at well below zero.

Arguably, rodents are the most successful order of mammals, and the squirrel family stands near the head of it. They are present in all the habitable continents except Australia, and fill widely varying niches wherever they occur. In the Upper Midwest they are fossorial (digging), arboreal, and aerial. The blocky, stolid woodchuck, the soft-eyed Flying Squirrel, and the skittering wee chipmunk are all squirrels. Some are among the world's most profound hibernators; others, like my frustrated friend in the oak tree, go at winter in high gear.

The Teeth Have It   Other admirable attributes aside, teeth are the rodents' key to success. These are mounted in a set of jaws hinged to switch instantly from cutting to grinding, with special sets of muscles to accomplish this change of gears. A set of cutting chisels are mounted prominently at the front of the muzzle, giving most rodents a kind of "buck-toothed" look, especially if, as in the case of beavers and porcupines, the teeth are deep orange.

The roots of these four incisors curve for an astonishing distance back into channels in the jaws. This is not only a very secure mounting; the roots are hollow and open at the bottom, a feature of teeth that grow constantly throughout the life of the owner. The rate of growth is constant, calibrated over evolutionary eons to match the average rate of wear the user imposes on them.

This, and the fact that wear automatically keeps the teeth chisel-sharp, permits rodents to cut through extremely tough and/or abrasive material and not wear out their tools. Rats can bore holes in concrete and cut through metal sheathing around wires, and Red Squirrels can chisel apart Jackpine cones for the seeds behind the locked, rock-hard scales. While at this, they close their lips behind the incisors, thus keeping concrete grindings, metal filings, and cone scales out of their mouths. This is possible due to a long, high-arched, toothless gap, a "diastema," in both jaws between the incisors and the molars.

Householders often note an aggravating habit of squirrels that seems to be nothing more than pointless gnawing, the better if it's on something valuable. The gnawing may indeed have no practical purpose, in our terms. What the squirrel is doing is honing off its ever-lengthening incisors, probably because the seeds it gets at feeders require nowhere near the amount of gnawing that shucking the hereditary diet of spruce cones demands. If it didn't keep them ground down, the teeth would grow to unmanageable lengths. Indeed, if accident or disease destroys one tooth, its opposite in the other jaw keeps growing, longer and longer until the animal cannot feed at all and dies of starvation.

I have noticed that many rodents, squirrels included, seem to love gnawing on old deer antlers, possibly gaining minerals as they hone down their teeth. Perhaps if you left a chunk of discarded antler, or a large bone, out where it could be chewed on by squirrels they'd be less likely to vandalize your trim.

Behind the diastema is a rank of grinding molars that process whatever the cutting incisors contribute in the way of food. In the cutting mode the lower jaw is shifted forward to engage the incisors, in which position the molars are disengaged. When the lower jaw is pulled back, the incisors are out of gear and the molars mesh into action.

There are a number of accessories and behaviors that various rodents have evolved to augment their teeth. Some squirrels store huge amounts of food to see themselves through the long winter. The chipmunks hibernate in a nest either built right on, or very close to, their stash. Every few days they begin to shiver violently to warm up and, aroused to a state of drowsy wakefulness, grope their way to the bathroom chamber, then eat a big snack out of stores and curl up again. Their hoard is often astonishingly huge. Banfield's *The Mammals of Canada* records a Least Chipmunk's cache of 478 acorns and 2,734 cherry pits.

The compulsive hoarding instinct and the great energy of the diminutive chipmunk are augmented by handy carrying pouches on each cheek, opening to the inside of the mouth. Their capacity is amazing. Banfield records a Least Chipmunk stuffed with thirteen prune stones at one time; Woods in *The Squirrels of Canada* records an Eastern Chipmunk with six chestnuts aboard.

There is more to the varied squirrel tribe than a fancy set of teeth and optional accessories. Conceited as we humans are about our own intelligence, it is a matter of particular interest that squirrels have the largest relative brain weight of any small mammal. Bird lovers, all too familiar with the feeling of defeat that follows every attempt to keep squirrels out of their feeders, have suspected it all along.

This brings me to the reason why, at all, squirrels should be treated seriously in a book about winter birds. Firstly, for most of us they are an unavoidable fact of life. Secondly, squirrels are card-carrying native species toughing out our relentless winters in ways that well merit our sympathetic attention. They are worthy foes if we insist on fighting them, fascinating guests if we choose to accept them.

The "Squirreliest" Squirrel   In the Upper Midwest the American Red Squirrel vies with the Gray Squirrel as the tree squirrel familiar to the greatest number of people. This noisy busybody is the most strident personality in the wild, the "squirreliest" of the squirrels. Except for rare moments of tranquility, its moods vary from mildly agitated to positively frenzied. In a human personality its pugnacious hysteria would be intolerable, and accordingly it is judged harshly, and unfairly.

The key to survival in the Red Squirrel's world is to be the sole, no-nonsense proprieter of a territory that includes food-producing trees. It will move quickly to stake out such a piece of property and fight desperately to keep it. The more times it fights successfully to keep its rights, the better its chances of keeping them. Should a wandering squirrel come by, there will be a frenzied confrontation which the homeless one almost invariably loses because the psychological and tactical advantages are mostly with the owner on his own turf. Established homeownership doesn't mean tranquility, however. As long as the squirrel is alive there will be constant frantic chases with neighbors as each tests the boundary lines of the others.

Although it is a familiar of farmland, parks, and yards, the Red Squirrel's real home is the vast forests of the North where, ultimately, his well-being depends on conifer seeds. About the end of August in a good year a squirrel with a grove of cone-bearing spruce in its territory goes to work as if possessed, cutting bunches of cones from the tops of the trees, letting them drop, then scurrying below to collect them.

In two weeks' work it will cut and cache as many as fifteen thousand, an astonishing heap if, as some squirrels do, it elects to pile them up before burying them. It buries "scatter hoards," single cones under the litter of spruce needles and in bunches in a labyrinth of tunnels under a big tree in the center of its territory. Burial keeps the under-ripened cones moist; otherwise the scales would dry out and open, losing the precious seeds. It also keeps them out of view, and in a more defensible stronghold against pilfering by neighboring squirrels. Piles of shuckings, "cone flakes," collect about stumps or logs where the squirrel perches in winter to take meals retrieved from his storehouse.

Red Squirrel motherhood is a tradeoff between conflicting imperatives. Mating is brief and tempestuous, after which the male is driven off. The young are given all that solicitous single parenthood could ask. But as a taste of things to come, before weaning them the female will often shift her pups to a den near the edge of her territory. After weaning, she becomes less and less tolerant of them until her own territoriality reasserts itself and they are all seen off, and kept off, violently.

Like many another squirrel-watcher, I have wondered why Red Squirrels are red. Unlike grays, which blend nicely into the bark of the trees they spend so much time in, the red's ruddy pelt stands out. Only on the mat of brick red needles on the ground, and in the clumps of rust-colored cones at the tops of spruce, does the Red Squirrel blend. Perhaps it is in these places, exposed and out of its safest element among the trapeze of branches, preoccupied with either cutting or caching, that the squirrel has most need of protective coloration.

Unhappy Wanderer   A full cone hoard is enough to last a Red Squirrel for two winters. It instinctively "knows" that spruce trees are capricious, that a bountiful year is followed by a lean one. In a winter following a bountiful crop, many squirrels will survive to multiply the following summer. The stage is thus set for massive misery, for the progeny of this ill-timed "baby boom" are a luckless lot. They are driven from their mother's territory into a world programmed for famine, where most of the claims are already staked, and where many contend for very few vacancies.

The landless are foredoomed to perish, facing starvation if they aren't caught by predators as they flee distracted from one territorial defender to another. Even for the lucky minority that find a place, the future is bleak; a store of dried mushrooms and rock-hard jackpine cones is a poor substitute for a larder full of spruce cones.

The dispersal of surplus squirrels on the eve of a winter of privation is, ironically, a long-term benefit to their species. Many of these refugees will be driven to seek homes far beyond the usual reach of squirreldom. A few—a very few—will reach uninhabited pockets of plenty and will there set up pioneering populations. They will thus play a small part in a grand plan, the dispersal of their species, a tradeoff for the sacrifice of the many refugees that won't make it.

Every now and then, in isolated farms and villages across the Red Squirrel's huge range, we may witness this process in action. After decades with no squirrels, one or two abruptly appear in late summer. If they could only talk, theirs would be tales of perilous runs over open ground, death-defying risks, hairbreadth escapes, and desperate battles. They would be among the rare ones, survivors thanks to a combination of luck, speed, and dauntless spirit. It is small wonder that their descendants are scrappy and strong and that they will defend their home with the last ounce of energy in their tough little bodies.

Red Squirrel *(Tamiasciurus hudsonicus)*

Squirrel family. "Squirrel" is from Greek *skiourus,* compounded from *skia,* "a shadow," plus *oura,* "tail," descriptive of animal's using tail as shade from sun; *Tamias* is from Latin "steward" or "one who stores" plus *sciurus,* "shade tail"; *hudsonicus,* "of hudson" (Bay) where first type specimen was described.

Description   Trim, muscular body about 6 in (15 cm) long, fluffy tail about same length; smooth, paprika-rufous coat in winter, especially bright in tail and along back; belly, throat, and chin silvery gray; in summer, body olive-brown, underparts white, with black line on side separating them; light eye-ring prominent at all seasons.

Behavior   Hyperactive, excitable, inquisitive; when alarmed runs, climbs with explosive speed; at rest on haunches coils tail closely over back and neck; noisy; territorial call is a scratchy, rattling "chrrrrr" usually delivered from elevated point; alarm call is a sharp, strident "k'cheek!-k'cheek!," often accompanied by agitated drumming of hind feet; drives other squirrels off territory in wild chases; often drives birds from feeder and vicinity.

Range   Truly northern; throughout boreal forest to tree limit, south wherever there are woodlands; through three Great Lakes states, northern portion of Iowa, eastern and northern North Dakota, all of Montana except northeast, and western South Dakota.

Food   Buds, shoots, fruit, seeds, insects, nuts, mushrooms, and occasional eggs and nestlings; in winter, relies on stored seeds, nuts in deciduous forests, and spruce or pine cones in coniferous forests; at feeder eats anything, but prefers sunflower seeds, baked scraps, and peanuts.

Nest   Favors tree holes, but will accumulate bulky ball of shredded grass, bark in buildings, rock piles, burrows, or in open branches where it is called a "drey."

Comment   In the hyperkinetic world of the Red Squirrel, territorial defense can be subject to nerve-frazzling compromises in the presence of a feeder. The unlimited supply of rich food may see the rules broken, particularly if the resident squirrel isn't overwhelmingly dominant. Driven by hunger, first one, then another prevails in a see-saw contest of wills. Adrenalin pumping, antagonists fume and shriek while cramming frantically. These nerve-wracking standoffs are often broken by high-speed scuffles in which significant dollops of blood get spilt.

Total peace is impossible, but with management the tension can be eased somewhat and the birds, at least, will benefit. If the main station is the focus of constant bickering, several others, preferably hanging feeders, can be deployed nearby. These will give the smaller birds, and perhaps even the beleaguered resident squirrel, a place to feed, out of the crossfire as it were.

Gray Squirrel *(Sciurus carolinensis)*

Squirrel family. "Squirrel" is from Greek *skiourus*, compounded from *skia*, "a shadow," plus *oura*, "tail," from animal's resting with tail over back as sunshade; *Sciurus* is Latin for "shade tail"; *carolinensis*, "of Carolina," where first type specimen was described.

Description Twice the size of Red Squirrel; body 8 to 12 in (20 to 30 cm) long, tail same or longer; smooth, grizzled gray coat with rusty shading on head and flanks; tail very full, longest hair tips frosty; belly silver-white; light buff eye-ring; short white tuft behind each ear; some local strains tending to black coats, others to ocher-buff.

Behavior Much calmer, quieter, and slower-moving than Red Squirrel; in sitting position curls tail against back and neck in graceful "question mark," when moving floats it out behind; when agitated thrashes tail; sometimes tolerates other grays at feeder; alarm calls variations on grating "kuk" sound.

Range Originally southeast U.S., expanding northwestward; present throughout all of regional Great Lakes states, all of Iowa except extreme southwest corner, northeast half of North Dakota; introduced to disjunct western cities, parks, and wooded areas as attractive addition to wildlife and/or for hunting.

Food   Buds, shoots, bark, seeds, flowers, nuts, fruit, and fungi; occasionally eggs and nestlings; "scatter hoards" nuts under forest litter, sniffs them out from under snow; omniverous at feeder, but prefers sunflower seeds, peanuts, and baked goods.

Nest   In tree hole or building; nest (drey) in crotch high in tree, a round, untidy clump of twigs, leaves, and grass with side entrance.

Comment   Despite their more pacific dispositions, grays can be more demanding guests around feeders than reds. They eat more, and in spite of their slower gait, can jump higher and farther. When confronting barriers intended to foil them they are much more persistent and can pull off astonishing acrobatics to get where they want. For bird feeders who can't accept squirrels and for whom armed intervention is distasteful and/or unlawful, there are ways of assuaging the humiliation of being outsmarted by a "dumb" animal; some of these are outlined in chapter 3, subsection "How High?," and chapter 4, "The Downside."

Gray squirrels communicate by voice and by tail signals. A rapid "kuk-kuk-kuk-kuk!" means serious danger, a nasal, rasping, drawn-out "raaaaaaaak!" at two-second intervals is a warning of pending danger, a slow, less intense "kuk kuk kuk" is an all-clear. If the tail is waggled jerkily it is a threat to other squirrels; if it is waved in a spasmodic, waggly circular motion it expresses agitation. Holding the tail against the back may signal that a threat has passed.

Northern Flying Squirrel *(Glaucomys sabrinus)*

Squirrel family. Occasionally "Canadian" Flying Squirrel or "Fairydiddle"; "Northern" as distinct from "Southern" (*Glaucomys volans*); "flying"is descriptive of ability to glide short distances; "squirrel" is from Greek *skiourus*, "shade-tail"; *Glaucomys* is Greek for "gray mouse," Latin *sabrinus*, "river nymph," refers to Severn River west of Hudson Bay where first type specimen was described.

Description   Smaller than Red Squirrel; body 5 to 7.5 in (13 to 18 cm), tail slightly shorter; large, dark eyes; very soft, gray-buff fur, cinnamon along back, shaded to light buff underparts; glide membrane dark-bordered; tail noticeably flat, especially on bottom surface.

Behavior   Strictly nocturnal, from an hour or more after dusk to an hour before dawn; swoops rapidly from high in tree to lower landing point, occasionally to ground; scampers up tree when alarmed and immediately turns to head-down launch posture; agile, but not as athletic, particularly on the ground, as red or gray; tolerant at feeders; quiet, voice is a soft chatter.

Range   Throughout boreal forest as far north as there are sizeable trees; around south of Great Lakes in mature mixed woodlands, south and

westward in river valleys, parks, wooded highlands, and well-treed urban areas.

Food   Prefers seeds and nuts; buds, flowers, lichens, fungi, berries, insects, and sweet sap; occasionally eggs and nestlings; caches winter food in den or nearby hollow trees.

Nest   Bed of finely shredded grass, bark in tree holes, occasionally buildings or bird houses; outside drey a ball of moss, grasses, and lichen, sometimes in disused bird nest or drey of Red Squirrel.

Comment   Many years before I ever saw a real live Northern Flying Squirrel I would occasionally find their light, fluffy, uniquely flattened tails, testimony to the previous owners' vulnerability to cats and owls. People living in well-forested regions often have no idea that they are kept company, well after dark, by these shy little gliders. Anonymous midnight scurryings on my cottage roof were resolved when I placed a small lightbulb, with an inside switch, over the window feeder. Turning it on when the squirrels were munching out didn't seem to bother them in the least, and neither did my obvious presence a few inches on the other side of the glass. A friend living in rural Manitoba reports that in a similar situation he was able to reach out through his opened window and pat a squirrel without alarming it.

Eastern & Least Chipmunks

(Tamias striatus and *Eutamias* [formerly *Tamias*] *minimus*
Squirrel family. "Chipmunk" is from Algonquian name; *Tamias*, Latin "steward," is a reference to zeal for storing food; *striatus* is Latin

for "striped"; *Eutamias,* Greek/Latin "true steward"; *minimus* is Latin for "least."

Description   Much smaller than Red Squirrel; long, slender tails not as full as tree squirrels'. **Eastern:** Compact, short body 5 to 6 in (13 to 15.3 cm), tail 2.75 to 4.25 in (7 to 11 cm); five dark stripes on back alternating with light buff lines; face striped, with light eye-ring; coat gray-tawny, but rump and hips rusty brown. **Least:** Light, short body, 4 to 5 in (10 to 12.7 cm), tail 4 to 4.5 in (10 to 11.5 cm); three prominent dark stripes on face separated by two buff stripes; very pointy nose, prominent, light-ringed eyes and large ears; five dark stripes full length of back, outer two on each side separated by light buff.

Behavior   Quick-moving, darting about on ground; Least Chipmunk especially dainty and beady-eyed; both usually run with long tail held straight up; occasionally climb trees, low bushes, but seek refuge in burrows, rock/trash/brush piles, or under buildings or roots; diligent hoarders of food, especially seeds and fruit pits; hibernate, but are early spring risers and venture out briefly during extended mild spells in winter. **Eastern:** voice a sharp "chip," followed in alarm by shrill chatter. **Least:** clear, high "chip-chip" and low, steady "wok," both with ventriloquistic quality making them hard to pinpoint; in alarm a slightly rasping "churrrr" followed by a trill issued in flight.

Range   **Eastern:** Through four eastern states in Upper Midwest, northeast North Dakota. **Least:** Northeast Minnesota, most of northern Wisconsin, Michigan's Upper Peninsula; western Dakotas, eastern and southern Montana, into extreme northwest Montana from western Alberta.

Food   Seeds, nuts, greens, and insects; at feeders fond of sunflower seeds, grains, baked scraps, and dried fruit.

Nest   A ball of shredded grass and fibers deep in a neat, hidden burrow in a rockpile, root tangle, or bank; nest often built near or on the main underground food cache.

Comment   These, particularly the Least Chipmunk, are the picnic-ground, four-legged equivalent of chickadees. Bold, pretty, and pert, they quickly turn their cute ways to good use in training humans to feed them on demand. Their eagerness for handouts is limitless; what they don't sit up and nibble on the spot, they jam into their bulging cheek pouches and scamper off with, a process their benefactors find endlessly comical. Good climbers, but not arboreal, at feeders they usually content themselves with gleaning fallout off the ground.

It is stretching things a bit to call chipmunks winter feeder species. But their busy late autumn and early spring charm are sufficient to give them at least honorary status.

Domestic Cats

Felis catus

The sunny, wintery scene at my study window is cheery and heart-warming. On the feeding tray at the sill, chickadees and nuthatches come and go in the manner of their kind, grabbing sunflower seeds and darting away with them, turn-about.

Abruptly there is a heavy thump, a shower of seeds, and an instant of frantic scrambling. On the feeder is a neighbor's cat with a chickadee jammed in its jaws. He fixes me with a momentary stare and is gone. He leaves behind some drifting feathers and two converging downstrokes smeared on the glass where his flailing paws trapped the bird.

Had my chickadee fallen prey to a full-time, wild predator I would have viewed the little casualty at my window with fascinated excitement quite untinged by resentment. But the cat is a subsidized predator that does not live by the ecological rules of the game. He does not need what he kills. He could not survive the winter on his own, but his depredations diminish the prey base of wild predators that do.

Having licked his chops and smoothed his fur, this on-again, off-again pet would have meowed for readmission to his keeper's cozy house and its unlimited supply of kitty-dins. Another mild day and the urge for some excitement and he would be back, as would my resentment at seeing my birds turned into cat treats.

Tooth-and-claw Genetics   The cat's nonprofessional status as a predator is no reflection at all on his efficiency as a killer. Cats, at least the "brand X" variety that constitute the overwhelming majority, have retained their physical and instinctual integrity despite generations of dependency on humans. They have done so because house cats, unlike their pedigreed counterparts, and almost all dogs, are not the products of arranged marriages. However pampered a suburban tom might be, he must still win his reproductive rights in tooth-and-claw brawls out behind the garage. He is thus prevented from passing on to his descendants anything but physical prowess of the winning kind.

This heritage includes dazzling athletic ability. The chickadee-hunter beneath my window pinpointed the location of his unseen victim by the sound of its feet on the wooden tray. He sprang five feet up, blasted over the edge of the platform and retained sufficient balance and control to make an accurate, lightning-fast grab in whichever direction the bird's own split-second reflexes launched it.

At one time, the keeping of cats was judged to be a matter of good domestic and barnyard management, to prevent the premises from being overrun with mice and rats. Mice, yes, and birds. But the average cat's reputation as a ratter is greatly overrated. Cats will rarely kill rats because they are difficult prey, tough and pugnacious. A study of feral cats in Sweden disclosed that they ate weasels more frequently than they did rats. Alley cats and rats in New York City have been photographed rummaging through garbage virtually shoulder-to-shoulder, ignoring each other.

But today's cat need claim no practical justification to be cherished; sentiment and affection rule the day. Good citizens aware of the effect of rainforest burning on our migrant birds think nothing amiss of the routine of putting the cat out every summer evening. If it tucks away an occasional bird, that's nature's way. Puss returns from the nightly forays, soft-furred and purring, its adventures cloaked in inscrutable mystery.

Inscrutability doesn't mystify scientists in search of truth. A couple of them in Britain, Peter Churcher and John Lawford, turned an analytical eye on just what impact pet cats have on the animal life around them. In a study begun in 1981 they monitored cat predation in a small Bedfordshire village by having owners tally all prey their pets brought home or were seen eating.

Their discoveries included some interesting insights into cat behavior: It appears to make no difference if a pet cat is well-fed; hunger is not the main motivator. The younger the cat, the more animals it catches; old cats get lazy. Sex and neutering did not appear to have much bearing on hunting success. Cats are fair-weather hunters, disinclined to go afield on cold, wet, or windy days.

Nevertheless, in the course of a year, from one-third to one-half of all

House Sparrow mortality in the study village was attributable to cats, even though this species accounted for only 16 percent of the total prey tallied. Cats living in the center of the village caught less prey, but the percentage of birds, relative to mice and other small mammals, increased. The heaviest months were June and July, due to the large proportion of easily caught baby birds, followed by September, the month of migration.

Massive Impact   What is sobering, from the figures tallied at the close of the study, is the collective impact of pet cats on small animals. Based on the annual tallied catch of the seventy-seven cats in the village, and assuming a population of five million cats in Britain, the total kill per year comes to about seventy million. Of this, from 30 to 50 percent would be birds, the higher figure applying to urban felines with less access to the meadow voles and mice their rural equivalents hunted.

Calculated strictly on the basis of the survey results of four birds per cat per year, domestic cats kill at least twenty million birds a year in Britain. However, an American study disclosed that cats bring home no more than half of what they catch, either eating the rest on the spot or leaving them behind. My own observations and that of friends support this finding; I regularly find feathers, wing-ends, flying-squirrel tails, and other remains around the yard. Churcher and Lawford therefore believe that a more accurate estimate of the cumulative bird kill in Britain would be forty million birds. This doesn't, of course, include ferals and strays whose depredations, one assumes, are much, much heavier than those of domestics.

If one makes a simple proportional estimate of the toll by cats in North America, the figures are appalling. There are some fifty million cats in the U.S. If they kill at the same rate as their British counterparts, they destroy 400 million birds a year.

The impact of cats in colder climates may by somewhat less, per cat, than in Britain or the Southern U.S., since northern winters keep the fair-weather felines indoors for part of the year. Still, the toll can't be that much less, since most bird losses are inflicted during the fledging and migrating seasons. In the balmy South cats can hunt all year, and there would be a proportionally much greater population of wild ferals.

Many devoted cat owners also maintain bird feeders, and many of these take active precautions to make sure that these interests don't conflict. Simply keeping family tabbys indoors, as breeders of show cats do as a matter of course, suffices. To turn them loose ensures the death of untold birds.

If one feels better about giving cats their liberty, declawing certainly has some effect on their ability to catch birds. But in intercat relations the loss is a physical handicap, particularly for males during mating competition. In good conscience, if one has a tom declawed, it should be neutered and given early retirement from the mating game.

There is room for serious consideration by bird lovers about whether owning a cat and turning it outdoors at all is an environmentally justifiable luxury.

CHAPTER 8

Census-taking

Feeding birds, and enjoying their proximity and trust during the course of the long winter, is usually considered an individual, if not even a rather solitary, pleasure. Some find their way into it through participation in the programs of local naturalists' clubs. Some do it the other way around, developing their private interests first and then joining a club to share ideas and rub shoulders socially.

Whatever the process, nature clubs foster a broader sharing of values on subjects like conservation and the environment. While most people share concerns over the environment, very few have the time, the resources, or the nerve to speak out individually. Joining forces with a group of like-minded folks can give direction and impact to those concerns when they are voiced in concert.

Christmas Bird Count

It was an issue dealing with environmental abuse that led to the organization, in 1900, of the Christmas Bird Count. Among naturalists of the day there was considerable anger over a barbarous custom among hunters, the Christmas "side hunt." In these, "sportsmen" would assemble on Christmas Day, choose sides, and fan out in teams over the countryside. According to Frank Chapman, the American Museum of Natural History's ornithologist, they shot "practically everything in fur or feathers that crossed their path." The team that killed the most, including piles of songbirds, hawks, and owls, was the winner and was given the routine hero's treatment in the sporting press.

To give positive vent to the outrage and frustration over this bloodthirsty ritual, Chapman organized a humane alternative. He summoned members of the Audubon Society to spend a portion of their Christmas Day "with the birds." The objective, which acknowledged a certain competitive bent in human nature, was to correctly identify, and count, as many species as possible. The time spent, the weather conditions, locality searched, and names of participants were recorded and handed in. In February of 1901 the results were published in *Bird Lore*, the then journal of the Audubon Society, which was edited by Chapman.

In the "CBC" of 1900, twenty-seven counters censused twenty-six localities. It was a small beginning, but the canny Chapman had started something that was to have lasting appeal and enduring value. Today's CBC draws around forty thousand counters and covers all the U.S., most of Canada, and localities in Central and South America and the Caribbean. Some guidelines for the count have changed: Area boundaries are more specific, and the counts are no longer limited to Christmas Day but can be done on any day within a two-week period around Christmas. But the methods remain essentially those laid down by Chapman, and this element of consistency means that there is a continuum of comparable statistics going back to 1900.

The CBC is still run by the Audubon Society, and the results, with the names of all the counters, are published in a substantial book distributed to all counters. Each counter pays a small fee ($5 as of 1991) which helps cover part of the cost of printing and distributing the results.

Today's CBCs are coordinated by local naturalist clubs or individuals. To get involved, contact your nearest naturalist club, state wildlife agency (see the Appendix), the nature columnist in your local paper, or a natural history museum. Or you can contact the Audubon Society directly (see National Organizations in the Appendix). You should, by the way, begin your enquiry no later than mid-September; *don't* leave it until a few weeks before Christmas.

Important Statistics   One of the most interesting results of CBCs is the variety of species that turn up, particularly after the counters have a few seasons under their belts and gain experience. Songbirds, hawks, owls, meadowlarks, and various waterfowl, some far north of their winter range, are tallied, along with hordes of House Sparrows and "Rock Doves" (pigeons).

At first acquaintance, a local CBC may seem a rather scattered and insignificant effort. How, after all, can the birds counted over eight hours (the required time period) in one day, by a half-dozen people, have any value? They can't possibly count *all* the birds!

Of course they can't. The value of what they find out is twofold: Firstly, each count is only a small part of a much larger effort that has been going on for decades; secondly, each set of findings, rated for each species on a birds-per-person-hour scale, can be compared with results elsewhere, for that species, for that year and many years previously. There is a rule of statistics that says the longer you accumulate data, and the more you gather, the less effect small errors will have if your methods remain consistent.

For example, it was the records compiled in the CBCs that revealed long-term, inexplicable declines in raptor populations that led to the investigations disclosing the impact of pesticides on the reproduction of birds of prey.

Project Feeder Watch

The forerunner of Project Feeder Watch was founded by Dr. Erica H. (Ricky) Dunn, its present coordinator. In 1976 she organized the Ontario Bird Feeder Survey and ran it through the Long Point Bird Observatory on Lake Erie. Encouraged by the response and realizing the value of expanding the survey to cover the continent, Ms. Dunn enlisted the cooperation of the Cornell University Laboratory of Ornithology in Ithaca, New York. It is now run by Cornell Laboratory and managed in Canada by Long Point.

As the name suggests, Project Feeder Watch collects the observations of people who feed birds. Participants observe their feeders on one or two days every two weeks from November to April and record their sightings. Results from close to ten thousand feeder watchers are summarized in a newsletter sent to all participants before the next winter. All that is required is the ability to identify the species that visit your feeders and the time to record your observations on computer-readable forms. This means filling in little circles with a soft-lead pencil, a simple exercise once you get the hang of it. The fee for joining Project Feeder Watch for one season is $12.00 (as of 1991). The Cornell address is under National Organizations in the Appendix.

I like the idea of Project Feeder Watch. It takes the fun we already have watching our birds and turns it painlessly into valuable information. It gives thousands of ordinary folks the chance to get involved in a higher scientific purpose. By encouraging people to participate in an organized way, Project Feeder Watch gets them into the habit of taking notes, which not only gives them a record of their observations, but also sharpens their powers of observation.

The Non-KISS Gourmet

Beef suet can be fed as is. Rendering it (melting it, straining out the tissue and "cracklings") makes it harder and less likely to turn rancid in warm weather. The following recipes call for rendered suet. Save the cracklings; they are excellent broken up and scattered on your feeder shelf along with the seeds.

Hot suet turns from a clear oil to soft white grease as it cools and then gradually turns hard. It is most conveniently handled if poured into molds before it sets. Fruit rinds, egg shells, paper cups, and stale ice cream cone shells have all been used to good effect as molds.

Suet/Peanut Butter Blend

2 parts rendered beef suet
1 part peanut butter
2 parts yellow cornmeal (optional)

Remelt suet (don't overheat), stir in peanut butter, and mix thoroughly. If desired, stir in cornmeal; let mixture harden. Hang out of reach of squirrels, since the scent of the peanut butter will attract them more than pure suet.

Protein Pemmican

3 parts rendered suet
1 part moist cat or dog food, or nonspiced processed meat
Raisins, chopped dried fruit, wild berries

Remelt suet, mash up the meat, and stir it into the suet. Add whole berries and dried fruit and stir mixture as it cools to get a consistent blend. Experiment with fruit to determine how much of any given kind you can add; too much, and the cooled block won't hold together. This mix adds a sweet kick from the fruit, which is good for any bird, and the protein could help a robin, blackbird, or other partially insectivorous holdover to make it through the winter.

Bread Pudding Block

Rendered suet
Stale bread, doughnuts, crackers, etc., and/or corn meal

Remelt suet, crush or grind up baked goods, and stir into hot suet. Stir again as it begins to cool to get uniform mix. Pour into molds and let set. Experience will dictate how much of any given baked product can be used and still have the block hold its shape.

Baron von Berlepsch's "Bird-stone"

"Bird-stone" is a term coined by old-time bird feeders for rendered, hard suet. This recipe, the ultimate concoction for the bird feeder who is into power feeding, was gleaned from a booklet published in 1923 by the National Parks of Canada. It is a lesson for those who might have thought such feeding was a latter-day compulsion. It would serve as a custom order for those wanting to see if their local pet-food dealer is *really* serious about good service.

White bread, dried and ground	4.5 oz
Meat, dried and ground	3 oz
Hemp (the *seeds*, of course)	6 oz
Crushed hemp	3 oz
Maw*	3 oz
Poppy flour	1.5 oz
Millet, white	3 oz
Oats	1.5 oz
Dried elderberries	1.5 oz
Sunflower seeds	1.5 oz
Ant's eggs	1.5 oz
Chopped nuts (various)	3 oz
Chopped green (unroasted) peanuts	3 oz
Ground bone**	2 oz
Sharp sand (for grit)***	2 oz

To the total quantity of dry food add about one and one-half times as much beef or mutton suet. The author of the booklet helpfully observes: "It will be found convenient to dry the bread before grinding it, but to grind the meat before drying it."

*My neighbors, Irvine and Gladys Jones, looked this up in an older edition of the Oxford English Dictionary where "maw" is defined as the seed of the opium poppy commonly used as food for caged birds. It is mentioned in some books on caged-bird care.

**Bone meal or perhaps cuttlebone would do nicely here.

***I know birds don't have teeth, but my own fillings incline me *not* to put the sand into the mixture, but to serve it instead as a side dish.

Feeders and Shelters

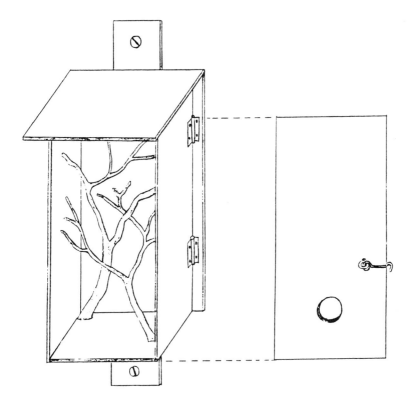

Roosting Box *Big isn't necessarily better, since it's also less snug. This is about bluebird-nestbox size. Tuck in a small branch for a perch, and put an inch or two of sawdust on the floor.*

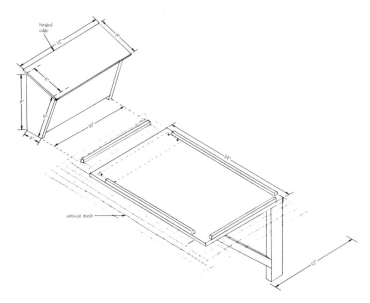

Window Shelf and Hopper *The dimensions are suggestions only. Sloping the hopper lid away from the shelf would prevent melting snow from dripping onto the feed.*

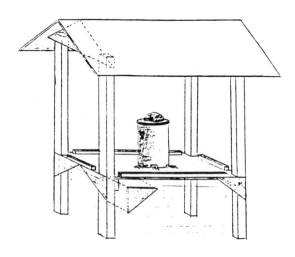

Roofed Table *Can be any size; this is two feet by four feet. The deck, roof, and side braces are half-inch plywood, the raised edges one-by-one inch pieces. Main deck supports are one-by-two inch, nailed between the two-by-two legs.*

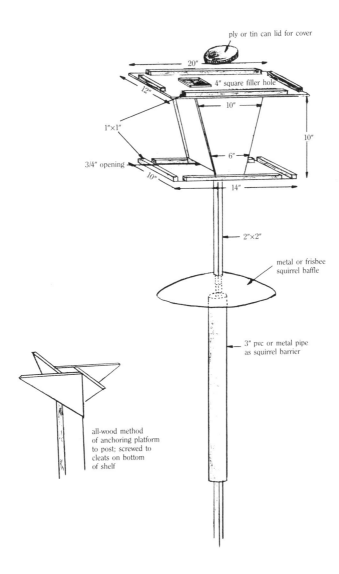

ply or tin can lid for cover

20″

4″ square filler hole

12″

10″

1″×1″

10″

3/4″ opening

6″

10″

14″

2″×2″

metal or frisbee
squirrel baffle

3″ pvc or metal pipe
as squirrel barrier

all-wood method
of anchoring platform
to post; screwed to
cleats on bottom
of shelf

Flat-topped Double-decker *The dimensions suggested give you a lower deck with a carrying capacity of several days, plus shelter from the larger, flat upper deck. Make sure the edge around the filler hole is waterproof; a generous layer of caulking compound under the pieces and at the corners will do this. Screw down one corner or edge of the filler hole lid, adjusting tension so you can swivel it aside for filling.*

Nature and Environmental Groups and Agencies

National Organizations

Aubudon Workshop
1501 Paddock Dr.
North Brook, IL 60062
(Bird feeding information & supplies)

Project Feeder Watch
Cornell Laboratory of Ornithology
159 Sapsucker Woods Rd.
Ithaca, NY 14850

American Birding Association
P.O. Box 6599
Colorado Springs, CO 80934

National Audubon Society
950 Third Ave.
New York, NY 10022

United States Fish & Wildlife Service
Washington, BC 20240

National Association of Interpretation
P.O. Box 1892
Fort Collins, CO 80522

The Nature Conservancy
Ste. 800, 1800 N. Kent St.
Arlington, VA 22209

Urban Wildlife Project
16018 Mill Creek Blvd.
Mill Creek, WA 98012

Sierra Club
730 Polk St.
San Francisco, CA 94109

Defenders of Wildlife
1244 19th St. NW
Washington, DC 20036

State and Local Organizations

Audubon Society
1313 SE 5th St.
Minneapolis, MN 55414

Carpenter St. Croix Valley Nature Center
12805 St. Croix Trail
Hastings, MN 55033

Eloise Butler Wildflower Garden & Bird Sanctuary
(Theodore Wirth Park)
Glenwood Ave. & Xerxes Ave., North
Minneapolis, MN 55422

James Ford Bell Museum of Natural History
17th Ave. & University Ave., Southeast
Minneapolis, MN 55455

Iowa Dept. of Natural Resources
Information-Education Bureau
E Ninth & Grand Ave., Wallace Bldg.
Des Moines, IA 50319–0034

Michigan Dept. of Natural Resources
Wildlife Div., Box 30028
Lansing, MI 48909

Minnesota Dept. of Natural Resources
Div. of Fish & Wildlife
Box 46, DNR Building
500 Lafayette Rd.
St. Paul, MN 55155

Montana Dept. of Fish, Wildlife & Parks
1420 East Sixth
Helena, MT 59620

North Dakota Parks & Recreation
Dept. 1424 W. Century Ave., Ste. 202
Bismarck, ND 58501

South Dakota Game, Fish & Parks Dept.
445 East Capitol
Pierre, SD 57501–3185

Wisconsin Dept. of Natural Resources
Bureau of Wildlife Management
Box 7921
Madison, WI 53707

REFERENCES

Field Guides

Bull, John, and John Farrand. *Audubon Society Field Guide to North American Birds* (Eastern Region). New York: Alfred A. Knopf, 1977.

Harrison, Colin. *A Field Guide to the Nests, Eggs and Nestlings of North American Birds*. New York: Collins, 1978.

Harrison, Hal H. *A Field Guide To Birds' Nests* (east of the Mississippi River), Peterson Field Guide Series. Boston: Houghton Mifflin Company, 1975.

Peterson, Roger Tory. *A Field Guide to the Birds* (Eastern and Central North America), Peterson Field Guide Series. Boston: Houghton Mifflin Company, 1980.

Robbins, Chandler S., et al. *Birds of North America*, Golden Guide Series. New York: Golden Press, 1983.

Scott, Shirley L., ed. *National Geographic Society Field Guide to the Birds of North America*. Washington, D.C.: National Geographic Society, 1987.

General References

Adler, Bill. *Outwitting Squirrels*. Chicago: Chicago Review Press, 1988.

Bent, Arthur Cleveland. *Life Histories of North American Birds*. New York: Dover Publications, Inc., 1964.

Bernstein, Chuck. *The Joy of Birding*. Santa Barbara: Capra Press, 1984.

Boswall, Jeffery. *Birds for all Seasons*. London: BBC Publications, 1986.

Burton, Robert. *Bird Behavior*. New York: Alfred A. Knopf, 1985.

Choate, Ernest A. *The Dictionary of American Bird Names*. Boston: Harvard, Common Press, 1985.

Corral, Michael. *The World of Birds*. Chester: Globe Pequot Press, 1989.

Ehrlich, Paul, et al. *The Birder's Handbook*. New York: Simon & Schuster, 1988.

Gooders, John. *The Practical Ornithologist*. New York: Simon & Schuster, 1990.

Mace, Alice E., ed. *The Birds Around Us*. San Francisco: Ortho Books, Chevron Chemical Company, 1986.

Martin, Brian. *World Birds*. Enfield: Guinness Superlatives Ltd., 1987.

Pasquier, Roger. *Watching Birds*. Boston: Houghton Mifflin Company, 1980.

Perrins, C. and A. Middleton, eds. *The Encyclopedia of Birds*. New York: Facts On File Publications, 1985.

Proctor, Noble. *Song Birds* (with cassette). London: Quarto Publishing, 1988.

Root, Terry. *Atlas of Wintering North American Birds*. Chicago: University of Chicago Press, 1988.

Savage, Candace. *Wings of the North*. Minneapolis: University of Minnesota Press, 1985.

Weidensahl, Scott. *The Birder's Miscellany*. New York: Simon & Schuster, 1991.

Regional References

Janssen, Robert B. *Birds in Minnesota*. Minneapolis: University of Minnesota Press, 1987.

Jehl, J., and B. Smith. *Birds of the Churchill Region*. Winnipeg: Manitoba Museum of Man and Nature, 1970.

McMillon, Bill. *Nature Nearby: An Outdoor Guide to 20 of America's Cities*. New York: John Wiley & Sons, 1990.

Manitoba Rare Bird Alert. *Birder's Guide to Southeastern Manitoba*. Winnipeg: Manitoba Naturalists' Society, 1980.

Zimmer, Kevin J. *A Birder's Guide to North Dakota*. Denver: L & P Press, 1979.

Feeds and Feeding

DeGraaf, R., and M. Witman. *Trees, Shrubs and Vines for Attracting Birds*. Amherst: University of Massachusetts Press, 1979.

Dennis, John. *Beyond the Bird Feeder*. New York: Alfred A. Knopf, 1986.

———. *A Complete Guide To Bird Feeding*. New York: Alfred A. Knopf, 1978.

Dobson, Clive. *Feeding Wild Birds in Winter*. Scarborough: Firefly Books, 1981.

How To Attract Birds. San Francisco: Ortho Books, Chevron Chemical Company, 1983.

Kress, Stephen. *The Audubon Society Guide to Attracting Birds*. New York: Charles Scribner's Sons, 1985.

Mahnken, Jan. *Feeding the Birds*. Pownal: Storey Communications, 1983.

Merilees, Bill. *Attracting Backyard Wildlife*. Stillwater, Minnesota: Voyageur Press, 1989.

Schutz. W. *How to Attract, House and Feed Birds*. New York: Collier Books, 1974.

Stokes, D., and L. Stokes. *The Bird Feeder Book*. Boston: Little, Brown and Company, 1987.

INDEX

Adaptability, 86
American Acclimatization Society, 124
American Crow, 92–94
American Goldfinch, 137, 151–52; cold tolerance, 50
American Robin, 112, 114–15
American Tree Sparrow, 130, 131–32
Ants, as food, 73, 74, 76, 82, 84
Arachis hypogaea. See Peanuts
Aspergillis, 15
Audubon Society, 172, 173

Baffles, cat, 28; squirrel, 25, 179; wind, 29
Baked goods, 20. *See also* Bread
Bald Eagles, 20
Banfield, A. W. F., 161
Bernstein, Chuck, 141
Bins. *See* Hoppers
Black-backed Woodpecker, 80–81
Black-billed Magpie, 91–92
Black-capped Chickadee, 95, 98–99
Black sunflower seed. *See* Sunflower
Blue Jay, 88
Body, fat, 52; mass, 51–52; temperature, 49, 51
Bohemian Waxwing, 115, 116, 117, 118–19
Bombycilla cedrorum. See Cedar Waxwing
Bombycilla garrulus. See Bohemian Waxwing
Bonasa umbellus. See Ruffed Grouse
Bones, as feed, 19; bird skeleton, 48
Boreal Chickadee, 51, 96, 99–100
Brassica napus. See Canola
Bread, 10. *See also* Baked goods
Brown Creeper, 51, 106, 107–9
Brown-headed Nuthatch, 103
Burrows. *See* Cavities, snow
"Bush partridge." *See* Ruffed Grouse
"Butcher bird." *See* Northern Shrike

Cage traps, 43–44
Canada Jay. *See* Gray Jay
Canary, 137
Canary seed, 14
Canola, 11, 15
"Cardinal bait." *See* Safflower
Cardinalis cardinalis. See Northern Cardinal
Cardinals, 128. *See also* Northern Cardinal
Carduelis flammea. See Common Redpoll
Carduelis hornemanni. See Hoary Redpoll
Carduelis pinus. See Pine Siskin
Carduelis tristis. See American Goldfinch
Carpodacus purpureus. See Purple Finch
Carrion, as feed, 19
Carthamus tinctorius. See Safflower
Cats, 169–71; at feeder, 11; predation study, 170–71; proofing, 45–47; stray, 45
Cavities: nests, 38, 74, 102, 125; roosts, 52–53, 74; snow, 51, 59; tree, 51
Cedar Waxwing, 112, 115, 116, 119–20
Certhia americana. See Brown Creeper
Chapman, Frank, 116, 172
Chickadees: accurate recall, 51; fat deposit, 52; torpor, 51. *See also* Black-capped Chickadee, Boreal Chickadee
Chicken, domestic, 52, 58
Chipmunks, 161. *See also* Eastern Chipmunk, Least Chipmunk
Choate, Ernest A., 56
Christmas Bird Count, 172–73
Churcher, Peter, 170–71
Clorox bottle feeder, 31
Coccothraustes vespertinus. See Evening Grosbeak

Oilseed sunflower. *See* Sunflower
Onion bag. *See* Suet, dispensers
Owls, 53

Panicum millaceum. See Millet
Paris, Matthew, 144
Parrot Crossbill, 142, 143
Partridges, 58–59. *See also* Gray Par-
tridge, Ruffed Grouse
Parus atricapillus. See Black-capped
Chickadee
Parus bicolor. See Tufted Titmouse
Parus hudsonicus. See Boreal Chickadee
Pasquier, Roger, 52
Passer domesticus. See House Sparrow
Passive obstruction. *See* Cat, proofing
Peanut butter, 17, 175; "hearts," 16
Peanuts, 15–16
Perdix perdix. See Gray Partridge
Perisoreus canadensis. See Gray Jay
Pests and problems, 39–47
Peterson, Roger Tory, 101, 133, 140
Phalaenoptilus nuttali. See Poorwill
Phalaris canariensis. See Canary Seed
Phasianus colchicus. See Ring-necked
Pheasant
Pheasants, 58–59. *See also* Ring-
necked Pheasant
Physiology, 48–49
Pica pica. See Black-billed Magpie
Picoides arcticus. See Black-backed
Woodpecker
Picoides pubescens. See Downy Wood-
pecker
Picoides tridactylus. See Three-toed
Woodpecker
Picoides villosus. See Hairy Wood-
pecker
Pigeons, 16, 20, 68–69
Pileated Woodpecker, 73, 83–84
Pine Grosbeak, 128, 139–40
Pine Siskin, 150–51; cold tolerance, 50;
food preference test, 12
Pinicola enucleator. See Pine Grosbeak
Pinshow, Berry, 121
Plectrophenax nivalis. See Snow
Bunting
Plywood, damage by woodpeckers, 42,
79
Poison, 43, 44

Poorwill, 51
"Prairie chicken." *See* Sharp-tailed
Grouse
Preference, of crushed sunflowers, 12;
of seeds, 12
Proctor, Noble, 107
Project Feeder Watch, 174
Purple Finch, 16, 140–41; cold toler-
ance, 50

Rabbits, 15
Raccoons, 15, 34
Rapeseed, 11, 15
Rats, 42, 170
Ravens, 20, 51, 86, 88. *See also* Com-
mon Raven
Recall interval, in chickadees, 51
Recipes, 175–76
Red-bellied Woodpecker, 75–76
Red-breasted Nuthatch, 102, 104–5
Red Crossbill, 142, 144–46
Red Jungle Fowl, 58
Redpolls, 51, 52, 147–48. *See also*
Common Redpoll, Hoary Redpoll
Red Squirrel, 88, 143, 160, 162, 163–65
Red-winged Blackbird, 112
Regulus satrapa. See Golden-crowned
Kinglet
Relocation, of pests, 44
Rescue, from injury, 41
Ring-necked Pheasant, 52, 60, 62–63,
155
Robin, 20. *See also* American Robin
Rock Dove, 68, 69–70, 155, 173. *See
also* Pigeons
Rodents, 160; as pests, 8–9. *See also*
Mice and Rats, 42; poison, 43
Roofs, on feeders, 37
Roosts, 57. *See also* Cavities, Nests,
Shelters
Rosy (Gray-crowned) Finch, 137–39
Ruby-crowned Kinglet, 109
Ruffed Grouse, 64–66

Safflower, 16
St. Francis of Assisi, 5
Salt, as feed, 21
Savage, Candace, 66, 72, 116
Sciurus carolinensis. See Gray Squirrel
Screenings, 14

About the Author

Born in Killarney, Manitoba, Bob Waldon has spent most of his life living and working in Manitoba. As a freelance writer, he has contributed to a number of periodicals, including *Harrowsmith*, *Maclean's*, and *Nature Canada*. A former president of the Manitoba Naturalists' Society and the Canadian Nature Federation, Bob presently works as an interpretive naturalist at Riding Mountain National Park. He lives with his wife, Carole, in Winnipeg.